W9-BXL-233

WITHDRAWN

Bloom's Modern Critical Views

Bloom's Modern Critical Views

Mary Wollstonecraft
  Shelley
Alexander Solzhenitsyn
John Steinbeck
Jonathan Swift
Amy Tan
Alfred, Lord Tennyson
Henry David Thoreau
J. R. R. Tolkien
Leo Tolstoy

Ivan Turgenev
Mark Twain
John Updike
Kurt Vonnegut
Derek Walcott
Alice Walker
Robert Penn Warren
H. G. Wells
Eudora Welty
Edith Wharton

Walt Whitman
Oscar Wilde
Tennessee Williams
Tom Wolfe
Virginia Woolf
William Wordsworth
Jay Wright
Richard Wright
William Butler Yeats
Émile Zola

Library & Media Ctr.
Carroll Community College
1601 Washington Rd.
Westminster, MD 21157

Bloom's Modern Critical Views

Emily Dickinson
New Edition

Edited and with an introduction by
Harold Bloom
Sterling Professor of the Humanities
Yale University

BLOOM'S
LITERARY CRITICISM
An imprint of Infobase Publishing

Editorial Consultant, Amanda Gailey

Bloom's Modern Critical Views: Emily Dickinson—New Edition

Copyright ©2008 by Infobase Publishing

Introduction ©2008 by Harold Bloom

All rights reserved. No part of this publication may be reproduced or utilized in any form or by any means, electronic or mechanical, including photocopying, recording, or by any information storage or retrieval systems, without permission in writing from the publisher. For more information contact:

Bloom's Literary Criticism
An imprint of Infobase Publishing
132 West 31st Street
New York NY 10001

Library of Congress Cataloging-in-Publication Data

Emily Dickinson / edited with an introduction by Harold Bloom. — New ed.
         p. cm. — (Modern criticial interpertations)
 Includes bibliographical references and index.
 ISBN 978-0-7910-9613-0 (hardcover : alk. paper)
  1. Dicksinson, Emily, 1830-1886—Criticism and interpretation. 2. Women and literature—United States—History—19th century. I. Bloom, Harold.

PS1541.Z5E38 2008
811'.4—dc22   2007045156

Bloom's Literary Criticism books are available at special discounts when purchased in bulk quantities for businesses, associations, institutions, or sales promotions. Please call our Special Sales Department in New York at (212) 967-8800 or (800) 322-8755.

You can find Bloom's Literary Criticism on the World Wide Web at
http://www.chelseahouse.com.

Cover design by Takeshi Takahashi/Jooyoung An

Printed in the United States of America
Bang BCL 10 9 8 7 6 5 4 3 2 1

This book is printed on acid-free paper.

All links and web addresses were checked and verified to be correct at the time of publication. Because of the dynamic nature of the web, some addresses and links may have changed since publication and may no longer be valid.

Contents

Editor's Note

My introduction meditates upon Emily Dickinson's astonishing cognitive originality, surpassed only by Shakespeare, among the poets.

The distinguished poet Richard Wilbur demonstrates Dickinson's insistence upon total consciousness, while Douglas Anderson shrewdly emphasizes that there is always more of her than we can expect.

Stylistic development in Dickinson is traced by Timothy Morris, after which Margaret Dickie urges us to take account of this poet's figurative excess which helps to constitute her self.

The revisionary element in Dickinson's manuscripts is analyzed by Domhnall Mitchell, while the great textual scholar G. Thomas Tanselle reviews what immediately became the definitive edition, done by R. W. Franklin.

Cynthia L. Hallen gives a helpful account of Dickinson's rhetoric, after which a major historical scholar, David S. Reynolds, charts the poet's relation to the popular culture of her era.

The curious emphasis upon the musical effect of Dickinson's work, during the initial reviews of the 1880's, is shown by Carolyn Lindley Cooley, while Logan Esdale rightly argues that the poet's personal letters are as fully *composed* as her poems.

Brilliantly argued by Shira Wolosky, the case is strongly made that Dickinson's Civil War poems are themselves battlefields between self and community, after which Dierdre Fagan centers upon the poet's obsessive use of the dash as punctuation.

Dickinson's idea of God, a very perplexing matter, is intimated by Jay Ladin to be an attempt to constitute her ideal reader in the deity, while the accomplished creative John Felstiner sensitively conveys her highly individual visions of death and dying.

HAROLD BLOOM

Introduction

EMILY DICKINSON (1830–1886)

I

It is not a rare quality for great poets to possess such cognitive strength that we are confronted by authentic intellectual difficulties when we read them. "Poems are made by fools like me," yes, and by Dante, Milton, Blake and Shelley, but only God can make a tree, to reappropriate a rejoinder I remember making to W.H. Auden many years ago, when he deprecated the possibilities of poetry as compared with the awful truths of Christian theology. But there are certainly very grand poets who are scarcely thinkers in the discursive modes. Tennyson and Whitman are instances of overwhelming elegiac artists who make us fitful when they argue, and the subtle rhetorical evasions of Wallace Stevens do not redeem his unfortunate essay, "A Collect of Philosophy."

Of all poets writing in English in the nineteenth and twentieth centuries, I judge Emily Dickinson to present us with the most authentic cognitive difficulties. Vast and subtle intellect cannot in itself make a poet; the essential qualities are inventiveness, mastery of trope and craft, and that weird flair for intuiting significance through rhythm to which we can give no proper name. Dickinson has all these, as well as a mind so original and powerful that we scarcely have begun, even now, to catch up with her.

Originality at its strongest—in the Yahwists, Plato, Shakespeare and Freud—usurps immense spaces of consciousness and language, and imposes contingencies upon all who come after. These contingencies work so as to conceal authentic difficulty through a misleading familiarity. Dickinson's strangeness, partly masked, still causes us to wonder at her, as we ought to wonder at Shakespeare or Freud. Like them, she has no single, overwhelming

1

precursor whose existence can lessen her wildness for us. Her agon was waged with the whole of tradition, but particularly with the Bible and with romanticism. As an agonist, she takes care to differ from any male model, and places us upon warning:

> I cannot dance upon my Toes—
> No Man instructed me—
> But oftentimes, among my mind,
> A Glee possesseth me,
>
> . . . .
>
> Nor any know I know the Art
> I mention—easy—Here—
> Nor any Placard boast me—
> It's full as Opera— [326]

The mode is hardly Whitmanian in this lyric of 1862, but the vaunting is, and both gleeful arts respond to the Emersonian prophecy of American Self-Reliance. Each responds with a difference, but it is a perpetual trial to be a heretic whose only orthodoxy is Emersonianism, or the exaltation of whim:

> If nature will not tell the tale
> Jehovah told to her
> Can human nature not survive
> Without a listener? [1748]

Emerson should have called his little first book, *Nature*, by its true title of Man, but Dickinson in any case would have altered that title also. Alas, that Emerson was not given the chance to read the other Titan that he fostered. We would cherish his charmed reaction to:

> A Bomb upon the Ceiling
> Is an improving thing—
> It keeps the nerves progressive
> Conjecture flourishing— [1128]

Dickinson, after all, could have sent her poems to Emerson rather than to the nobly obtuse Higginson. We cannot envision Whitman addressing a copy of the first *Leaves of Grass* to a Higginson. There is little reason to suppose that mere diffidence prevented Miss Dickinson of Amherst from presenting her work to Mr. Emerson of Concord. In 1862, Emerson was still Emerson; his long decline dates from after the conclusion of the War. A private unfolding remained necessary for Dickinson, according to laws of the spirit and of poetic reason that we perpetually quest to surmise. Whereas Whitman masked his delicate, subtle and hermetic art by developing the outward self of the rough Walt, Dickinson set herself free to invest her imaginative exuberance elsewhere. The heraldic drama of her reclusiveness became the cost of her confirmation as a poet more original even than Whitman, indeed more original than any poet of her century after (and except) Wordsworth. Like Wordsworth, she began anew upon a *tabula rasa* of poetry, to appropriate Hazlitt's remark about Wordsworth. Whitman rethought the relation of the poet's self to his own vision, whereas Dickinson rethought the entire content of poetic vision. Wordsworth had done both, and done both more implicitly than these Americans could manage, but then Wordsworth had Coleridge as stimulus, while Whitman and Dickinson had the yet more startling and far wilder Emerson, who was and is the American difference personified. I cannot believe that even Dickinson would have written with so absolutely astonishing an audacity had Emerson not insisted that poets were as liberating gods:

> Because that you are going
> And never coming back
> And I, however absolute,
> May overlook your Track—
>
> Because that Death is final,
> However first it be,
> This instant be suspended
> Above Mortality—
>
> Significance that each has lived
> The other to detect
> Discovery not God himself
> Could now annihilate
>
> Eternity, Presumption
> The instant I perceive
> That you, who were Existence
> Yourself forgot to live—

These are the opening quatrains of poem 1260, dated by Thomas Johnson as about 1873, but it must be later, if indeed the reference is to the dying either of Samuel Bowles (1878) or of Judge Otis Lord (1884), the two men Richard Sewall, Dickinson's principal biographer, considers to have been her authentic loves, if not in any conventional way her lovers. The poem closes with a conditional vision of God refunding to us finally our "confiscated Gods." Reversing the traditional pattern, Dickinson required and achieved male Muses, and her "confiscated Gods" plays darkly against Emerson's "liberating gods." Of Emerson, whose crucial work (*Essays*, *The Conduct of Life*, *Society and Solitude*, the *Poems*) she had mastered, Dickinson spoke with the ambiguity we might expect. When Emerson lectured in Amherst in December 1857, and stayed next door with Dickinson's brother and sister-in-law, he was characterized by the poet: "as if he had come from where dreams are born." Presumably the Transcendental Emerson might have merited this, but it is curious when applied to the exalter of "Fate" and "Power" in *The Conduct of Life*, or to the dialectical pragmatist of "Experience" and "Circles," two essays that I think Dickinson had internalized. Later, writing to Higginson, she observed: "With the Kingdom of Heaven on his knee, could Mr. Emerson hesitate?" The question, whether open or rhetorical, is dangerous and wonderful, and provokes considerable rumination.

Yet her subtle ways with other male precursors are scarcely less provocative. Since Shelley had addressed *Epipsychidion* to Emilia Viviani, under the name of "Emily," Dickinson felt authorized to answer a poet who, like herself, favored the image of volcanoes. Only ten days or so before Judge Lord died, she composed a remarkable quatrain in his honor (and her own):

> Circumference thou Bride of Awe
> Possessing thou shalt be
> Possessed by every hallowed Knight
> That dares to covet thee [1620]

Sewall notes the interplay with some lines in *Epipsychidion*:

> Possessing and possessed by all that is
> Within that calm circumference of bliss,
> And by each other, till to love and live
> Be one:— [549–552]

Shelley's passage goes on to a kind of lovers' apocalypse:

> One hope within two wills, one will beneath
> Two overshadowing minds, one life, one death,
> One heaven, one Hell, one immortality,
> And one annihilation . . . [584–587]

In his essay, "Circles," Emerson had insisted: "There is no outside, no inclosing wall, no circumference to us." The same essay declares: "The only sin is limitation." If that is so, then there remains the cost of confirmation, worked out by Dickinson in an extraordinary short poem that may be her critique of Emerson's denial of an outside:

I saw no Way—The Heavens were stitched
I felt the Columns close—
The Earth reversed her Hemispheres—
I touched the Universe—

And back it slid—and I alone
A Speck upon a Ball—
Went out upon Circumference—
Beyond the Dip of Bell— [378]

"My Business is Circumference—" she famously wrote to Higginson, to whom, not less famously, she described herself as "the only Kangaroo among the Beauty." When she wrote, to another correspondent, that "The Bible dealt with the Centre, not with the Circumference—," she would have been aware that the terms were Emerson's, and that Emerson also dealt only with the Central, in the hope of the Central Man who would come. Clearly, "Circumference" is her trope for the Sublime, as consciousness and as achievement or performance. For Shelley, Circumference was a Spenserian cynosure, a Gardens of Adonis vision, while for Emerson it was no part of us, or only another challenge to be overcome by the Central, by the Self-Reliant Man.

If the Bible's concern is Centre, not Circumference, it cannot be because the Bible does not quest for the Sublime. If Circumference or Dickinson is the bride of Awe or of the authority of Judge Lord, then Awe too somehow had to be detached from the Centre:

No man saw awe, nor to his house
Admitted he a man
Though by his awful residence
Has human nature been.

Not deeming of his dread abode
Till laboring to flee
A grasp on comprehension laid
Detained vitality.

> Returning is a different route
> The Spirit could not show
> For breathing is the only work
> To be enacted now.
>
> "Am not consumed," old Moses wrote,
> "Yet saw him face to face"—
> That very physiognomy
> I am convinced was this. [1733]

This might be called an assimilation of Awe to Circumference, where "laboring to flee" and returning via "a different route" cease to be antithetical to one another. "Vitality" here is another trope for Circumference or the Dickinsonian Sublime. If, as I surmise, this undated poem is a kind of proleptic elegy for Judge Lord, then Dickinson identifies herself with "old Moses," and not for the first time in her work. Moses, denied entrance into Canaan, "wasn't fairly used— ," she wrote, as though the exclusion were her fate also. In some sense, she chose this fate, and not just by extending her circumference to Bowles and to Lord, unlikely pragmatic choices. The spiritual choice was not to be post-Christian, as with Whitman or Emerson, but to become a sect of one, like Milton or Blake. Perhaps her crucial choice was to refuse the auction of her mind through publication. Character being fate, the Canaan she would not cross to was poetic recognition while she lived.

Of Dickinson's 1,775 poems and fragments, several hundred are authentic, strong works, with scores achieving an absolute aesthetic dignity. To choose one above all the others must reveal more about the critic than he or she could hope to know. But I do not hesitate in my choice, poem 627, written probably in her very productive year, 1862. What precedents are there for such a poem, a work of un-naming, a profound and shockingly original cognitive act of negation?

> The Tint I cannot take—is best—
> The Color too remote
> That I could show it in Bazaar—
> A Guinea at a sight—
>
> The fine—impalpable Array—
> That swaggers on the eye
> Like Cleopatra's Company—
> Repeated—in the sky—
>
> The Moments of Dominion
> That happen on the Soul

And leave it with a Discontent
Too exquisite—to tell—

The eager look—on Landscapes—
As if they just repressed
Some Secret—that was pushing
Like Chariots—in the West—

The Pleading of the Summer—
That other Prank—of Snow—
That Cushions Mystery with Tulle,
For fear the Squirrels—know.

Their Graspless manners—mock us—
Until the Cheated Eye
Shuts arrogantly—in the Grave—
Another way—to see—

It is, rugged and complete, a poetics, and a manifesto of Self-Reliance. "The poet did not stop at the color or the form, but read their meaning; neither may he rest in this meaning, but he makes the same objects exponents of his new thought." This Orphic metamorphosis is Emerson's, but is not accomplished in his own poetry, nor is his radical program of un-naming. Dickinson begins by throwing away the lights and the definitions, and by asserting that her jocular procreations are too subtle for the Bazaar of publication. The repetition of colors (an old word, after all, for tropes) remains impalpable and provokes her into her own Sublime, that state of Circumference at once a divine discontent and a series of absolute moments that take dominion everywhere. Better perhaps than any other poet, she knows and indicates that what is worth representing is beyond depiction, what is worth saying cannot be said. What she reads, on landscapes and in seasons, is propulsive force, the recurrence of perspectives that themselves are powers and instrumentalities of the only knowledge ever available.

The final stanza does not attempt to break out of this siege of perspectives, but it hints again that her eye and will are receptive, not plundering, so that her power to un-name is not Emersonian finally, but something different, another way to see. To see feelingly, yes, but beyond the arrogance of the self in its war against process and its stand against other selves. Her interplay of perspectives touches apotheosis not in a Nietzschean or Emersonian exaltation of the will to power, however receptive and reactive, but in suggestions of an alternative mode, less an interpretation than a questioning, or an othering of natural process. The poem, like so much of Dickinson at her strongest, compels us to begin again in rethinking our relation to poems, and to the equally troubling and dynamic relation of poems to our world of appearances.

RICHARD WILBUR

Sumptuous Destitution

At some point Emily Dickinson sent her whole Calvinist vocabulary into exile, telling it not to come back until it would subserve her own sense of things.

Of course, that is not a true story, but it is a way of saying what I find most remarkable in Emily Dickinson. She inherited a great and over-bearing vocabulary which, had she used it submissively, would have forced her to express an established theology and psychology. But she would not let that vocabulary write her poems for her. There lies the real difference between a poet like Emily Dickinson and a fine versifier like Isaac Watts. To be sure, Emily Dickinson also wrote in the metres of hymnody, and paraphrased the Bible, and made her poems turn on great words like Immortality and Salvation and Election. But in her poems those great words are not merely being themselves; they have been adopted, for expressive purposes; they have been personally, and therefore redefined.

The poems of Emily Dickinson are continual appeal to experience, motivated by an arrogant passion for the truth. "Truth is so rare a thing," she once said, "it is delightful to tell it." And, sending some poems to Colonel Higginson, she wrote, "Excuse them, if they are untrue." And again, to the same correspondent, she observed, "Candor is the only wile"—meaning that the writer's bag of tricks need contain one trick only,

Richard Wilbur, Louise Bogan, and Archibald MacLeish, *Emily Dickinson: Three Views* (Amherst: Amherst College Press, 1960): pp. 127–136. Copyright © 1960 by the Amherst College Press.

the trick of being honest. That her taste for truth involved a regard for objective fact need not be argued: we have her poem on the snake, and that on the hummingbird, and they are all small masterpieces of exact description. She liked accuracy; she liked solid and homely detail; and even in her most exalted poems we are surprised and reassured by buckets, shawls, or buzzing flies.

But her chief truthfulness lay in her insistence on discovering the facts of her inner experience. She was a Linnaeus to the phenomena of her own consciousness, describing and distinguishing the states and motions of her soul. The results of this "psychic reconnaissance," as Professor Whicher called it, were several. For one thing, it made her articulate about inward matters which poetry had never so sharply defined; specifically, it made her capable of writing two such lines as these:

> A perfect, paralyzing bliss
> Contented as despair.

We often assent to the shock of a paradox before we understand it, but those lines are so just and so concentrated as to explode their meaning instantly in the mind. They did not come so easily, I think, to Emily Dickinson. Unless I guess wrongly as to chronology, such lines were the fruit of long poetic research; the poet had worked toward them through much study of the way certain emotions can usurp consciousness entirely, annulling our sense of past and future, cancelling near and far, converting all time and space to a joyous or grievous here and now. It is in their ways of annihilating time and space that bliss and despair are comparable.

Which leads me to a second consequence of Emily Dickinson's self-analysis. It is one thing to assert as pious doctrine that the soul has power, with God's grace, to master circumstance. It is another thing to find out personally, as Emily Dickinson did in writing her psychological poems, that the aspect of the world is in no way constant, that the power of external things depends on our state of mind, that the soul selects its own society and may, if granted strength to do so, select a superior order and scope of consciousness which will render it finally invulnerable. She learned these things by witnessing her own courageous spirit.

Another result of Emily Dickinson's introspection was that she discovered some grounds, in the nature of her soul and its affections, for a personal conception of such ideas as Heaven and Immortality, and so managed a precarious convergence between her inner experience and her religious inheritance. What I want to attempt now is a rough sketch of the imaginative logic by which she did this. I had better say before I start that I shall often seem demonstrably wrong, because Emily Dickinson, like many poets, was consistent in her concerns but inconsistent in her attitudes. The following, therefore, is merely an opinion as to her main drift.

Emily Dickinson never lets us forget for very long that in some respects life gave her short measure; and indeed it is possible to see the greater part of her poetry as an effort to cope with her sense of privation. I think that for her there were three major privations: she was deprived of an orthodox and steady religious faith; she was deprived of love; she was deprived of literary recognition.

At the age of 17, after a series of revival meetings at Mount Holyoke Seminary, Emily Dickinson found that she must refuse to become a professing Christian. To some modern minds this may seem to have been a sensible and necessary step; and surely it was a step toward becoming such a poet as she became. But for her, no pleasure in her own integrity could then eradicate the feeling that she had betrayed a deficiency, a want of grace. In her letters to Abiah Root she tells of the enhancing effect of conversion on her fellow-students, and says of herself in a famous passage:

> *I* am one of the lingering bad ones, and so do I slink away, and pause and ponder, and ponder and pause, and do work without knowing why, not surely, for this brief world, and more sure it is not for heaven, and I ask what this message *means* that they ask for so very eagerly: *you* know of this depth and fulness, will you try to tell me about it?

There is humor in that, and stubbornness, and a bit of characteristic lurking pride: but there is also an anguished sense of having separated herself, through some dry incapacity, from spiritual community, from purpose, and from magnitude of life. As a child of evangelical Amherst, she inevitably thought of purposive, heroic life as requiring a vigorous faith. Out of such a thought she later wrote:

> The abdication of Belief
> Makes the Behavoir small—
> Better an ignis fatuus
> Than no illume at all—(1551)

That hers *was* a species of religious personality goes without saying; but by her refusal of such ideas as original sin, redemption, hell, and election, she made it possible for herself—as Professor Whicher observed—"to share the religious life of her generation." She became an unsteady congregation of one.

Her second privation, the privation of love, is one with which her poems and her biographies have made us exceedingly familiar, though some biographical facts remain conjectural. She had the good fortune, at least once, to bestow her heart on another; but she seems to have found her life, in great part, a history of loneliness, separation, and bereavement.

As for literary fame, some will deny that Emily Dickinson ever greatly desired it, and certainly there is evidence, mostly from her latter years, to support such a view. She *did* write that "Publication is the auction/Of the mind of man." And she *did* say to Helen Hunt Jackson, "How can you print a piece of your soul?" But earlier, in 1861, she had frankly expressed to Sue Dickinson the hope that "sometime" she might make her kinfolk proud of her. The truth is, I think, that Emily Dickinson knew she was good, and began her career with a normal appetite for recognition. I think that she later came, with some reason, to despair of being understood or properly valued, and so directed against her hopes of fame what was by then a well-developed disposition to renounce. That she wrote a good number of poems about fame supports my view: the subjects to which a poet returns are those which vex him.

What did Emily Dickinson do, as a poet, with her sense of privation? One thing she quite often did was to pose as the laureate and attorney of the empty-handed, and question God about the economy of His creation. Why, she asked, is a fatherly God so sparing of His presence? Why is there never a sign that prayers are heard? Why does Nature tell us no comforting news of its Maker? Why do some receive a whole loaf, while others must starve on a crumb? Where is the benevolence in shipwreck and earthquake? By asking such questions as these, she turned complaint into critique, and used her own sufferings as experiential evidence about the nature of the deity. The God who emerges from these poems is a God who does not answer, and unrevealed God whom one cannot confidently approach through Nature or through doctrine.

But there was another way in which Emily Dickinson dealt with her sentiment of lack—another emotional strategy which was both more frequent and more faithful. I refer to her repeated assertion of the paradox that privation is more plentiful than plenty; that to renounce is to possess the more; that "The Benquet of abstemiousness / a Defaces that of wine." We all know how the poet illustrated this ascetic paradox in her behavior—how in her latter years she chose to live in relative retirement, keeping the world, even in its dearest aspects, at a physical remove. She would write her friends, telling them how she missed them, then flee upstairs when they came to see her; afterward, she might send a note of apology, offering the odd explanation that "We shun because we prize." Any reader of Dickinson biographies can furnish other examples, dramatic or homely, of this prizing and shunning, this yearning and renouncing: in my own mind's eye is a picture of Emily Dickinson watching a gay circus caravan from the distance of her chamber window.

In her inner life, as well, she came to keep the world's images, even the images of things passionately desired, at the remove which renunciation makes; and her poetry at its most mature continually proclaims that to lose or forego what we desire is somehow to gain. We may say, if we like, with some of the poet's commentators, that this central paradox of her thought is a rationalization of her neurotic plight; but we had better add that it is also a discovery of something about the soul. Let me read you a little poem of psychological observation which, whatever its date of composition, may logically be considered as an approach to that discovery.

Undue Significance a starving man attaches
To Food—
Far off—He sighs—and therefore—Hopeless—
And therefore—Good—
Partaken—it relieves—indeed—
But proves us
That Spices fly
In the Receipt—It was the Distance—
Was Savory—(439)

This poem describes an educational experience, in which a starving man is brought to distinguish between appetite and desire. So long as he despairs of sustenance, the man conceives it with the eye of desire as infinitely delicious. But when, after all, he secures it and appeases his hunger, he finds that its imagined spices have flown. The moral is plain: once an object has been magnified by desire, it cannot be wholly possessed by appetite.

The poet is not concerned, in this poem, with passing any judgment. She is simply describing the way things go in the human soul, telling us that the frustration of appetite awakens or abets desire, and that the effect of intense desiring is to render any finite satisfaction disappointing. Now I want to read you another well-known poem, in which Emily Dickinson was again considering privation and possession, and the modes of enjoyment possible to each. In this case, I think, a judgment is strongly implied.

Success is countered sweetest
By those who ne'er succeed.
To comprehend a nectar
Requires sorest need.

Not one of all the purple Host
Who took the Flag today
Can tell the definition
So clear of Victory

As he defeated—dying—
On whose forbidden ear
The distant strains of triumph
Burst agonized and clear! (67)

Certainly Emily Dickinson's critics are right in calling this poem an expression of the idea of compensation—of the idea that every evil confers some balancing good, that through bitterness we learn to appreciate the sweet, that "Water is taught by thirst." The defeated and dying soldier of this poem is compensated by a greater awareness of the meaning of victory than the victors themselves can have: he can comprehend the joy of success through its polar contrast to his own despair.

The poem surely does say that; yet it seems to me that there is something further implied. On a first reading, we are much impressed with the wretchedness of the dying soldier's lot, and an improved understanding of the nature of victory may seem small compensation for defeat and death; but the more one ponders this poem the likelier it grows that Emily Dickinson is arguing the *superiority* of defeat to victory, of frustration to satisfaction, and of anguished comprehension to mere possession. What do the victors have but victory, a victory which they cannot fully savor or clearly define? They have paid for their triumph by a sacrifice of awareness; a material gain has cost them a spiritual loss. For the dying soldier, the case is reversed: defeat and death are attended by an increase of awareness, and material loss has led to spiritual gain. Emily Dickinson would think that the better bargain.

In the first of these two poems I have read, it was possible to imagine the poet as saying that a starving man's visions of food are but wish fulfillments, and hence illusory; but the second poem assures us of the contrary—assures us that food, or victory, or any other good thing is best comprehended by the eye of desire from the vantage of privation. We must now ask in what way desire can define things, what comprehension of nectars it can have beyond a sense of inaccessible sweetness.

Since Emily Dickinson was not a philosopher, and never set forth her thought in any orderly way, I shall answer that question by a quotation from the seventeenth-century divine Thomas Traherne. Conveniently for us, Traherne is thinking, in this brief mediation, about food—specifically, about acorns—as perceived by appetite and by desire.

The services of things and their excellencies are spiritual: being objects not of the eye, but of the mind: and you more spiritual by how much more you esteem them. Pigs eat acorns, but neither consider the sun that gave them life, nor the influences of the heavens by which they were nourished, nor the very root of the tree from whence they came. This being the work of Angels, who in a wide and clear light see even the sea that gave them moisture: And feed upon that acorn spiritually while they know the ends for which it was created, and feast upon all these as upon a World of Joys within it: while to ignorant swine that eat the shell, it is an empty husk of no taste nor delightful savor.

Emily Dickinson could not have written that, for various reasons, a major reason being that she could not see in Nature any revelations of divine purpose. But like Traherne she discovered that the soul has an infinite hunger, a hunger to possess all things. (That discovery, I suspect, was the major fruit of her introspection.) And like Traherne she distinguished two ways of possessing things, the way of appetite and the way of desire. What Traherne said of the pig she said of her favorite insect:

Auto da Fe and Judgment—
Are nothing to the Bee—
His separation from His Rose—
To Him—sums Misery—(620)

The creature of appetite (whether insect or human) pursues satisfaction, and strives to possess the object in itself; it cannot imagine the vaster economy of desire, in which the pain of abstinence is justified by moments of infinite joy, and the object is spiritually possessed, not merely for itself, but more truly as an index of the All. That is how one comprehends a nectar. Miss Dickinson's bee does not comprehend the rose which it plunders, because the truer sweetness of the rose lies beyond the rose, in its relationship to the whole of being; but she would say that Gerard Manley Hopkins comprehends a bluebell when, having noticed its intrinsic beauties, he adds, "I know the beauty of Our Lord by it." And here is an eight-line poem of her own, in which she comprehends the full sweetness of water.

We thirst at first—'tis Nature's Act—
And later—when we die—
A little Water supplicate—
Of fingers going by—

It intimates the finer want—
Whose adequate supply
Is that Great Water in the West—
Termed Immortality—(726)

Emily Dickinson elected the economy of desire, and called her privation good, rendering it positive by renunciation. And so she came to live in a huge world of delectable distances. Far-off words like "Brazil" or "Circassian" appear continually in her poems as symbols of things distanced by loss or renunciation, yet infinitely prized anad yearned-for. So identified in her mind are distance and delight that, when ravished by the sight of a hummingbird in her garden, she calls it "the mail from Tunis." And not only are the objects of her desire distant; they are also very often moving away, their sweetness increasing in proportion to their remoteness. "To disappear enhances," one of the poems begins, and another closes with these lines:

The Mountain—at a given distance—
In Amber—lies—
Approached—the Amber flits—a little—
And That's—the Skies—(572)

To the eye of desire, all things are seen in a profound perspective, either moving or gesturing toward the vanishing point. Or to use a figure which may be closer to Miss Dickinson's thought, to the eye of desire the world is a centrifuge, in which all things are straining or flying toward the occult circumference. In some such way, Emily Dickinson conceived her world, and it was in a spatial metaphor that she gave her personal definition of Heaven. "Heaven," she said, "is what I cannot reach."

At times it seems that there is nothing in her world but her own soul, with its attendant abstractions, and, at a vast remove, the inscrutable Heaven. On most of what might intervene she has closed the valves of her attention, and what mortal objects she does acknowledge are riddled by desire to the point of transparency. Here is a sentence from her correspondence: "Enough is of so vast a sweetness, I suppose it never occurs, only pathetic counterfeits." The writer of that sentence could not invest her longings in any finite object. Again she wrote, "Emblem is immeasurable—that is why it is better than fulfilment, which can be drained." For such sensibility, it was natural and necessary that things be touched with infinity. Therefore her nature poetry, when most serious, does not play descriptively with birds or flowers but presents us repeatedly with dawn, noon, and sunset, those grand ceremonial moments of the day which argue the splendor of Paradise. Or it shows us the ordinary landscape transformed by the electric brilliance of a storm; or it shows us the fields succumbing to the annual mystery of death. In her love-poems, Emily Dickinson was at first covetous of the beloved himself; indeed, she could be idolatrous, going so far as to say that his face, should she see it again in Heaven, would eclipse the face of Jesus. But in what I take to be her later work the beloved's lineaments, which were never very distinct, vanish entirely; he becomes pure emblem, a symbol of remote spiritual joy, and so is all but absorbed into the idea of Heaven. The lost beloved is, as one poem declares, "infinite when gone," and in such lines as the following we are aware of him mainly as an instrument in the poet's commerce with the beyond.

> Of all the Souls that stand create—
> I have elected—One—
> When Sense from Spirit—files away—
> And Subterfuge—is done—
> When that which is—and that which was—
> Apart—intrinsic—stand—
> And this brief Tragedy of Flesh—
> Is shifted—like a Sand—
> When Figures show their royal Front—
> And Mists—are carved away,
> Behold the Atom—I preferred—
> To all the lists of Clay! (664)

In this extraordinary poem, the corporeal beloved is seen as if from another and immaterial existence, and in such perspective his earthly person is but an atom of clay. His risen spirit, we presume, is more imposing, but it is certainly not in focus. What the rapt and thudding lines of this poem portray is the poet's own magnificence of soul—her fidelity to desire, her confidence of Heaven, her contempt of the world. Like Cleopatra's final speeches, this poem is an irresistible demonstration of spiritual status, in which the supernatural is so royally demanded that skepticism is disarmed. A part of its effect derives, by the way, from the fact that the life to come is described in an ambiguous present tense, so that we half-suppose the speaker to be already in Heaven.

There were times when Emily Dickinson supposed this herself, and I want to close by making a partial guess at the logic of her claims to beatitude. It seems to me that she generally saw Heaven as a kind of infinitely remote bank, in which, she hoped, her untouched felicities were drawing interest. Parting, she said, was all she knew of it. Hence it is surprising to find her saying, in some poems, that Heaven has drawn near to her, and that in her soul's "superior instants" Eternity has disclosed to her "the colossal substance / Of immortality." Yet the contradiction can be understood, if we recall what sort of evidence was persuasive to Emily Dickinson.

"Too much of proof," she wrote, "affronts belief"; and she was little convinced either by doctrine or by theological reasoning. Her residual Calvinism was criticized and fortified by her study of her own soul in action, and from the phenomena of her soul she was capable of making the boldest inferences. That the sense of time is subject to the moods of the soul seemed to her a proof of the soul's eternity. Her insanity of grief for the dead, and her feeling of their continued presence, seemed to her arguments for the reunion of souls in Heaven. And when she found in herself infinite desires, "immortal longings," it seemed to her possible that such desires might somewhere be infinitely answered.

One psychic experience which she interpreted as beatitude was "glee," or as some would call it, euphoria. Now, a notable thing about glee or euphoria is its gratuitousness. It seems to come from nowhere, and it was this apparent sourcelessness of the emotion from which Emily Dickinson made her inference. "The 'happiness' without a cause," she said, "is the best happiness, for glee intuitive and lasting is the gift of God." Having foregone all earthly causes of happiness, she could only explain her glee, when it came, as a divine gift—a compensation in joy for what she had renounced in satisfaction, and foretaste of the mood of Heaven. The experience of glee, as she records it, is boundless: all distances collapse, and the soul expands to the very circumference of things. Here is how she put it in one of her letters: "Abroad is close tonight and I have but to lift my hands to touch the 'Hights of Abraham.'" And one of her gleeful poems begins,

> 'Tis little—I could care for Pearls—
> Who own the ample sea—

How often she felt that way we cannot know, and it hardly matters. As Robert Frost has pointed out, happiness can make up in height for what it lacks in length; and the important thing for us, as for her, is that she constructed the experience as a divine gift. So also she thought of the power to write poetry, a power which, as we know, came to her often; and poetry must have been the chief source of her sense of blessedness. The poetic impulses which visited her seemed "bulletins from Immortality," and by their means she converted all her losses into gains, and all the pains of her life to that clarity and repose which were to her the qualities of Heaven. So superior did she feel, as a poet, to earthly circumstance, and so strong was her faith in words, that she more than once presumed to view this life from the vantage of the grave.

In a manner of speaking, she *was* dead. And yet her poetry, with its articulate faithfulness to inner and outer truth, its insistence on maximum consciousness, is not an avoidance of life but an eccentric mastery of it. Let

me close by reading you a last poem, in which she conveys both the extent of
her repudiation and the extent of her happiness.

> The Missing All, prevented Me
> From missing minor Things.
> If nothing larger than a World's
> Departure from a Hinge
> Or Sun's extinction, be observed
> 'Twas not so large that I
> Could lift my Forehead from my work
> For Curiosity. (985)

DOUGLAS ANDERSON

Presence and Place in Emily Dickinson's Poetry

Departed – to the Judgment –
A Mighty Afternoon –
Great Clouds – like Ushers – leaning –
Creation – looking on –

The Flesh – Surrendered – Cancelled –
The Bodiless – begun
Two Worlds – like Audiences – disperse –
And leave the Soul – alone

—Emily Dickinson

As more than one reader has observed, Emily Dickinson's poetry reaches its maturity almost immediately. Beginning with the verse valentine of 1850 (P–1), she is in full possession of the technical and thematic powers that distinguish her finest lyrics.[1] In particular, Dickinson is ready at the outset of her creative life to give memorable expression to what E. M. W. Tillyard has called the conflicting claims of two worlds—claims that will fully occupy her attention through almost forty years of writing. Certainly her fondness for contrasting the earthly with the heavenly, the artificial with the natural, is clear to the most casual reader. In some things, even this lover of indirection is direct: "I taste a liquor never brewed– / From

The New England Quarterly, Vol. 57, No. 2. (June, 1984): pp. 205–224. *The New England Quarterly* is currently published by The New England Quarterly, Inc.

Tankards scooped in Pearl–"; "Some keep the Sabbath going to Church– /
I keep it, staying at Home–";

> The Pedigree of Honey
> Does not concern the Bee–
> A Clover, any time, to him,
> Is Aristocracy–

Lines like these do not cry out for commentary. Their exuberance and icon-
oclasm are delightful in part because they are reassuringly familiar assertions of the availability of a higher life, in comparison with which ordinary
social existence seems trivial.

Dickinson's poetic power derives in large measure from the unfamiliar range she gives to this familiar duality, a range achieved by providing
the two contrasting poles—transcendent life and circumstantial, daily existence—with new names and new locations in human experience. Solitude
was in Dickinson's own life increasingly the precondition for this exploration
of transcendence, though the extent of her personal withdrawal from society
is usually exaggerated. The reason she sought isolation was not because she
found it peaceful, or even safe, but because she found it "brimfull."[2] This singular experience of amplitude Dickinson came to embody in her poetry as
"presence," a term the full meaning of which—along with that of its corollar-
ies—most clearly emerges from the poems themselves.

The short prose poem addressed to her brother Austin, "There is another
sky," is a good early example of how Dickinson was prepared to bring her personal idiom to bear upon the poetic perception of two worlds that had been
commonplace in America since Anne Bradstreet's beautifully conventional
"Verses on the Burning of Our House." In the letter that accompanies the
poem, Dickinson has been trying, half in fun and half seriously, to lure her
brother back to Amherst from the harsh environs of Boston, where he had
gone to study law. In Johnson's edition, her poetic "sentence" takes the form
of these lines:

> There is another sky,
> Ever serene and fair,
> And there is another sunshine,
> Though it be darkness there;
> Never mind faded forests, Austin,
> Never mind silent fields–
>
> *Here* is a little forest,
> Whose leaf is ever green;

Here is a brighter garden,
Where not a frost has been;
In its unfading flowers
I hear the bright bee hum;
Prithee, my brother,
Into *my* garden come!

[P–2]

The strategy of consolation is roughly the same as that Bradstreet employed in 1666: a permanent world waits to comfort us for the losses we experience in the present, painfully mutable one. Such a reduction to strategy, of course, overlooks the chief purpose of Bradstreet's poem, which is, I think, to dramatize not the desirability but the difficulty of placing confidence in the permanent "house on high erect" that cannot burn. Bradstreet's imagination clings in loving detail to the objects and places she lost when her home was consumed. At heart, she is unable to give up the mutable world—an inability that Emily Dickinson would understand—and this nostalgic pull gives Bradstreet's lines their poignancy.

Dickinson's poem is far more radically committed to the mutable world than is Bradstreet's, or so it may seem at first. The consolation she offers Austin for the faded forests and silent fields of autumn is not a vision of perpetual spring "on high" but a personal garden, free from frost, unfading, and distinctly hers, not heaven's. Dickinson has deliberately (and deviously) crafted the poem to lead us to anticipate the more conventional, heavenly consolation. The first four lines with their emphasis on the permanence of "another" sky and "another" sunshine—Dickinson underscored both "anothers" in the version of the poem she mailed to Austin—clearly invite us to expect the sort of pious message characteristic of contemporary hymns: there is another changeless world ... etc. In customary Dickinson fashion, the lines even comprise a reasonably regular, hymnlike quatrain and bear a more or less familial resemblance to the popular verses from Isaac Watts that Herman Melville chose to have Captain Bildad sing as he piloted the *Pequod* out of Nantucket harbor:

There is a land of pure delight,
    Where saints immortal reign;
Infinite day excludes the night,
    And pleasures banish pain.

There everlasting spring abides,
    And never / with'ring flowers:
Death, like a narrow sea, divides
    This heavenly land from ours.

Sweet fields, beyond the swelling flood,
  Stand dress'd in living green;
So to the Jews old Canaan stood,
  While Jordan roll'd between.[3]

Despite its pious associations, however, anyone giving Dickinson's poem even a cursory reading might be a bit puzzled by the "there" at the end of the fourth line (the "darkness," after all, ought to be "here") and still more unsettled by the emphatic "here" at the beginning of the seventh line, precisely where in a good hymn one would expect to be envisioning the eternal "there." The changeless climate that Dickinson in fact has in mind is heterodoxically convenient—*my* garden—rather than a remote region of pure delight, the attainment of which is contingent upon grace, good works, or prayer. Her world of transcendent consolation is wonderfully at hand, complete with homely bee; no narrow sea of death, no savior, and no apocalypse required.

Dickinson may, of course, only have been indulging in a little private humor about the herbarium of which she was so fond and which could certainly be described, somewhat impishly, as frost / free. I think it likely that she was doing just that, but she also skillfully set her joke in a context that calls attention to the closeness she felt for Austin—they were able to share a bit of wicked humor—and to the profound importance she placed in her life on family warmth. The consolatory vision Dickinson offers is rooted in human affections every bit as stable and permanent (the poem argues) as heavenly refuges.

Compared to Bradstreet's more straightforward piety, Dickinson's poem is, in some sense, worldly, but Dickinson has divided experience just as decisively as did Bradstreet or Watts into the mutable and the immutable, the inessential and the deeply significant. More important, she has modified the spiritual geography that Watts and Bradstreet both transmit unmodified from their religious contexts. The critical difference is presence. Dickinson's unfaded forest may be "little," her garden merely "brighter" rather than full of infinite day, but her landscape of promise is *here,* as close as a bee is when we can hear the hum. This sense of the intimate proximity of transcendent experience reappears again and again in dozens of disguises in Dickinson's poetry, sometimes as a subject of celebration, sometimes as a source of pain, but always central to the experience of the poem. It seems useful to me to refer to this proximity as "presence" because Dickinson herself often did in contexts that help illuminate her meaning.

The most direct of these references immediately links the idea of "presence" with those of "place" and "circumference."

At Half past Three, a single Bird
Unto a silent Sky

Propounded but a single term
Of cautious melody.

At Half past Four, Experiment
Had subjugated test
And lo, Her silver Principle
Supplanted all the rest.

At Half past Seven, Element
Nor Implement, be seen—
And Place was where the Presence was
Circumference between.

                                        [P–1084]

Like much of Dickinson's poetry, these lines allow for a certain latitude of interpretation, but their central thrust is clear. For an unusually specific period of time, the neutrality of space and "silent Sky" is transformed by the song of a bird. "Presence" is the word Dickinson gives to this musical interlude. Its opposite condition—the silence that precedes and follows—is not (as common sense might suggest) "absence" but "place," not a condition of emptiness but a setting into which the bird's song has already once introduced itself and where it may yet again at any time.

"Place" is Dickinson's reservoir of the possibilities that "absence" too completely excludes. In many respects this invisible bird is a good example of one of the countless visitors that David Porter finds throughout Dickinson's poetry and that initiate, in Porter's view, the experience of "aftermath" that pervades it. By half past seven the bird certainly seems to be gone—though Dickinson is careful only to tell us that it cannot "be seen"—and the last stanza seems clearly to evoke the experience of "living after things happen," which Porter characterizes as the crucial experience in Dickinson's life and art.[4] The problem with applying the term "aftermath" to a poem like "At Half past Three, a single Bird," however, is that it carries with it the assumption that something is irrevocably finished. Not only does the use of "place" seem to hold that sense of "finish" at bay, but Dickinson's exultant "circumference" in the last line suggests a special amplitude in the silence that follows the song. Presence yields to Place, but the outcome of the exchange is fullness rather than deprivation, and Dickinson characterizes that fullness with the same word she used in a well-known letter to Thomas Wentworth Higginson describing her sense of poetic purpose and accomplishment: "My Business is Circumference."

In fact, the whole sequence of song and silence may be closely related to the exhilaration of successful writing. There is no reason why the singing bird might not be Dickinson herself, "implement" in hand, beginning a poem rather cautiously in mid-afternoon, progressing with a growing sense of power and mastery, and finishing some hours later. I am privately suspicious of readers who find Dickinson repeatedly writing poems about "poems" and "poetry," but the possibility that she is doing so here is worth raising only because it helps us recognize the feeling of complete possession with which these lines close. The music of the bird provides one sort of luminous "presence" for the speaker, but the sheer joy of listening—of a sensibility that is immediate, active, resolutely "present"—is the poem's genuine subject. The units of time (half past three, half past four) remind us of the flight of the mutable world at the same time that the sense of circumference contains that flight—in a poem, in the unique case of Emily Dickinson, but more generally in the alert and susceptible human consciousness. Moreover, Dickinson's emphasis on the clock magnifies the suddenness with which the last line bursts upon us. She prepares the reader, in some sense, for failure; the hours seem relentless and irreversible in their movement. In the space of a line, however, that movement folds itself into a completed circle, without beginning or end, without the disturbing segmentation that divides and numbers the day. The transformation is refreshingly immediate. "Circumference" has much of the force of Dickinson's emphatic *"here"* in "There is another sky."

In a poem that Thomas Johnson dates three years earlier than this one, Dickinson had described the singing of birds at dawn in much the same way that she treats the single song in "At Half past Three, a single Bird." A specific interval of time again measures the experience. The birds begin their "Music numerous as space" at four o'clock and quit just as the sun fully asserts itself at six. Instead of the terms "presence" and "place," Dickinson emphasizes the sense of closeness the music inspires—"neighboring as noon"—and the surprising suddenness with which it concludes.

> The Birds begun at Four o'clock–
> Their period for Dawn–
> A Music numerous as space–
> But neighboring as Noon–
>
> I could not count their Force–
> Their Voices did expend
> As Brook by Brook bestows itself
> To multiply the Pond.
>
> Their Witnesses were not–
> Except occasional man–

In homely industry arrayed–
To overtake the Morn–

Nor was it for applause–
That I could ascertain–
But independent Exstasy
Of Deity and Men–

By Six, the Flood had done–
No Tumult there had been
Of Dressing, or Departure–
And yet the Band was gone–

The Sun engrossed the East–
The Day controlled the World–
The Miracle that introduced
Forgotten, as fulfilled.

[P–783]

As with the solitary singer earlier, this morning chorus is transient; it passes unnoticed except by the occasional alert listener and ends with disconcerting, unceremonious swiftness. But each experience leaves its residue of fulfillment. In "The Birds begun at Four o'clock" Dickinson augments the special nature of the moment with the religious associations of "Flood" and "Miracle," but like the little garden she offers Austin, this musical gift is free of the weight of sacred institutions: it is "independent Exstasy / Of Deity and Men–." The more manipulative powers of "Sun" and "Day" work on a vast scale over great distances. The "Force" exerted by the birds, on the other hand, is intimate and "homely." What distinguishes the miraculous dawn is not any special sanctity but common availability—its closeness.

It should be clear even from this brief look at a few poems that Dickinson's understanding and use of the idea of "presence" as a synecdoche for transcendent experience can be unusually subtle. In the message to Austin, the impersonal reassurances of the first lines yield first to a surprisingly accessible forest refuge and then, abruptly, to the poet's own person in an invitation that seems strikingly intimate. The progression is from the public cadences of a hymn to warm, human privacy. In "At Half past Three, a single Bird," the movement, rising to the fulfillment of "silver Principle" before lapsing into the suspenseful mystery of Place and the final satisfactions of Circumference, is a bit more complex. Dickinson overcomes the obstacles of vacancy and distance by means of a direct application of personal charm in the first instance and by means of an attentive and appreciative ear in the second. Both strategies replace a deadening vacuity with vivid presence. Elsewhere she is still more explicit about the restorative virtues of this kind of circumferential awareness.

> Conscious am I in my Chamber,
> Of a shapeless friend—
> He doth not attest by Posture—
> Nor Confirm—by Word—
>
> Neither Place—need I present Him—
> Fitter Courtesy
> Hospitable intuition
> Of His Company—
>
> Presence—is His furthest license—
> Neither He to Me
> Nor Myself to Him—by Accent—
> Forfeit Probity—
>
> Weariness of Him, were quainter
> Than Monotony
> Knew a Particle—of Space's
> Vast Society—
>
> Neither if He visit Other—
> Do He dwell—or Nay—know I—
> But Instinct esteem Him
> Immortality—

[P–679]

Dickinson has no obstacles to overcome here, for the shapeless friend is neither absent like Austin nor transient like the song of a bird. On the other hand, neither does "He" offer any physical assurances of his existence beyond a certain, sociable intuition. A sense of simple "Presence" absorbs the speaker here—a presence without open communion, without weariness, without any guarantees of constancy, but with no sense of departure. Negatives dominate the poem but bring with them no accompanying puzzlement or frustration. That, indeed, appears to be Dickinson's point: the instinct of immortality is peace without knowledge.

Reducing the lines to such a religious homily, however, deprives them of their air of ghostly romance. Until the final stanza—and practically until the poem's final word—the relationship between the poet and her visitor seems anything but momentous. A deep, domestic peace fills them, the sort of word-less companionability of very old, very contented (and perhaps imaginary) married couples. Dickinson seems to whisper to us of her complete connubial satisfaction, when suddenly we find we have been lured to the hearthside with an abstraction. The poem asserts the speaker's full intimacy with "Immortal-ity," at least for the moment, and in the process draws the reader along, again momentarily, into the same intimate circle. "Presence" in these lines is both a metaphor and strategy.

Equally "strategic," perhaps, but a far more delicate and appealing poem is the short piece in which the speaker explains why she adopts the gentle ec-centricity of saying "Goodnight" even at daytime partings. Dickinson builds these lines around a series of three verbal disjunctions, each of which is de-signed to reduce the distance between people, to keep them more completely in one another's company: "goodnight" rather than "goodbye," "presence" as an equally eccentric opposite to "parting," and finally simply a condition of light rather than the name of "morn."

> Some say goodnight–at night–
> I say goodnight by day–
> Goodbye–the Going utter me–
> Goodnight, I still reply–
>
> For parting, that is night,
> And presence, simply dawn–
> Itself, the purple on the height
> Denominated morn.
>
> [P–1739]

In the first stanza, the speaker's stubbornness is both amusing and pa-tiently tender. The "Going" "utter" their fateful syllables with all the sense of self-conscious ceremony that that verb implies, and "Goodbye," spoken with such gravity, is full of associations of great finality, time, and distance. "Good-night," by contrast, is much more of a household word; the vision of separa-tion it evokes is comfortably brief, like a night's sleep, rather than protracted and ceremonial. Moreover, the quiet persistence with which the speaker sticks to this word is openly solicitous. "Goodnight" holds the "Going" closer and resists the formality of departure.

The explanation for the speaker's peculiarity of speech is the beauty of presence. The simple opposition of night and day in the first stanza leads us to expect an equally simple opposite for "parting" at the beginning of the second—"returning," perhaps, or "coming," to keep the meter. Dickin-son, however, leaps immediately from the sense of departure in "parting" not to the anticipatory joy of returning but to a full and stable "presence"—a presence as direct as simple experience is in comparison with the mediated experience of words, as direct as "purple on the height" is in comparison with "morn." The formal poise of "Goodbye," which met with such polite resistance in the first stanza, meets with a more resolute opposition in the second. Dickinson declines balanced syntax and then "denomination" itself as instruments of distance and obstacles to unmediated intimacy. Here too, as in a number of the other poems involving presence, an element of suddenness captured in carefully paced and structured lines reproduces, in the reading, the sense of vivid immediacy upon which Dickinson placed such stress. The eccentricities of speech that shape the poem are engaged, once again, in the sort of affectionate struggle with mutability that we began by noticing in the message to Austin.

The struggle with mutability is by no means always affectionate in Dickinson, nor is the sense of presence always redemptive in the ways that it clearly is in "Some say goodnight—at night" or "Conscious am I in my Chamber." "Place" alone is an unstable state that can yield as easily to a sense of isolation as to the exhilaration of circumference. Indeed, in many of Dickinson's finest poems "presence" itself takes the form of such an acute degree of loneliness and loss that it too erases time, though not in the triumphant way that circumference is able to contain the evanescent beauty of a bird's song. In the short poem "Pain—has an Element of Blank," the past and the future disappear into an infinite sensation of suffering, which is a perpetual "presence," or an inescapable "presentness." The eight lines begin and end with the word "pain," as if Dickinson meant us to see a cruel parody of "circumference" in the endless imprisoning circle the poem actually makes.

> Pain—has an Element of Blank—
> It cannot recollect
> When it begun—or if there were
> A time when it was not—
>
> It has no Future—but itself—
> Its Infinite contain
> Its Past—enlightened to perceive
> New Periods—of Pain.

[P–650]

The extremity of suffering is, of course, a frequent subject of Dickinson's, but the remarkable quality of her treatment of it is the relentless closeness she insists upon. Perhaps the most memorable of all such poems begins with the most intense, face-to-face inspection—"I like a look of Agony"

(P–241)–and in yet another exploration of this apparently most lonely of human states, Dickinson emphasized not the supreme isolation of pain but its "nearness to Tremendousness" (P–963). "Departed—to the Judgment" (P–524), explicitly addressing the subject of mutable and immutable worlds, portrays one individual's surrender of the flesh and assumption of spirit in the company of two vast audiences that represent all mutable creation and the immutable heavens. At the end of the transformation—which, by Dickinson's personal standards, ought to be glorious and an occasion for joy—the great audiences simply dissolve, leaving an isolated "Soul—alone," without clear membership in either of the cosmic communities. The cryptic "alone" may signify "only" and refer to the soul's liberation from the body, or it may indeed represent "alone" in the more terrifying sense of complete loneliness. The poem's sudden descent from crowded spectacle to single presence leaves no decisive clue to its meaning; what begins in apparent triumph ends in an uncertainty all the more profound given the religious intensity with which Dickinson has approached it.

An equally swift descent into suffering "presence" occurs in "I shall know why–when Time is over" (P–193). This poem opens with much the same kind of naive consolation that Dickinson employed in the hymnlike sections of "There is another sky"; the speaker looks forward with some complacency to the full and satisfactory explanation of human anguish that Christ will offer after the Last Judgment. The complacent tone, however, is no sooner established than shattered by an outcry that forces its way twice through the formulaic, distant pieties.

> I shall know why when Time is over—
> And I have ceased to wonder why
> Christ will explain each separate anguish
> In the fair schoolroom of the sky—
>
> He will tell me what "Peter" promised—
> And I–for wonder at his woe—
> I shall forget the drop of Anguish
> That scalds me now–that scalds me now!
>
> [P–193]

The power of poems like these derives in large measure from their ability to capture a sense of the instant, to insist on the subject's full presence even at moments when such presence is scarcely bearable. Mutability—deeply personal loss—is the unspoken background of all of these poems, but their force is a direct result of the artistic restraint of time. Just such a restraint has some bearing on many of the well-known (and often analyzed) poems about death, or more precisely about the act of dying: "Because I could not stop for Death" (P–712), "I heard a Fly buzz–when I died" (P–465), "I felt a Funeral, in my Brain" (P–280).[5] In each of these three pieces, Dickinson establishes some sort of plot—a funeral service and procession, a carriage journey, the formal deathbed rituals of farewell and bequest—which creates in the reader a subtle sense of expectation, the anticipation of closure. We are waiting for Dickinson's carriage to arrive or half expect the King himself to give some evidence of his triumphant presence, but in each case the climax is curiously truncated. The plots all stop short or wander from their course, hinting at continuations in which we do not participate or which we cannot fully grasp. Readers remain in very much the same situation as that in which Dickinson's speakers often find themselves: we have received a miraculous visitor (in this case from just beyond the instant of death) who just as miraculously abandons us in a state of acute susceptibility. None of these poems can be said precisely to end, since they perpetually maintain themselves at the instant and in the condition in which they stopped. We are, in a way, between breaths, much as we were in "At Half past Three, a single Bird" between the last and the next-to-last lines before place gave way to the stable closure of circumference.

Not only the cataclysms of death or sorrow have the capacity to maintain us in presence. Dickinson sent a beautiful quatrain to Mrs. Josiah Holland, in celebration of her daughter's wedding, that turns the language of the marriage ceremony into a delightful chronological joke.

> The Clock strikes one that just struck two–
> Some schism in the Sum–
> A Vagabond from Genesis
> Has wrecked the Pendulum–
>
> > [P–1569]

That the poem is also an incomparably graceful reminder of Dickinson's faith in the timelessness of human love scarcely needs to be said. In the message to Austin with which we began, Dickinson herself was the vagabond from Genesis who wrecked the pendulum and called a halt to seasons. In one of the first of the more than one hundred poems she sent to Thomas Wentworth Higginson, perhaps in gratitude for his willingness to enter into correspondence with her, Dickinson captures through the simplest of technical means the outburst of joy at the instant a very precious gift is recognized and received.

> As if I asked a common Alms,
> And in my wondering hand
> A Stranger pressed a Kingdom,

And I, bewildered, stand–
As if I asked the Orient
Had it for me a Morn–
And it should lift its purple Dikes,
And shatter me with Dawn!

[P–323]

Both of these exultant poems are still, vaguely, cataclysmic: time is left in
wreckage; the impact of dawn is shattering. Presence, in its very unmediated
intensity, can be destructive. The mysterious bird songs that we considered
earlier have a force that subjugates as it delights and that leaves us, abruptly,
in a state not far removed from ignorance, though impossibly remote from
emptiness.

Dickinson's finest poems of presence invariably seem to incorporate an
element of incomplete human participation. The observing consciousness
tantalizingly (or perhaps wisely) remains "the term between," contemplating
miracle before, miracle behind, "And Maelstrom / in the Sky" (P–721). This
peculiar status, however, is anything but neutrality.

Before I got my eye put out
I liked as well to see–
As other Creatures, that have Eyes
And know no other way–

But were it told to me–Today–
That I might have the sky
For mine–I tell you that my Heart
Would split, for size of me–

The Meadows –mine–
The Mountains –mine–
All Forests–Stintless Stars–
As much of Noon as I could take
Between my finite eyes–

The Motions of the Dipping Birds–
The Morning's Amber Road–
For mine–to look at when I liked–
The News would strike me dead–

So safer–guess–with just my soul
Upon the Window pane–

Where other Creatures put their eyes—
Incautious—of the Sun—

[P–327]

The condition of perception that Dickinson describes here is both something less and something more than ordinary human power. The speaker is apparently sightless, not just reduced to a single eye, and as a result utterly deprived of visual experience. But the speaker has learned to see another way, and nature remains so vividly (if mentally) present that a fuller exposure seems frightening. Indeed the sightless speaker's vulnerability to "sight" is greater than that of "other Creatures" because less intervenes between herself and the brilliance of noon. She exposes her soul directly where others expose only their eyes, but the power of vision is ecstatically alive in the images of stintless stars, the motion of birds, the morning's amber road—which present themselves to us not nostalgically but with an immediacy that is to be approached only warily. To maintain its poise between the remembered fact and the present miracle of memory is the poem's chief objective.

An equally ambiguous present miracle is recorded in the poem that Thomas Johnson places immediately after, "A Bird came down the Walk" (P–328). The dangers as well as the beauty represented by nature at large in "Before I got my eye put out" are here concentrated in a single bird that exhibits a complex mix of qualities: ferocity, fastidiousness, courtesy, fear, and grace.

A Bird came down the Walk—
He did not know I saw—
He bit an Angleworm in halves
And ate the fellow, raw,

And then he drank a Dew
From a convenient Grass—
And then hopped sidewise to the Wall
To let a Beetle pass—

He glanced with rapid eyes
That hurried all around—
They looked like frightened Beads, I thought—
He stirred his Velvet Head

Like one in danger, Cautious,
I offered him a Crumb
And he unrolled his feathers
And rowed him softer home—

Than Oars divide the Ocean,
Too silver for a seam—
Or Butterflies, off Banks of Noon
Leap, plashless as they swim.

[P–328]

The human observer approaches with all the caution of the sightless soul in "Before I got my eye put out," but the bird makes a marvelous departure that Dickinson renders in a series of oddly incompatible, and inappropriate, but wholly engrossing motions: unrolling, rowing, dividing, leaping, swimming. This is the flight of a bird seen, in some respects, with the soul, rather than finite eyes, upon the windowpane. Presence is elusive and, in a small way, dangerous here—just as it is invisible and dangerous to its blind "observer" earlier—but it is also deeply captivating. Though the bird leaves, the poem itself never runs the risk of lapsing into the experience of aftermath or even the temporary hiatus of place. The feeling of circumference, like the magic circle that captures the precious "Principle" of "At Half past Three, a single Bird," is direct and unsegmented: "Too silver for a seam."

In both of these poems, and in many of those we have looked at here, transcendent presence offers itself directly to the human consciousness, its manifestations for the most part spectacularly clear. Dickinson could work without such clarity, for she found even in ignorance that is nearly total some evidence of forces waiting quietly for a moment of fuller illumination. In "Four Trees—upon a solitary Acre" (P–742) her subject seems, merely, place, but here too is a nearness to tremendousness that the trees themselves effortlessly "maintain" in a kind of modest readiness. The deeds and plans of "General Nature" seem in one respect hopelessly out of reach; in another respect, they are our nearest neighbors.

Four Trees—upon a solitary Acre—
Without Design
Or Order, or Apparent Action—
Maintain—

The Sun—upon a Morning meets them—
The Wind—
No nearer Neighbor—have they—
But God—

The Acre gives them—Place—
They—Him—Attention of Passer by—

Of Shadow, or of Squirrel, haply–
Or Boy–

What Deed is Theirs unto the General Nature–
What Plan
They severally–retard—or further–
Unknown–

One particularly regrettable assumption that proceeds from the Dickinson myth is that her work possesses some grand unity, that all the poems are but episodes of one long poem. Most readers, tempted perhaps by the distinctive character of form and language throughout the Dickinson canon, have felt the effects of this assumption at one time or another. A Dickinson lyric is unmistakable and unlikely to be confused with the work of any other poet. This singleness of voice seems to hint at an equally singleminded vision, but so far no reader to my knowledge has been equal to the synoptic feat of uncovering it. In many respects, then, the best way of approaching the collected poems is to adopt a version of Dickinson's own youthful enthusiasm for the considerable resources of her family library. She recalled for Thomas Wentworth Higginson the childish wonder with which she discovered reading: "This then is a book! And there are more of them!"[6]

One of the chief rewards of reading Dickinson is that there is always more of her. The idea of "presence" in Dickinson's poetry does not diminish that sense of plenitude; no sooner do we apply it than we begin to be aware of its limitations and to discover striking exceptions among the poems themselves. Presence, to some extent, is no more than one of the generic givens of a lyric poem, as Sandra Gilbert and Susan Gubar have recently reminded us: "The novelist in a sense says 'they': she works in a third-person form even when constructing a first-person narrative. But the poet, even when writing in the third person, says 'I.'"[7] For Emily Dickinson, however, the act of saying "I" is not just an inescapable consequence of picking up her pen. It is part of the experience of intimacy that gives her solitude its fullness.

Notes

1. Citations to the poems refer to the numbering in *The Poems of Emily Dickinson*, ed. Thomas Johnson, 3 vols. (Cambridge: Harvard University Press, 1955).

2. From a letter to her brother Austin, quoted by Richard Sewall, in *The Life of Emily Dickinson* (New York: Farrar, Straus, & Giroux, 1974): p. 431.

3. From *The Psalms, Hymns, and Spiritual Songs of the Reverend Isaac Watts*, ed. Samuel M. Worcester (Boston, 1838): p. 413. Dickinson quoted from this hymn directly in P–112 (see *Poems*, 1:83). See also David Porter, *The Art of Emily Dickinson's Early Poetry* (Cambridge: Harvard University Press, 1966): pp. 55–74.

4. David Porter, "The Crucial Experience in Emily Dickinson's Poetry," *ESQ* 20 (Fourth Quarter, 1974): pp. 280–90.

5. "I felt a Funeral, in my Brain" (P–280) is not necessarily about dying but about the breaking of a "Plank in Reason." For the purposes of the point I am trying to make, this difference is less important than the poem's overall similarity to the other two poems.

6. See Sewall, *Life of Dickinson*, p. 566.

7. Sandra Gilbert and Susan Gubar, *The Madwoman in the Attic* (New Haven: Yale University Press, 1979): p. 548.

TIMOTHY MORRIS

The Development of Dickinson's Style

It has become a given of Dickinson criticism that the poet's style never changed. A recent study begins: "As more than one critic has observed, Emily Dickinson's poetry reaches its maturity almost immediately. Beginning with the verse valentine of 1850 (P–1), she is in full possession of the technical and thematic powers that distinguish her finest lyrics."[1] Most critics in the last twenty years have accepted this view; several of the most distinguished writers on Dickinson agree that her style was unchanging, including Barbara Antonina Clarke Mossberg, David Porter, and Robert Weisbuch.[2] The thesis that Dickinson's style never developed owes a great deal to Charles R. Anderson. In 1960 Anderson wrote: "The chronological arrangement of the new edition [Thomas H. Johnson's 1955 variorum] has been useful in minor ways, but not for selecting or ordering the poems. There are no marked periods in her career, no significant curve of development in her artistic powers, such as might furnish the central plan for a book on Milton or Yeats."[3] Hence, Anderson arranged his readings by theme, an approach that has been followed by many of Dickinson's interpreters.

The thematic reading of Dickinson's poetry has produced a great deal of valuable and provocative criticism; it is not my purpose to argue with the fine readings of Mossberg and Weisbuch, or to undermine the method that led

American Literature, Vol. 60, No. 1. (March 1988): pp. 26–41. Copyright © 1988 by the Duke University Press.

to those readings. But the development of Dickinson's style deserves more critical attention.

By measuring Dickinson's patterns of rhyme and enjambment, we can see that these formal contours of her verse changed over time, especially from 1858 to 1865. As Dickinson refined her verse technique, her approach to the subjects of her poems changed as well. But her poetry did not develop in the ways we are accustomed to see with poets whose work is published during their lifetimes and subjected to criticism and editorial advice.

Dickinson's poetic development consists mainly of two achievements that mark her work as unique and have established her as a great and difficult poet. First, she revised the hymn quatrain and made of it a more purely literary genre than it had ever been before. By "literary genre" I mean one where the work is intended to exist on the page alone and to be read silently. Dickinson's quatrain poems go even farther beyond the musical hymn of Isaac Watts than the literary ballad of Cowper, Coleridge and others goes beyond the sung ballad. Far from being constrained by her form or immured within the tradition of the hymn, she escaped that tradition completely, to the point where most of her poems no longer bear even a parodic or contrasting relationship to hymns.

Dickinson's second achievement is even more radical. In moving to her late manner she commented on her own texts, producing poems that were adaptations of earlier texts in her growing collection of manuscript fascicles. Having created a genre unique to her own work, she spent her career exploring and redefining that genre. Her reworkings of the subjects of her earlier poems show her concern with the interrelations between texts and with the effects of her own characteristic diction on her subjects. Her use of later poems to comment on earlier ones gives rise to those problems of interpretation that confront any reader of reworked material—except that here the poet is not adapting another's work but her own.

The most striking thing about Dickinson's work is that it is not directed outward. Although her letters teem with references to and talk about literature, there are hardly any uses in her poetry of the language of other poets. Even her few allusions to Shakespeare are mostly character names, except for "Mail from Tunis" in 1463, used for an impossibly long haul, as in *The Tempest*.[4] One of her poems, 960—"Lay this Laurel on the One"—is an adaptation of T. W. Higginson's "Decoration." There is one possible use of Emerson (214), one of Percy Shelley (1620). Her only use of the language of Elizabeth Barrett Browning is in 449, "I died for Beauty—"; and it is a commonplace equation of Beauty and Truth which obviously owes at least as much to Keats, or to dozens of other poets.[5] Criticism has traced powerful undercurrents of the influence of Dickinson's wide reading on her poetry, and of the implicit relation of her style to that of her precursors.[6] But in the language of her poems, Dickinson never appropriated the language of another poet and never used the characteristic diction of a school or movement.

The state of Dickinson's surviving manuscripts confirms this picture of her as an inward-directed artist. There are no prose jottings on the construction of poems, no notebooks on art. We have no idea what her philosophy of composition was. We know that she revised carefully, sometimes taking great pains to find the right word.[7] But she left no explicit clue to her creative process. Her fair copies, bound into fascicles, are a vast and enigmatic book that has evoked many competing interpretations. But that book is not externally a record of artistic experiment. Aside from changes in handwriting over the years, the fascicles are uniform in presentation. They are featureless aside from the texts of the poems and variant readings recorded, without comment, by the poet herself.

But of course this very featurelessness of the fascicles is silent testimony to Dickinson's concern with the status of her texts. Many of the fair copies contain text alone. But the fair copies that contain variant readings are problematic. Johnson considers these manuscripts to be poems in "the semifinal stage"; the variants, carefully written at the end of each poem and keyed to crosses over the words in the poem's text, seemed to him to be suggested changes.[8] This may be true; but it may just as well be true that Dickinson was preserving not future possibilities but stages in the composition of the poem, recording alternatives she had considered but rejected. Most semifinal drafts of a poet's work contain crossings-out and lists of alternatives; many of Dickinson's manuscripts are in this state. But the variants in the meticulously transcribed fair copies do not seem like intermediate draft alternatives but like part of the poet's attempt to preserve her own handwritten variorum edition. It is possible that the careful preservation of variants indicates great attention by Dickinson to versions of her poems and to the consequent refinements in diction that different versions entail.

The manuscript books offer a blank face in terms of the poet's own discussion of her poetics; but they do allow for the establishment of a chronology of Dickinson's poems from 1858 to 1865 (nearly all the fascicles are from these years). The chronology, in turn, can be used to show how Dickinson's use of rhyme and enjambment developed over time. The efforts of Johnson, Theodora Ward, and R. W. Franklin have established a sound, approximate dating of the fascicle poems.[9]

Table I presents this chronology. Only the years 1850–1865, the crucial ones for Dickinson's poetic development, are included.

Table I

Chronology of Dickinson's Poems

1850–54	1–5
1858	6–57, 323, 1729–1730
1859	58–151, 216
1860	152–215, 318, 324
1861	217–298, 317, 319, 322, 325, 330, 687, 1737
1862	299–316, 320–321, 326–329, 332–432, 434–608, 610–664, 678, 683, 688, 712–717, 759–770, 1053, 1072, 1076, 1181, 1710, 1712, 1725, 1727, 1739
1863	665–667, 679–682, 684–686, 689–711, 718–758, 771–807
1864	808–981, 1114
1865	433, 982–991, 993–1052, 1054–1066, 1070, 1073, 1177, 1540

The analysis of Dickinson's rhymes is made straightforward by the conventionality of her poems in terms of meter and rhyme-scheme. She did write a small number of poems in a "free-rhyming" verse that rhymes erratically, with no regular meter or rhyme-scheme, and I have excluded those poems from this analysis.[10] And of course some of her poems are fragmentary or in very rough drafts; these have also been excluded. But apart from these exceptions, all of her poems are in hymn stanzas and rhyme in one of the basic hymn rhyme-schemes: *aab ccb* or *xaxa*. Nearly all the places where rhyme would be expected in these poems have some type of rhyme; Dickinson wrote very little unrhymed or free verse (she approaches free verse only in 690 and in parts of 252, 253, 352, and 1720).

Eighty-eight percent of Dickinson's rhymes are of three phonetic types: exact, consonantal, and vowel rhymes.[11] Exact rhyme is the most common type, as in 67:

> Success is counted sweetest
> By those who ne'er *succeed*.
> To comprehend a nectar
> Requires sorest *need*. (Italics mine here
> and in the next two examples.)

Nearly as common is consonantal rhyme, where the final consonants, but not the preceding vowels, are identical:

One dignity delays for all—
One mitred After*noon*—
None can avoid this purple—
None evade this *Crown*! (98)

Dickinson also frequently uses vowel rhyme, where any vowel rhymes with any other:

I stepped from Plank to Plank
A slow and cautious *way*
The Stars about my Head I felt
About my Feet the *Sea*. (875)

Table 2

Dickinson's Rhymes by Year and Rhyme-Type

	Exact	Consonantal	Vowel
1850–54	80.4	10.7	—
1858	68.1	14.4	7.5
1859	57.7	19.1	10.0
1860	45.5	25.8	13.4
1861	40.0	34.6	13.1
1862	34.5	33.8	17.2
1863	30.5	36.1	18.8
1864	28.3	35.5	17.5
1865	29.9	36.5	16.8

(The percentages given are of all rhymes in a given sample, and exclude less common types of rhyme, so totals are less than 100%.).[12]

Table 2 shows the development of Dickinson's technique in terms of rhyme. For each year, the percentage of all rhymes is given for each of the three most common phonetic types. In her earliest surviving poems (1–5, from 1850–54) Dickinson uses mainly exact rhymes; the poems are Valentines, or bits of verse incorporated into letters, and are highly conventional in diction. By the time when she was first binding poems into fascicles, in 1858–59, she had developed a much less conventional rhyming technique. Unfortunately, we have no evidence about how she created these early fascicle poems; none of her manuscripts from the years 1855–57 survive. We see her now in the manuscripts, after four years of silence, as a poet who had broken with the conventional rhyming of her earliest verse.

After 1865, Dickinson wrote so little poetry that analysis of trends is not reliable. There are few fascicles from 1866 and after; most of the later poems survive in isolated copies and transcripts. Dickinson stopped her great out-pouring of poetry in 1866, and the technique she had developed through so many hundreds of poems shows no strong growth in any direction thereafter.

Even more than her rhyme, Dickinson's characteristic enjambment is probably the one formal element that makes her quatrains sound so distinctive. Hymn quatrains are always end-stopped. The hymns of Watts, though they employ inexact rhyme, are entirely unenjambed. In performance, it would be intolerable for a syntactic phrase to be broken at the end of one stanza and picked up at the beginning of the next after an instrumental passage or chorus. But the quatrains of purely literary poems that are meant to be read silently or recited in a speaking voice need not be end-stopped. And in Dickinson's hands, the quatrain became a form meant to be read silently, similar in diction to that of the unenjambed couplets of Keats (as in "Sleep and Poetry") or Browning (*Sordello* or "My Last Duchess"). With their frequent inexact rhyme and their true syntactic verse-paragraphs, Dickinson's quatrains are a new genre, one unique to her own poetry.

Table 3 shows how Dickinson's use of enjambment developed from her earliest verse until 1865. (The final quatrains of poems are not included, as it makes no sense to speak of them as being enjambed or not.)

Table 3

Dickinson's Enjambment

	percentage of enjambed quatrains
1850–54	5.6
1858	16.7
1859	14.6
1860	15.4
1861	20.4
1862	29.8
1863	27.1
1864	34.1
1865	36.7

Dickinson began by using conventional hymn-like endstopping. Her earliest poems are heavily end-stopped, and the first fascicle poems, in 1858–59, show only infrequent enjambment. But from 1860 to 1865, the amount of enjambment in her poetry grows steadily. By 1864, more than one-third of her quatrains are enjambed.

Dickinson used her later style, enjambed and using frequent inexact rhyme, to write adaptations of her earlier poems. The themes and subjects of these earlier poems reappear in the late style, but Dickinson adapts them by compressing or expanding the diction, changing the amount and nature of subordinate detail, and shifting—or often suppressing—key symbolic references.

Several readers have noticed compression in Dickinson's later poetry. George Frisbie Whicher discusses the condensation of the hummingbird poem "Within my Garden, rides a Bird" (500, dated 1862) into the famous "A Route of Evanescence" (1463, dated 1879).[13] Richard B. Sewall notes the impact of the boiling-down of the nine-stanza "I watched the Moon around the House" (629, dated 1862) into the two-stanza "The Moon upon her fluent Route" (1528, dated 1881).[14] The ultimate of this compressing process is what Gérard Genette calls *haïkaïsation*.[15] No matter how far haïkaïsation goes, the central referent of the original text (hummingbird, moon) remains present in the rewritten text. And so, the essential element of what Genette calls the "hypotext," the original version, is still present in the "hypertext," the revised version.

But Dickinson did not always condense; she often chose more complex ways of adapting her earlier work. Particularly problematic is the kind of hypertext produced by what Genette calls demotivation.[16] In this type of adaptation, the presence of the hypotext is absolutely necessary for the reading of the hypertext. There is no sense in which otiose material has been removed from the hypotext; or rather, the otiose and the essential are both removed, or essential material is replaced by new otiose material. In Flaubert's tale "Hérodias," Genette explains, the author retells the Biblical story. But he omits a vital part of the story, the crucial act of Hérodias that dooms John the Baptist. When adapting a Biblical story, Flaubert takes advantage of the fact that every reader knows the hypotext. But it is entirely possible for an author to practice demotivation of a text that is not well known, or that is unknown to every reader but herself; and this is what Dickinson does in reworking 72, "Glowing is her Bonnet" (about 1859) into 978, "It bloomed and dropt, a Single Noon—" (about 1864). Here is the earlier poem:

Glowing is her Bonnet,
Glowing is her Cheek,
Glowing is her Kirtle,
Yet she cannot speak.

Better as the Daisy
From the Summer hill
Vanish unrecorded
Save by tearful rill—

Save by loving sunrise
Looking for her face.

Save by feet unnumbered
Pausing at the place.

These quatrains are typical in form for an early Dickinson poem. They
rhyme exactly, and the only enjambment comes between the second and
third stanzas, at a break between paratactic phrases.

The first stanza establishes that someone is dead. It does so indirectly;
but the central referent is clear. The following two stanzas express a preference for the way flowers die. The diction of the poem is characteristically
Dickinson's, especially in its terse obliqueness; many of her early poems are
terse and telegraphic in a similar way.

This early poem is marked strongly by the absence of tension. The poem,
with its stock metrical phrases—"tearful rill," "loving sunrise"—and its conventional meter, rhyme, and end-stopping, is a metaphoric cliché. This is
true despite Dickinson's metonymic evasiveness, her reluctance to name the
central referents. And it is also clear that no amount of compression could
complicate the poem much. In fact, not much compression is possible, given
the poem's already small bounds.

In reworking the material of this poem, then, Dickinson elaborated
rather than compressed it. But as she elaborated the detail and the rhetorical
structure of the poem (by adding "I," in this case), and as she loosened the
prosody by means of inexact rhyme and enjambment, she also removed the
initial reference to a human death that motivates the consideration of the
flower. The result is the demotivated text of 978.

It bloomed and dropt, a Single Noon—
The Flower—distinct and Red—
I, passing, thought another Noon
Another in its stead

Will equal glow, and thought no More
But came another Day
To find the Species disappeared—
The Same Locality—

The Sun in place—no other fraud
On Nature's perfect Sum—
Had I but lingered Yesterday—
Was my retrieveless blame—

Much Flowers of this and further Zones
Have perished in my Hands

For seeking its Resemblance—
But unapproached it stands—

The single Flower of the Earth
That I, in passing by
Unconscious was—Great Nature's Face
Passed infinite by Me—

In contrast to 72, 978 contains all the features of Dickinson's later style. In the variation of rhyme and enjambment and in its verse-paragraphing, the poem avoids the stock phrases that fill out 72.

Poem 72 compares a human death and the death of a flower; 978 expands on the death of the flower and removes the human death altogether. Dickinson expands the terseness of the narrative detail in the earlier poem; "Vanish unrecorded" becomes "came another Day / To find the Species disappeared— / The Same Locality— / The Sun in place—no other fraud / On Nature's perfect Sum—." But no similar refinement is applied to the first stanza of 72. It is simply dropped. The result of this demotivation is to throw great emphasis on the disappearance of the flower, and to demand a symbolic referent for it. But the poem refuses to associate the flower with anything else. The extremity of the speaker's emotions becomes extremely puzzling: "retrieveless blame" and "Great Nature's Face / Passed infinite by me" suggest a psychological depth that the literal situation doesn't call for. The reader is left wondering what so extreme an emotion could be evoked by, and what the hidden connection between the flower and the unknown symbolic referent could be. One is led, when reading such a poem, to a state of *presque vu* about the poet's intentions and private associations. The powerful suggestiveness of the poem results from its being a demotivation of a hypotext that was more explicit about these associations.

Over the course of Dickinson's career, she returned again and again to the basic themes that figure in her early poems—hence the observation by many critics that her subject matter remained static. But while the early poems tend to be simply descriptive or to present stock conclusions (even when they are paradoxical or ironic stock conclusions), the later poems employ compression, or demotivation, or a shift in symbolic direction, to cause problems of interpretation. Dickinson's later style demands that the intricacy of her early hymn-like poems be doubled back on itself to produce a problem of interpretation every time the poem is read. The style in itself becomes the argument. This pattern can be observed in the large clusters of poems on death, marriage, loneliness, and other subjects; one small cluster of poems that shows it well is on Indian Summer, the period of warm weather after the first frost. Dickinson's first Indian Summer poem is 130:

These are the days when Birds come back—
A very few—a Bird or two—
To take a backward look.

These are the days when skies resume
The old—old sophistries of June—
A blue and gold mistake.
Oh fraud that cannot cheat the Bee—
Almost thy plausibility
Induces my belief.

Till ranks of seeds their witness bear—
And softly thro' the altered air
Hurries a timid leaf.

Oh Sacrament of summer days,
Oh Last Communion in the Haze—
Permit a child to join.

The sacred emblems to partake—
Thy consecrated bread to take
And thine immortal wine!

The poem is far from being a simple appreciation of the season. Even though the final stanza seems like an ecstatic acceptance of Indian Summer, the poem is, centrally, ambiguous. Indian Summer is a "Sacrament," but it is also a "fraud" and a "mistake": it is a repetition of the "sophistries of June." And if June itself, the real summer, is full of sophistries, a false June must be even falser. The speaker seems weary of the summer itself, because it is necessarily transient, and even wearier of the final deceit of the Indian Summer.

And yet, paradoxically, the speaker regains her faith at the very moment when she is made certain that the false summer is false: when "ranks of seeds their witness bear." Now that the season has stopped pretending to be anything other than summer's last gasp, she is ready to participate, and the poem slips into the devotional language of the last two stanzas. Or maybe it doesn't; maybe the last two stanzas are a satire on a type of attitude toward faith that embraces faith despite a deep-rooted skepticism. This satiric logic is papered over by the end-stopped hymn stanzas and the light tone. The satirical level is there, but it remains smirking, not serious; mock-devotional, not anti-devotional. Above all, the poem does not confront the problem of faith. It poses outside the problem, and we can either appreciate or reject that pose, but not engage it in an argument.

Poem 130 was written about 1859. Five years later, Dickinson returned to the theme of Indian Summer to write a more problematic poem, 930:

There is a June when Corn is cut
And Roses in the Seed—
A Summer briefer than the first
But tenderer indeed
As should a Face supposed the Grave's
Emerge a single Noon
In the Vermillion that it wore
Affect us, and return—

Two Seasons, it is said, exist—
The Summer of the Just,
And this of Ours, diversified
With Prospect, and with Frost—

May not our Second with its First
So infinite compare
That We but recollect the one
The other to prefer?

The problems of interpretation in this poem come from its piling up of comparisons, comparisons that at each level embody paradoxes. The enjambment from the first stanza to the second makes the first comparison, between Indian Summer and the brief reappearance of someone buried. Indian Summer itself is presented paradoxically, as a "June when Corn is cut," instead of simply as "the days when Birds come back." And the season is not merely accused of sophistry, as in 130; it is directly compared to an experience that is impossible: someone coming back from the dead not as a ghost but "in the Vermillion," in the flesh. Most similes present the unfamiliar in terms of the familiar, but this one presents the familiar in terms of the impossible. In the third stanza, Indian Summer, in its impossible beauty, is compared to the bliss of heaven, the "Summer of the Just." Which is better? The fourth stanza should tell us, but it doesn't quite manage to; its syntax is as baffling as anything Dickinson ever wrote. "Our Second" is Indian Summer, and "its First" is heaven, but which of these is "the other" that we have recollected "the one" to prefer?

The answer, I think, lies not in any internal evidence, but in an echo of 130 that the whole situation of 930 brings to mind. Remember that both June and Indian Summer in the earlier poem are accused of "sophistries," in an offhand way that the speaker does not elaborate. The speaker instead

drifts into a formulaic appreciation of the season she has accused. Here in
930, though, the sophistry is examined and explained. The reappearance of
someone buried in the second stanza is, of course, only humanly impossible;
there is a notable example of it, beyond human power, in the Resurrection.
And we are certainly reminded of the Resurrection in the second stanza, because the very impossibility of the simile demands it. After the end-stopping
at the end of the second stanza, the poem picks up the same comparison that
it made in that second stanza, because the Resurrection and the "Summer of
the Just" are, after all, identical. The Resurrection defeated death and made
this summer that is not "diversified" possible.

So when we "recollect the one," we are recollecting that Resurrection
and its promise of eternal summer. But we are preferring "the other," the
Indian Summer that so paradoxically can only be appreciated because it is
false—palpably, not metaphysically, false. Poem 930, welded together out of
a tremendous tension of style and symbol, is a rejection of the whole mystery
of immortality in favor of a confidence trick by Nature that seems honest in
comparison. But the poet is not merely expounding a position here; she is ar-
riving at it by the process of adapting an earlier text. In another poem or set
of poems she may very well—she certainly did—arrive at other conclusions
about Christ and about immortality. But here, she takes what is only hinted
at in the contradictions of 130, and by pressing those contradictions to their
limit, she arrives at the agonizing puzzle of 930.

Dickinson continued to rework the theme of Indian Summer, and
her 1364, written about 1876, is a late haïkaïsation of the subject. As in
many of these extremely compressed poems, the central term has become
enigmatic:

> How know it from a Summer's Day?
> Its Fervors are as firm—
> And nothing in its Countenance
> But scintillates the same—
> Yet Birds examine it and flee—
> And Vans without a name
> Inspect the Admonition
> And sunder as they came—

The first five lines of the poem are a simple compression of Dickinson's
earlier descriptions of Indian Summer. The speaker knows that it is not summer; the only difficulty is in proving it, and this is accomplished by noting
that the birds aren't fooled. (In 130, the proof was the "ranks of seeds." Also
in that poem, it was the bees, not the birds, that couldn't be fooled; but bees
actually are very active on warm autumn days, perhaps leading Dickinson

to drop that element of the treatment.) The problem of the poem lies in lines 6–8. "Vans without a name" is an impossibly obscure phrase, and deliberately so. These Vans are only named by their lack of a name, and their only action in the poem is to refuse to appear in it. They might be insects; the vaguely visual evocation of them makes them "look" like insects; but why would insects lack a name when birds are given one? As they appear, nameless, almost in the poem, they are spiritual presences of some sort, hovering on the edge of the poem's consciousness. Their sundering, in the last line, is a melting into silence of all the sarcasm and anguish that surrounded Indian Summer in 130 and 930, and 1364 is eerier and more cryptic than either of its predecessors.

The Indian Summer poems chart, in miniature, the development of Dickinson's style, from something resembling a hymn, at least in formal outline, to a far more individual treatment of the same subjects, made possible by inexact rhyme, enjambment, verse-paragraphing, haïkaïsation, demotivation—in general, by a ceaseless reworking of the one book that meant more to Dickinson than any other, even the Bible: the book of her own poetry. R. P. Blackmur accused Dickinson of "revolving in a vacuum" when she wrote her unconventional verse, and the accusation is true.[17] She never adopted conventional technique, but started very early with something idiosyncratic and then revised her own idiosyncrasies. Probably it is fortunate that she did, as she was led to complicate rather than to polish her early work. An editor would have noted very early on that she had gotten the bees and birds mixed up in 130, and while she was smoothing that out, she might never have composed 930.

Picasso is supposed to have said that he didn't care who influenced him, so long as he didn't influence himself. Dickinson proceeded oppositely; she was vigorously anti-eclectic. This leads to the difficulty of considering her work as a single integrated corpus. In the Indian Summer poems, Dickinson certainly has her earlier poems—carefully preserved in the fascicles—in mind as a context for the later ones. But for other sequences of poems, such as the many that affirm faith and immortality, her manuscript books provide different contexts. It is customary to think of lyric poems as being strictly independent utterances, or as being elements in a narrative or meditative sequence. But Dickinson's fascicles are neither. The logic of clusters on different themes—or even, sometimes, of different poems within a cluster on the same theme—develops in different directions. When interpreters attempt to capture her thought on a given subject by referring to poems written over a twenty-five-year period, they are not proceeding incorrectly—very often there is no other way to proceed if we want to make sense of Dickinson—but they are compiling provisional indexes to what was still, in its final "edition," very much a work in progress.

So was *Leaves of Grass,* of course, but the difference is that Dickinson was not making a book for anyone but herself. Her work is inward-directed to a unique extent, and not just in its lack of appropriation of the language of others and in her lack of interest in publication. The most distinctive thing about her poetry is, finally, the intensely problematic nature of her painstaking and often enigmatic adaptation of her private texts.

NOTES

1. Douglas Anderson, "Presence and Place in Emily Dickinson's Poetry," *New England Quarterly,* 57 (1984): p. 205.

2. See Mossberg, *Emily Dickinson: When a Writer Is a Daughter* (Bloomington: Indiana University Press, 1982); Porter, *Dickinson: The Modern Idiom* (Cambridge: Harvard University Press, 1981); Weisbuch, *Emily Dickinson's Poetry* (Chicago: University of Chicago Press, 1975)

3. *Emily Dickinson's Poetry: Stairway of Surprise* (New York: Holt, Rinehart, and Winston, 1960): p. xii.

4. All quotations from Dickinson's poetry are from *The Poems of Emily Dickinson,* ed. Thomas H. Johnson (Cambridge: Harvard University Press, 1955). They are referred to by the numbers given them in that edition.

5. See Jack L. Capps, *Emily Dickinson's Reading: 1836–1886* (Cambridge: Harvard University Press, 1966): pp. 147–188.

6. See Joanne Feit Diehl, *Dickinson and the Romantic Imagination* (Princeton: Princeton University Press, 1981), which treats Dickinson's responses to her major Romantic precursors; Susan Howe, *My Emily Dickinson* (Berkeley, Cal.: North Atlantic Press, 1985), which examines far-reaching networks of associations between Dickinson's reading and her poetry; A. R. C. Finch, "Dickinson and Patriarchal Meter: A Theory of Metrical Codes," *PMLA,* 102 (1987): pp. 166–176, looks at Dickinson's choice of the quatrain in relation to the tradition of pentameter in English verse.

7. See *Poems,* I: pp. xxxiii–xxxviii.

8. *Poems,* I: p. xxxiii.

9. The chronology of Dickinson's poems is from *Poems* with corrections from *The Manuscript Books of Emily Dickinson,* ed. R. W. Franklin (Cambridge: Harvard University Press, 1981).

10. See Timothy Morris, "The Free-Rhyming Poetry of Emerson and Dickinson," *Essays in Literature,* 12 (1985): pp. 225–240.

11. Of 4,840 rhymes in Dickinson's poems, 2,006 (41.4%) are exact (of the type see/me, 1732); 167 (3.5%) pair a vowel with a reduced version of itself (me/immortality, 712); 80 (1.6%) are assonantal (breath/quench, 422); 731 (15.1%) are vowel (blew/sky, 354); 1,535 (31.7%) are consonantal (mean/sun, 411); 164 (3.4%) pair a consonant with a cluster containing that consonant (night/erect, 419); 23 pair a cluster with another cluster that shares one consonant with it (disclosed/blind, 761); 2 rhyme a cluster with the same cluster reversed (used/birds, 430); 84 (1.7%) rhyme one nasal consonant with another (thing/begun, 565); 20 rhyme one fricative with another (breeze/divorce, 896); 2 rhyme one voiced stop with another (sob/wood, 45); 5 rhyme one unvoiced stop with another (frock/night, 584); 21 rhyme-positions show less close approximations to exact rhyme, and cannot be considered rhyme at all (for instance, blaze/forge in 365).

12. I have not found it worthwhile to give a fascicle-by-fascicle analysis of Dickinson's rhymes. The broad trends of the change in her style do show, of course, in such an analysis: for example, she uses 78.1% exact rhyme in Fascicle I and only 24.3% exact rhyme in Fascicle 24. But the trend would only be obscured by noting the very small variations from fascicle to fascicle. The dating of the fascicles can never be precise enough to permit statements about development over very brief intervals of time anyway; the year-by-year dating shows Dickinson's stylistic development in general terms, which is my aim here.

13. *This Was a Poet* (New York: Scribners, 1939): p. 262.

14. *The Life of Emily Dickinson* (New York: Farrar, Straus, and Giroux, 1974), I: pp. 240–243.

15. *Palimpsestes* (Paris: Seuil, 1982), chap. 9.

16. "Demotivation in *Hérodias*," in *Flaubert and Postmodernism*, ed. Naomi Sekori and Henry F. Majewski (Lincoln: University of Nebraska Press, 1984): pp. 192-201. Trans. Marlena Corcoran.

17. "Emily Dickinson: Notes on Prejudice and Fact," *Southern Review*, 3 (1937): pp. 323–347.

MARGARET DICKIE

Dickinson's Discontinuous Lyric Self

It is the habit of our times to read poetry as if it were prose perhaps because recent strategies for reading derive from and are most easily applied to prose. Psychoanalytic, Marxist, feminist models for reading all depend to one extent or another upon a plot, upon character, and upon extended development. When these models are applied to a form such as a lyric poem that is brief, repetitive, and figurative, they fit uneasily and most usefully only when the lyric form itself is neglected in favor of the narrative that can be derived from joining together a number of poems. It must be admitted that the brevity of the lyric poses an obstacle to a critical argument because it is equally difficult to make a compelling point on the basis of a single brief lyric and, for different reasons, to discuss a series of poems as one continuous work. Perhaps then what is needed is a critical argument that will start by noticing that the properties of the lyric—its brevity, its repetition, its figuration—obstruct readings that are determined by a socially limited understanding of the self or the subject, by a view of character as expressed in a cause and effect logic, by an insistence that the poet can be understood by certain representative attitudes. The lyric poem resists the totalizing ambition of such readings.

In trying to formulate a new model for reading the lyric poem, Emily Dickinson's poetry may be instructive especially because it has been given

American Literature, Vol. 60, No. 4. (December, 1988): pp. 537–553. Copyright ©1988 by the Duke University Press.

a recent and vigorous reading by American feminist critics who have been reading it for plot, character, and the extended argument of the work.[1] For example, Alicia Ostriker has commented: "Dickinson genuinely despises publicity and power, prefers the private and powerless life—and the reverse is equally true. We may say the same about many of her poems in praise of deprivation: they reject what they commend, commend what they reject. Their delight, their strength derives from their doubleness" (p. 41). Power and deprivation are themes that interest Ostriker, issues central to feminist criticism; but Ostriker's own claims would suggest that they are not issues equally central or politically determined to Dickinson.

The brevity with which the lyric "I" is presented in Dickinson's poems should suggest that that "I" is not to be known in terms such as publicity and power that might define a character in a novel.[2] The longer life of an individual in the novel, and especially in the nineteenth-century novel, tends inevitably toward steadfastness of character. Even an effort such as Edgar Allan Poe's to undermine the stalwartness of fictional characters by the use of unreliable narrators relies upon a consistency of representation that is foreign to the lyric "I." In a lyric poem, the "I" is known only in limited detail. For a lyric poet of consistent productivity such as Dickinson, this limitation is a deliberate choice of self-presentation, expressive of a particular sense of the self (of herself or a self) as shifting, changing, reforming. Such a self will be distorted in being described in terms appropriate for either a real-life or novelistic character.

But what terms can be used then? Brevity, repetition, and figuration, I repeat. These qualities articulate a sense of the self as particular, discontinuous, limited, private, hidden. Such a concept of self directly subverts the idea that the self is a publicly knowable, organized, single entity. Thus, it challenges all kinds of narrative explanations of character, not only the feminist and psychoanalytic reading of Dickinson's work but the dominant ideology of self-reliance expressed in the prose of nineteenth-century American culture.[3] Dickinson's poetry has been read typically as an expression of that ideology when actually it is far more revolutionary in its understanding of the self. Its chief means of revolt is its choice of the publicly degraded lyric form.

Only in America, where there was no great lyric tradition and thus no great tradition of reading the lyric, would this easily conventionalized genre be available for subversive expression. Despite Poe's claim for its importance, the lyric was a woman's form, considered insufficient to express the grandness of America and the American individual, the central mission of the nineteenth-century American literary establishment. This insufficiency of form was coextensive with the insufficiency of a self conceived as incomplete, unsure, recalcitrant, and—it must be admitted—female. The precariousness of identity, the un-mappable privacy, and the unacknowledged limitations of individuality could be suggested, evoked, tentatively recognized in the lyric form which shared the very qualities it was called upon to express. Furthermore, the lyric was uniquely available for self-expression in a society where other literary forms for such expression (the diary, the letter, for example) had been conventionalized and absorbed by the cultural imperatives of the Puritan tradition.

Dickinson's exclusive choice of the lyric genre separated her from Emerson and Thoreau, but she was also distanced from them in time. She wrote the bulk of her poems in the early years of the Civil War at the very juncture when the ideology of individualism established by its links to an American destiny was beginning to reveal the limits not of its optimism, which was much later in developing, but of its comprehensiveness. The individualism of Emerson and Thoreau was male, white, middle class, and Protestant. It did not extend to the work of a woman. It is no surprise then that in this woman writer, individualism as a concept gave way to the expression of individuality.

The two are not commensurate as we know from reading Emerson, but it is perhaps Nietzsche who most fully articulates the idea that the word individuality is always spoken with a forked tongue. The concept of individuality with its sense of commonality threatens the claims to individuality. Discussing Nietzsche, Werner Hamacher argues:

> Individuality is so fully determined as incommensurability that no individual could correspond to its concept if it were at one with and equal to itself, if it were a thoroughly determined, whole form. *Human, All Too Human* proposes, in the interests of knowledge, that one not uniformize oneself into rigidity of bearing and that one not treat oneself "like a stiff steadfast, *single* individual." Only the individual's nonidentity with itself can constitute its individuality. Measured against itself as concept, bearing, and function, the individual proves to be other, to be more—or less—than itself. Its individuality is always only what reaches out beyond its empirical appearance, its social and psychological identities, and its logical form. Individuality is unaccountable surplus.[4]

This unaccountable surplus is what cannot be made uniform, narrated, and organized into a single individual. It is best expressed not in prose but in lyric poetry where a brief and repeated form depends upon the exposure of particularity and peculiarity. Such limited details rather than extended narrative development will provide relief from the self-defeating ambitions of a coherent and definitive presentation of the self. The lyric poem does not mythologize the individual as a readable organization, making coherence out of isolated moments and fragmentary experience as the novel does;

rather the lyric makes isolated moments out of coherence and restores with words the contingency of the self that has been lost to experience.[5] Unlike the novel, the lyric's "significant form" does not signify social viability.[6]

The brevity of the lyric focuses the sharp edges of details that will be necessarily scant. But the pressure of the brief form also attenuates the detail until it changes under scrutiny. Thus, the lyric's brevity enlarges rather than contracts the possibility of the detail. Such presentation relies on the profligacy of details rather than on their coherence.

The value of profligacy is the subject of Poem 634 where Dickinson represents not a human being but a bird. A riddle or more accurately a quasi-riddle since it is evident from the start that the subject is a bird, the poem demonstrates the way in which the lyric strains the techniques of representation by rendering clear details opaque and then creating out of that opacity the central clarity. The poem's riddling quality is an important element of its representation because it allows Dickinson to present one thing in terms of another as an image and in the instability of the image to suggest thereby the paradox of identity.[7] What we see best, we see least well; what we cannot see or refuse to see becomes clearest evidence. Offering instruction on how to know a bird, Dickinson provides too an inquiry into self-representation.

She starts with alarming confidence in the brief detail: "You'll know Her – by Her Foot." And that particularity presents itself as immediately obstructive since to know *her* by her foot is to know nothing of the conventional feminine beauty of her face or figure. Nor is it to know much by symbolic extension. The foot, unlike the hand or the heart, does not stand for anything except standing. But, curiously, the first stanza insists on its own particular way of knowing by metaphorical extension, developing in apposition:

> You'll know Her – by Her Foot –
> The smallest Gamboge Hand
> With Fingers – where the Toes should be –
> Would more affront the Sand –

No poet could make these connections without thinking of how she herself is known by her poetic foot, and in the apposition of the foot/hand Dickinson makes a whimsical connection between bird and poet, hand writing and poetic foot, which will be developed in the final stanza where she meditates on an idea close to the Nietzschean surplus in individuality.

Before that, however, the poem appears to be a detailed taxonomy of the bird, identified by particular details—her foot, her vest, her cap. But these typical parts lose their immediate force in the poet's efforts to maintain the metaphor of bird and woman. The bird's foot described as "this Quaint Creature's Boot" is rendered unknowable as either foot or boot when the speaker says it is "Without a Button – I could vouch." That testimony guarantees enigma. Without a button, it is not a boot, and so the vouching undoes the knowledge it would confirm. The excursion seems merely decorative, as does the admission that inside her tight-fitting vest she wore a duller jacket when she was born. This wandering bird-knowledge appears inappropriately applied to a figure described as small, snug, tightly encased, finely plumed.

Like Nietzsche's individual, this bird is something other than its type. Its foot is a boot but not a boot; its orange-brown vest is the opposite of its original jacket; its cap appears from a distance no cap at all and then closer up proves to be a cap that is no cap since it has no band or brim. By the sixth stanza, Dickinson has demonstrated convincingly the extent to which details do not represent the whole, and concomitantly the uncertainty of ever knowing the whole either by knowledge of parts as in synecdoche, by knowledge derived from identifying one thing in terms of another or relating the familiar to the unfamiliar as in metaphor, or by personal testimony or by precise description and careful distinction. Even in combination, such ways do not lead to a satisfactory representation of the whole. But the poem does not end with this conclusion toward which it appears to be drawing. Rather, it presents the bird presenting herself:

> You'll know Her – by her Voice –
> At first – a doubtful Tone –
> A sweet endeavor – but as March
> To April – hurries on –
>
> She squanders on your Ear
> Such Arguments of Pearl –
> You beg the Robin in your Brain
> To keep the other – still –

The "doubtful Tone" that turns into "Arguments of Pearl" is an excessive presentation. And it is perhaps the excess from which the poet imagines the recipient retreating, preferring the idea to this reality.

Such self-presentation as the bird's is always more than enough. It must be excessive if it is to be the expression of an individual, of the "unaccountable surplus" of individuality. This bird of doubtful tone exemplifies Hamacher's description of the Nietzschean individual: "The individual does not live. It outlives. Its being is being out and being over, an insubstantial remainder and excess beyond every determinable form of human life. Instead of being a social or psychic form of human existence, the individual—the self surpassing of type, or genius—is the announcement of what, generally translated as 'superman' or 'overman,' is best translated in this context as 'outman'" (p. 119).

Leaving aside for the moment the absurdity of considering Dickinson's bird an "outman," I draw attention to the way in which the poet presents a bird by brief details and then obliterates these details in the verb "Squanders" where the bird surpasses the type. Thus, the bird is profligate in Nietzschean terms. And the poet behind the bird knows too that, in its squandering, it is casting pearls before swine, claiming individuality in a world that prefers types.

Thus, the brevity of the lyric allows a certain kind of knowing. It demands the excessive patience and attention that only a poet would possess, and it requires an indulgence that Dickinson had every reason to believe her readers would lack. To know by the foot is not a simple knowledge nor is it a different way of knowing something that exists outside the poem; it is rather a form of knowing by excesses only available in brief and metrical form.

Such excesses figure in the brevity of lyric representation by distorting syntax and sense. Knowing by the foot means fitting language to form as in the lines, "Nor is it Clasped unto of Band – / Nor held upon – of Brim." Extracted from the poem, these lines fail to signify anything; they can signify only in an arrangement of language that prizes apposition, parallel structures, or periphrasis, in short, that prizes excessive statement. Or, another example, the opening quatrain with its comparison of foot to a hand that "Would more affront the Sand" is a deictic chaos, made necessary and then managed by the only full rhyme in the poem—"Sand" holds "hand" in place. Here, Dickinson seems to be underscoring the whimsy of knowing in rhyme and rhythm. Like the bird, the poet too is a squanderer and, like the bird's, her squandering is permitted and limited by brief form and the formal repetition it requires.

The lyric's repetition derives from its brevity, but repetition is curiously essential both *to* and *in* the lyric poem. As a way of representation, repetition brought Dickinson's lyrics into conflict with Romantic conceptions of form and subject in nineteenth-century America. A form that depends upon the repetition of its formal elements will not be free nor will it necessarily grow by the principle of organic form. Moreover, the subject presented in repetitive images will not be original and new. It will always be a copy and a copy of a copy.

The vulnerability of the lyric to conventional form and subject is well documented in the history of literature. But for Dickinson, it posed a particular problem. She shared with her fellow Romantics a suspicion of convention. She knew, as they did, the limits of the self that was made and the character that was formed in large and in little by repeating familiar patterns of behavior, by repeated professions of faith, by copying over moral precepts both in school books and in embroidery lessons at home, by duties performed and performed again. She resisted in her own life these means through which one generation inculcated into the next its values, its identity, its way of life, and forced the self through repetition to grow into a presentable self. It was this self that Thoreau hoped to wash off each morning in his dips into Walden Pond. It was this self that Emerson intended to escape by writing "Whim" on his lintel post and departing from family and friends for a day. And it was this self that Dickinson drew and satirized in several poems. But while Thoreau believed in the natural man beyond the social man and Emerson relied on the genius within, Dickinson as a lyric poet had no access to these plots of redemption.

Rather, she was tied by the repetition in and of the lyric to use repetition as the constituent of character. Again, the limits of the genre enlarged her understanding, and when in Poem 443, for example, she takes repetition as her subject she uses it to express ranges of experience inaccessible to narrative organization. The poem has been enforced into such organization by Barbara Mossberg, who reads it as evidence of the duplicity imposed upon women by the dominant patriarchal culture (p. 197). The repetitive language and strate gies of the poem reveal, however, a miserable lack of duplicity or division between inner and outer actions.

The repetition in the verb tense—"I tie my Hat," "I crease my Shawl," "I put new Blossoms in the Glass," "I push a petal from my Gown," "I have so much to do"—describes particular habits by which the lyric "I" prepares herself and her house for presentation to the world. Yet they are not aids in self-making so much as subterfuges behind which she hides both from the world and from herself. More crucially, the theatricality of these acts is doubled by the theatricality within; the outer self acting is in danger at every point of being upstaged by the dramatic, even melodramatic, inner self who "got a Bomb − / And held it in our Bosom." By this convergence of outer show and inner show, Dickinson calls into question the nature of identity. What is real? What is cover-up? Or, more to the point, do these questions even apply? Is the self only show?

The repetitive gestures of putting on hats and taking off shawls may be obsessive acts, but no more so than the "stinging work − / To cover what we are," the effort of holding a bomb in the bosom. The speaker justifies her "life's labor" by claiming that it holds "our Senses − on." But on to what? What is the center? What is the periphery here? The speaker's sense that she must "simulate" is, as it must be in the lyric, unexplained. Her boast that she only trembles at the bomb that would make others start suggests a fondness for her own dilemma. She is holding on to "Miles on Miles of Nought" by the same effort of will that nullified the self. Both her inner and her outer life reflect a willingness to act as if "the very least / Were infinite − to me."

Often accused of speaking from beyond the grave, here Dickinson brings the grave into the center of life. This is not a poem in which life as disruption of stasis "seems like an outbreak around which control keeps trying, unsuccessfully, to close" or where "meaning disrupts both vacuous action and the sentential in which such action takes refuge," as Sharon Cameron would have it.[8] It is rather a poem about a life in which control is the only meaning and meaning the only control.

In this poem where the inner self is fashioned by the same patterns of repetition that fashion the outer self, the collapse of the division between inner and outer in the speaker makes it possible to collapse the division between self and other. "I" becomes "we" at the very point in mid-poem where the speaker turns from her daily duties to announce the unique errand that should have distinguished her from all others. It is not that the catastrophe deprives her of individuality but that she divests herself of her individuality by surrendering to this single event. "*We* came to flesh" and "*we* got a Bomb," the speaker boasts, as if she were somehow made more grand, indeed "completed," by this dwindling of life into a single purpose which it is now her duty to memorialize.

In life lived as a duty, there can be no difference between private and public. The repetitive strategies of the lyric are used here to express the dilemma of the self ensnared in its own trap of meaning. The clotting of the lines with internal rhymes, assonance, consonance, alliteration, anaphora, and phrases in apposition suggests the way in which language can be used to impede change, to repeat sameness, even as it seems to press forward.

"I tie my Hat" is not about loss but about the refusal to give up loss. The speaker in this poem wants to account for the unaccountable surplus of individuality, to explain it in terms of a single completed "errand." But insofar as that "errand" appears undetailed and only abstractly named, it will require endless repetition.

The "Bomb" in the bosom that somehow mysteriously never goes off, that is paradoxically "calm," is pure melodrama, an image that loses its power the second it fixes itself in the imagination or should lose its power. In fact, in critical commentary, it has not. The restitution of order around the bomb evident in the persistent present of the verb "we do life's labor" has come to signify the speaker's martyrdom for critics who want to see in the poem a cause and effect explanation of character, a narrative that will contrast the liveliness of the bomb to the deadliness of routine existence (Mossberg, p. 197). But such a reading provides a plot where plot has been deliberately suppressed by repetitive action; it finds biography where Dickinson has placed only habit.

Dickinson's poems have been particularly vulnerable to narrative explanation, specifically to biographical explication. Vivian R. Pollak justifies this practice by arguing that Dickinson's art of self-display and self-advertisement draws attention to the person behind the poems and so calls for an examination of biographical relationships.[9] What Pollak terms self-display and self-advertisement could as easily be called repression as in "I tie my Hat," where the staged performance of daily duties is an evasion of self-knowledge and even the inner faithfulness to the bomb in the bosom has its element of ritual—a display perhaps, but not of the bared self.

The relationship of poet to speaker is not a simple equation; it is always mediated through and suppressed by the lyric's figurative language. Dickinson wrote to Thomas Wentworth Higginson, the editor who advised her against publishing, "When I state myself, as the Representative of the Verse—it does not mean—me—but a supposed person" (II 412). In these terms, she points us in a different direction to ask questions that lead away from biography and toward figuration and supposition or, as in Poem 505, the person supposing. Dickinson's art of self-presentation depends on supposition in "I would not paint – a picture."

The relationship of speaker to Dickinson is intricate and inadequately understood in Adrienne Rich's powerful reading of the poem that identifies Dickinson with the speaker and with the fear of her poetic power.[10] All that is known about the actual person who wrote this poem, about her difficulties in reaching the kind of appreciative audience she imagines in this speaker, about the doubts that she might have entertained over the breathlessness of this speaker, about her attitude toward art in general and her own poetry in particular, all this information must be added to the poem when it is read as a political and social tract. But if such reading seems reductive in its extraneousness, equally reductive is the view of the speaker here as purified of contingency by the lyric. It is a poet, after all, who is writing "Nor would I be a Poet" and imagining what the dower of art would be. Hers is a mixed voice, contaminated by its source and, as we shall see, easily blending into its circumstances.

The speaker of this poem is a person supposing, dwelling in supposition, and, as such, she moves in and out of identities. She figures, refigures, and figures again. Now audience, now artist, she is a creature without a core, free to dwell on and in the creator's feelings and the feelings that creation inspires, as open to elevation as to fixity, both impotent and privileged. The speaker is all feeling here, and her feeling is dependent on what will arouse it. But it is a productive and willing dependency that drives her to superfluous denials and extravagant affirmations. "I would not paint," "I would not talk" are excessive protestations. Denying herself what she most wants, the speaker intensifies its pleasures by doubling them in creating the occasion for the poem. Sweet torment and sumptuous despair are moods of desire prolonged and longingly anticipated, not evidence of Dickinson's passivity as Rich has argued. The speaker's relishing of her own relishing cannot fit into Rich's narrative of female repression because it is perversely an unrepressed narrative—a desire that is always for something else, always reaching out toward something, never satisfying itself except in its repetition and perpetuation. The poet is not frustrated in her desire to be a painter but rather thrilled by the desire to feel what the painter feels. She is not denied art; she has after all "fingers" of her own which stir, as we read, evoking both in the writer and in the reader their own sweet torment.

Again, in the second stanza, the speaker repeats her rapture. Just as in the first stanza where there was an odd disproportion between the "bright impossibility" of paintings and the "fingers" of the painter, so here the speaker as "endued Balloon" launched by "a lip of Metal" presents herself as soaring high from rather low inspiration. The talk of cornets is banal by comparison to the speaker's elevation through "Villages of Ether." The transport of art and the ability to be transported by art thrill the speaker who marvels at her own powers to be moved by "*but* a lip." The cornet player is a performer, not a creator, and his performance is rendered remarkable by the response of the "One / Raised softly to the Ceilings." She, too, is a performer–and on a higher wire.

The final stanza narrows the gap between creator/performer and audience/performer by endowing the speaker with the "Ear" *for* the poet and *of* the poet. Identities blur. The ear of the poet as of her audience is "Enamored – impotent – content," a passive receiver and willing receptacle. It is through the ear that both will be inspired and stunned by "Bolts of Melody." The separate identities of the creator and the reverent appreciator of poetry compose a fantasy that had started disingenuously in the speaker's wondering how the painter's fingers feel and how the musician's lips could inspire her, but it is a fantasy of self-empowerment, not self-diminishment. The speaker also has fingers, also has lips, even as she has "the Ear." "What would the Dower be, / Had I the Art to Stun myself," she speculates, but only after she has presented herself as stunned and stunnable. She has the "Art."

The supposed person that Dickinson might have called the representative of this verse is less a person than the power of supposition. Drawing up a *dramatis personae* for the poem or outlining a narrative continuity of envy and renunciation both diminishes and mislocates the power which names itself only in repetition. "I would not paint," "I would not talk," "Nor would I be a Poet" are repeated affirmations of the always unsatisfied, always to be satisfied desire to create. They celebrate themselves in prolonging the moment of desire just before it is satisfied. If a narrative of sexual longing and consummation cannot be easily generated from these unanchored images, the eroticism of the language here has its oddity.

The description of a painter creating a picture by the "rare – celestial – stir" of fingers is not mimetic. The words move from perceiver to perceived, from effect to affect, along a wayward path that zigzags between sound and sense. Sound alone seems to require the preposterous metaphor "Pontoon" for the self. And finally the wish to know what the dower would be if one could electrify oneself seems willful semantic wandering.

The excess in this language cannot do more than point to the excessiveness in the speaker's fantasy of self. She would be *sweetly* tormented, *sumptuously* despaired, raised and endued, awed and stunned, moved beyond sense. In her state of elevated and extravagant longing, the speaker is wanton with language, disposing lines with abandon as if they were impediments to rather than expressions of anticipated ecstasy. If language cannot speak itself, it must appropriate a channel for its transmission. The channel in lyric poetry need not be a fully developed character defined by birth and death dates, by family and a maturation plot; it can be, as here, a voice that speaks from shifting perspectives, that inhabits various frequencies, that has no center but rather many circumferences.

From the robin to the woman of melodramatic routine to this disembodied power of supposition, the examples I have chosen appear—when placed together—random, discontinuous, and uncentered. They are intentionally so because I want to suggest something of Dickinson's profligacy. It is possible to set the poem about the robin in the context of Dickinson's riddles or of her bird poems and to discuss Poem 505 with other poems in which Dickinson sets out her poetics. Or all three poems could be adapted to one or more narratives of social repression, artistic restriction, romantic deprivation. But although such order and explanation might justify critical discourse, even my own, it would have to be superimposed and designed to suppress or ignore the fact that the poems are discrete forms, perhaps part of a larger whole that is the poet's imaginative world but deliberately brief, separate, disconnected units of expression.

Even as I insist on that aspect of the work, I am aware of the misfit between the brevity of the lyric and the length of my own commentary. Little can be concluded from one brief lyric or three. Only the fact that Dickinson chose this form consistently makes it possible to argue that the form itself is an important confirmation or creation of her sense of self. Thus, I return once more to consider the properties of the lyric: brevity, repetition, and figuration.

The brevity of the lyrics she wrote is a form of artistic restraint that relies paradoxically on excess. In an age of sprawling masterpieces that followed the laws of nature, chapters proliferating as branches grow from trunks, in Melville's terms, the brevity, compactness, and convention of the lyric form appear unnecessarily restrictive. Yet Dickinson could use the brevity of the lyric to suggest even more freely than Melville the unaccountability of individuality. Although the lyric speaker can be conventionalized by the form itself, insofar as she is imaged in details rather than as a whole, particularized rather than totalized, she appears not conventional at all.

Such a speaker presents herself partially, not fully; her whole existence is, for us, partial. Measured against Ahab, for example, the lyric speaker suggests a sense of self that is certainly limited and yet remains paradoxically free from the restraints of social viability that will be exerted on the novelistic character. The partial may be, if not all there is, more than we realize. Brevity, then, may be the soul of character.

The brevity of the lyric form enforces its repetition. It encourages a refiguration of the already figured, and so it permits a concept of the self not only as partial but as excessive. In composing over a hundred poems that start with "I," Dickinson could create and recreate a supposed person supposing one way and then another. No single "errand" for her, the lyric speaker is singular, unique, isolated, changeable, not to be made into one composite person by joining poems together. The lyric "I" is not the real-life poet or even part of her because she will not share her beginning or her end, her history. She is not a copy of that original either because she is always and conventionally partial.

Formally, repetition encourages a predictability that nonetheless permits disruption and gaps. Dickinson establishes a repetitive rhythm or rhyme scheme or organizing grammar and then breaks it, as she does in "I tie my Hat" when she breaks the rhythm with "Stopped – struck – my ticking – through" and the rhyme in "Too Telescopic Eyes / To bear on us unshaded – / For their – sake – not for Ours" and the grammar in "But since we got a Bomb – / And held it in our Bosom." The disruption, only made possible by the expectations of repetitive form, allows the brief lyric to expand its space, to incorporate blanks, to open indeterminately.

Repetition in the lyric as, for example, in the anaphora of "I would not paint – a picture –" becomes a means of obstructing narrative explanation. It also precludes the organization of events in a causal series. And it leaves open the question of what is original, what copy, as, for example, in "I tie my Hat" in which the repetitive routine gestures of the speaker may imitate a deadened inner life or may be themselves the originator of that life.[11]

Finally, the figurative language of a lyric poem represses one term under another and suggests again the profligacy of such repression. The self is not exposed in figurative language but hidden and shielded and thus freed from social definition. Such freedom allows for the whimsy always available in self-presentation. The lyric character may be called "Pontoon" perhaps only to rhyme with "Balloon" or stuck in the improbable pose of holding a bomb in the bosom or singing not a tune but a "tone." The lyric "I" is free because its relationship to even the "I" of a supposed person is of copy to copy. It can proliferate endlessly. Although Dickinson describes one speaker acting "With scrupulous exactness – / To hold our Senses – on," she actually calls into question the center around which such exactness would accrue both in that particular poem and in a lifetime's accumulation of such poems.

In concentrating on the brevity, the repetition, and the figuration of the lyric form, I have attempted to read Dickinson's poems by the qualities they possess. These terms may only be useful for Dickinson's work; they will not all serve Wordsworth's lyrics or Milton's or Shakespeare's, for example. Thus, they cannot be worked into a model for reading all lyric poetry. But they are important here because they point to the essential qualities of Dickinson's work: its interest in the unaccountable surplus of individuality, in repetition as constituent of character, and in figurative excess as essential to self-presentation.

The problems of interpretation that Dickinson's poetry poses are essentially problems of narrative readability which have usually been resolved by the imposition of a master narrative on the work and the life. Feminist critics of Dickinson who have brought so much new energy to the reading of her poetry are only the latest version of this tendency; they have been preceded by psychoanalytic critics, biographers, and cultural historians. Dickinson's work evades them because it represents a much more radical understanding of the self than American feminists, tied as they are to a social explanation of character, can allow. Dickinson's lyric speakers have no narrative continuity, no social viability, no steadfast identity. In their squandering, melodrama, and excesses, they express an individuality that resists final representation and the control that signifies. Yet Dickinson's lyric presentation of a self that obstructs narrative reading because it is discontinuous, profligate, and excessive may be the nineteenth century's most revolutionary expression of individuality. Thus, it may offer not only a new model for reading the lyric but a new and perhaps persuasively feminist model of self-presentation.

NOTES

1. It is not only the feminists who have read for the plot. Early and late, narrativizing critics have worked on Dickinson. See for example Clark Griffith's *The Long Shadow: Emily Dickinson's Tragic Poetry* (Princeton: Princeton University Press, 1964) which traces her traumatic relationship with her father as the source of her tragic poetry or John Cody's *After Great Pain: The Inner Life of Emily Dickinson* (Cambridge: Harvard University Press, 1971) which uses the poetry as a psychoanalytic case study. Among representative feminist readings of Dickinson are Margaret Homans, *Women Writers and Poetic Identity* (Princeton: Princeton University Press, 1980), Joanne Feit Diehl, *Dickinson and the Romantic Imagination* (Princeton: Princeton University Press, 1981), Barbara Antonina Clarke Mossberg, *Emily Dickinson: When a Writer Is a Daughter* (Bloomington: Indiana University Press, 1982), Sandra M. Gilbert and Susan Gubar, *The Madwoman in the Attic* (New Haven: Yale University Press, 1979), and Alicia Suskin Ostriker, *Stealing the Language: The Emergence of Women's Poetry in America* (Boston: Beacon Press, 1986). Based on a model of binary opposition, these varied readings of Dickinson

stress the extent to which she was different because she was made to be by a society that restricted or repressed women's expression. Sacvan Bercovitch in *The Puritan Origins of the American Self* (New Haven: Yale University Press, 1975) explores the strain on the individual from the demands of American individualism in terms that explain some of the difficulties of reading Dickinson's poetry.

References to Dickinson's work are to *The Complete Poems of Emily Dickinson,* ed. Thomas H. Johnson (Boston: Little, Brown & Company, 1957),and *The Letters of Emily Dickinson,* ed. Thomas H. Johnson and Theodora Ward, 3 vols. (Cambridge: Harvard University Press, 1958). References will appear in the text in parentheses.

2. In talking about the brevity of Dickinson's poems, I mean only to suggest a general characteristic of all lyric poems and not to stress the particular ways in which Dickinson exploited brevity or limitation as a theme. For such treatment, see Jane Donahue Eberwein's *Dickinson: Strategies of Limitation* (Amherst: University of Massachusetts Press, 1985).

3. See Sacvan Bercovitch's discussion of Emerson for a complete treatment of his sense of the public self. The whole question of privacy is a central concern of Dickinson. For example, in Poem 1385, she deals directly with the impossibility of publishing the private, making public the secret. Dickinson's privacy is an issue of some debate among her critics. She is charged with being too private by Elinor Wilnor, "The Poetics of Emily Dickinson," *ELH,* 38 (1971): pp. 126–154, and David Porter, *Dickinson: The Modern Idiom* (Cambridge: Harvard University Press, 1981). Robert Weisbuch has defended her habit of privacy in *Emily Dickinson's Poetry* (Chicago: University of Chicago Press, 1975). More recently, Christopher E. G. Benfey has discussed the issue of privacy and secrecy as a longing for invisibility in *Emily Dickinson and the Problem of Others* (Amherst: University of Massachusetts Press, 1984).

4. "'Disintegration of the Will': Nietzsche on the Individual and Individuality," in *Reconstructing Individualism: Autonomy, Individuality, and the Self in Western Thought,* ed. Thomas C. Heller et al. (Stanford: Stanford University Press, 1986): p. 110.

5. For more on Nietzsche, the self, and contingency, see Richard Rorty, "The Contingency of Self," *London Review of Books,* 8 (8 May 1986): pp. 11–15.

6. I am indebted here to the arguments of Leo Bersani in *The Freudian Body: Psychoanalysis and Art* (New York: Columbia University Press, 1986): pp. 82–83.

7. I rely here on Andrew Welsh's discussion of riddle in *Roots of Lyric: Primitive Poetry and Modern Poetics* (Princeton: Princeton University Press, 1978): p. 30.

8. "'A Loaded Gun': Dickinson and the Dialectic of Rage," *PMLA,* 93 (1978): p. 431.

9. *Dickinson: The Anxiety of Gender* (Ithaca: Cornell University Press, 1984): pp. 18–19.

10 "Vesuvius at Home: The Power of Emily Dickinson," in *On Lies, Secrets, and Silence: Selected Prose 1966-1978* (New York: Norton, 1979): p. 169. Rich gives this much repeated reading its most palatable form because she does understand that for Dickinson there is no split between masculine creativity and feminine receptivity. Other feminists have taken up the split that Rich identifies and then denies and have made much of it. See Diehl, pp. 19–20.

11. I am indebted here to Gilles Deleuze's discussion of repetition in *Différence et Répétition* (Paris: Presses Universitaires de France, 1968): pp. 96–168.

DOMHNALL MITCHELL

Revising the Script: Emily Dickinson's Manuscripts

Emily Dickinson's poetry presents particular challenges, difficulties, and opportunities for a number of reasons; chief among them in the current critical climate is the fact that her poems remained largely unpublished (in the sense of being typographically fixed in a printed text) in her own lifetime. This essay deals with individual versions of poems in manuscript and examines the extent to which levels of meaning are or are not lost for particular poems when they are transposed from the author's handwritten originals to printed translations. For the majority of published writers, manuscripts may be understood as notes towards a final, printed version, but for Dickinson print has been seen as seriously misrepresenting a very different, and potentially more sophisticated, medium. It has been suggested that print, with its blank background and uniformity of typescript, regularizes her poetry much as her first editors regularized her "idiosyncrasies" of grammar, punctuation, meter, and rhyme—in this case by erasing its graphic aspects. For Martha Nell Smith, the most visible and outstanding of a new generation of Dickinson textual scholars, physical or chirographical features of Dickinson's work are part of the poet's project of "destabilization."[1] One of the purposes of this essay is to test the accuracy of that observation—and to look also at what the manuscripts' material attributes might tell us about Dickinson's relationship to commercial culture and ideology. Clearly, any

American Literature, Vol. 70, No. 4. (December, 1998): pp. 705–737. © 1998 by Duke University Press.

study that claims that Dickinson's poems generate meaning from the manner of their inscription has serious implications for all her works. At least potentially, such studies call into question the validity of all printed editions of Dickinson's poems and letters.

That Dickinson *intended* the printed versions of her works to reproduce all the details of her manuscripts is not at all clear. She left no explicit instructions on how her texts were to be assembled and presented after her death, and the evidence contained in the manuscripts themselves is not always consistent. Nevertheless, there is, broadly speaking, a consensus of international scholarly opinion that holds that a return to the manuscripts is necessary to the establishment of a reliable corpus of her poems; by and large, I agree. But I have misgivings about the positivistic assumptions that underpin such a project, or, more accurately, misgivings about the lack of published opinion opposing this impulse. It is not that I think it is wrong but that certain problems of approach (and some of the conclusions already drawn) have not yet been thought through or sufficiently debated. I am therefore testing the assertion that Dickinson's manuscripts are the most reliable guide to her meaning(s)—and that they demonstrate a proleptic textual radicalism—by looking closely at how Dickinson presented her work to others and by examining the evidence on how her closest friend and literary ally, her sister-in-law Susan Huntington Gilbert Dickinson, appears to have interpreted formal aspects of Dickinson's poetry. Details of punctuation, capitalization, indentation, and lineation, as well as the relationships between lines, and between words at the end of a line and the right-hand edge of the page, will also be examined in an attempt to provide readers with enough detail to draw abstract or theoretical conclusions independent of my own.

* * *

Voices opposed to the contemporary emphasis on the manuscripts as agents of a new poetic and scriptural enterprise are too often dismissed as anachronistic. Ironically, one of those voices belongs to the man who, perhaps more than anyone else, was responsible for generating much of the new interest in the manuscripts with *The Editing of Emily Dickinson: A Reconsideration* (1967) and *The Manuscript Books of Emily Dickinson* (1981).[2] Ralph Franklin does not believe that Dickinson's work sheets, drafts, and fair copies possess the detailed aesthetic significance attributed to them by later scholars, though his comments have often been interpreted as if they support such a view.[3] In *The Birth-mark*, Susan Howe paraphrases her correspondence with Franklin on this question, in which he expresses antipathy to the project of making manuscripts the primary object of Dickinson scholarship:

He [Franklin] told me the notebooks were not artistic structures and were not intended for other readers; Dickinson had a long history of sending poems to people—individual poems—that were complete, he said. My suggestion about line breaks depended on an "assumption" that one reads in lines; he asked, "what happens if the form lurking in the mind is the *stanza?*" [Howe's italics][4]

Another conscientious objector is David Porter. In a review of William Shurr's *New Poems of Emily Dickinson,* Porter contests Jerome McGann's claim that Dickinson's "surviving manuscript texts urge us to take them at face value, to treat all scriptural forms as potentially significant *at the aesthetic or expressive level*":[5]

In the aesthetics of her scriptural forms, then, what is the function of Dickinson's disabling eye trouble and the probability that, as she wrote in pen then pencil, her impaired peripheral vision could not measure out spaces or reliably ascertain a sheet's edges where her hand-written lines began or finished or were interrupted?[6]

Porter and Franklin, as I understand them, appear to unite in resisting Howe's observation that after "the first nine fascicles, lines break off, interrupting meter" and the implication that this represents a deliberate strategy on Dickinson's part.[7] But if the manuscripts *do* include significant features that are normalized or even excluded (accidentally or purposely) from the published editions of Dickinson's work, then the printed versions of some poems (perhaps even of the majority) misrepresent essential parts of their meaning(s). Such at least is the argument put forward by McGann in *Black Riders: The Visible Language of Modernism,* in which he illustrates his conclusions by taking as examples two versions of the opening stanza of P650; the first is the version that appears in Johnson's one-volume edition, the second McGann's transcription of Dickinson's manuscript form:

1.

Pain—has an Element of Blank—
It cannot recollect
When it begun—or if there were
A time when it was not—

2.

Pain has an Element
of Blank—

It cannot recollect
When it began—or if
there were
A time when it was not[8]

McGann says that it "does no good to argue, as some might, that these odd lineations are unintentional—the result of Dickinson finding herself at the right edge of the page, and so folding her lines over. Her manuscripts show that she could preserve the integrity of the metrical unit if she wanted."[9] Whether McGann's certainty derives from empirical research (a statistical study of the number of times Dickinson divides a given metrical unit into two lines for reasons that can be construed to be conscious, as opposed to the number of divisions made necessary by the length of a word and/or its proximity to the right edge of the page) is not stated. One does not even know if such a scientific approach could be objectively sustained. But one would want, nevertheless, to question some of McGann's conclusions. Does it follow, for example, that the "integrity of the metrical unit" is compromised by having it occupy two lines of a manuscript rather than one? And while there is no reason to doubt his claim that the blank space that follows the word "Blank" is a kind of pun, is it not possible that the same pun exists in the "regularized" version? Moreover, if this pun is truly intentional, why did Dickinson not accentuate it by omitting the dash, which interposes itself between the noun and the space that follows, and which may be read as leading us to the next line rather than to that space? Finally, if McGann is so concerned with the misrepresentation of Dickinson's technique entailed by any failure to present her texts exactly as she wrote them, why does he ignore the plus sign (+) after "A" in line 6 of the manuscript version, which signals the presence of a variant ("Day") for the word that comes after it ("time")? Indeed, why not point out that "began" in line 4 looks very much like the "begun" which Johnson transcribed it as? Are we to assume that this ambiguity is accidental where all the rest are not? And why omit the dash that appears to follow "not" in the manuscript version? Where are we to stop when it comes to judging what is deliberate?

Peter Campbell makes many of the same points in his review of *Black Riders,* and he goes on to suggest that Dickinson's line breaks may indicate that she was not at all interested in the physical properties of the poem, a possibility that may be difficult for twentieth-century editors and readers to accept but that cannot be dismissed.[10] In this context, Dickinson's correspondence with Thomas Wentworth Higginson, the manuscripts of which are presently lodged at the Boston Public Library, can be instructive for a number of reasons. The correspondence was carried on from 1862, the peak year of Dickinson's creative enterprise, to 1886, the year of her death, and is therefore quite comprehensive. At the same time, it comprises a limited number of texts and a manageable yet reliable body of evidence for close textual investigation. Finally, it combines both poems and letters, which one can compare for common characteristics to determine whether any conclusions can be drawn from these commonalities. As Ralph Franklin has argued, "any special theory of Dickinson's mechanics will have to fit both poems and letters."[11] And there are common features. For example, in the manuscript of L441, written in July 1875, Dickinson twice splits words (ironically enough, given the criticism of Johnson for not reproducing these features, both occur in his transcription of the letter): on the second page, she writes, "She asks / for my / Father, con- / stantly," and on the third page, "I am pleased / that what / grieves our- /self so much."[12] On the first and second pages of her January 1876 letter to Higginson she tells him, "I had read [page-break] 'Childhood,' / with compunc- / tion that / thought so / fair-fall / on foreign / Eyes—" (*L*, 2:546–547; GC, Ms. Am. 1093 [581]). In February or March of the same year she asks, "Could you / pardon the / Elderly gentle- / man, who/ entrusted / the circumstan- / ces to you" (*L*, 2:549; GC, Ms. Am. 1093 [66]). Again, in L458 (spring 1876), she writes:

Dear Friend,
    Your
thought is
so serious
and cap-
tivating, (*L*, 2:552–553; GC, Ms. Am. 1093 [69])

In L486 (about 1877) she writes on the second page, "In a dissem- / bling hue" and "Please re- / member me" (*L*, 2:571–572; GC, Ms. Am. 1093 [78]). These two word breaks are especially interesting because the first forms part of a poem, while the second is in the letter itself. Of the two, the second might seem to have the most semantic potential, though it seems likely that it was accidental. Dickinson is asking to be remembered to Mrs. Higginson, and there would seem to be very little point in punning on the letter as a kind of *disjecta membra,* which is then reconstituted in the living speech of the recipient to his wife. On the fourth page of the same letter, she talks of how "I thought / your appro- / bation Fame– / and it's with- / drawal Infamy." In L488 she refers on the third page to looking in vain for Higginson "in the Mag- / azines, where" once he wrote (*L*, 2:573; GC, Ms. Am. 1093 [79]). The examples continue (and I have not included all of] them): "per- / haps" on the third page of L622 (December 1879, *L*, 2:649– 650; GC, Ms. Am. 1093 [99]), "con- / venient" on the second page of L674 (November 1880, *L*, 3:680; GC, Ms. Am. 1093 [101]), "can- / not" on the third page of L735 (about 1881, *L*, 3:716; GC, Ms. Am. 1093 [106]), "im- / measurable" on the second page of L819 (late April 1883, *L*, 3:773; GC, Ms. Am. 1093 [107]), "Biogra- / phied" on the second page of L972 (February 1885, *L*, 3:863–864; GC, Ms. Am. 1093 [111]), "Super- / scription" on the second page of L1007 (August 1885, *L*, 3:884; GC, Ms. Am. 1093 [112]), "en- / tered" on the first page and "no- / tices" on the third page of L1042 (spring 1886, *L*, 3:903; GC, Ms. Am. 1093 [113]), and (finally) "acclama- / tion" in L1043, written in late April 1886 (*L*, 3:904; GC, Ms. Am. 1093 [114]). The patterns are clear enough. In the years I have looked at in which word separation occurs in Dickinson's correspondence, the ratio of letters with instances of division to letters without is about one to two.[13] However, if we add the years between 1876 and 1886 when there is no division at all, the ratio is closer to two to five (twenty with, forty-eight without). The occurrences seem largely accidental, however; they do not appear to have been deliberately manipulated for semantic purposes.

Now letters are not poems, even though a great deal of thought (and sometimes revision) went into Dickinson's correspondence. There were frequently drafts of letters (and even of short notes), and Dickinson seems to have kept little scraps with images and phrases that she subsequently incorporated into her communications when the occasion allowed. In 1863 she included this version of the concluding stanza of "That after Horror—that 'twas us" (P286) in a note to Higginson:

> The possibility to pass
> Without a Moment's Bell—
> Into Conjecture's pres-
> ence—
> Is like a face of Steel
> That suddenly looks into
> Our's
> With a Metallic Grin— [page break]
> The Cordiality of Death
> Who Drills his
> welcome—in— (HL, MS Am 1118.3 [33]).

McGann claims that Dickinson's manuscripts urge us "to treat all scriptural forms as potentially significant," and one can, in fact, construct (or reconstruct) a possible strategy behind the splitting of "pres-ence." It delays the encounter between the speaker and Death—heightening the sense of dreadful anticipation—and perhaps also performs the desire to postpone that final meeting. It would be nice to believe that Dickinson intended such an effect, but it is impossible to say with any certainty that she did, for the photostat shows that she broke the word at this point because she did not have room enough to complete it.[14] What is relevant for my discussion is this: Almost any feature of Dickinson's manuscripts can be interpreted to suggest a proleptic concern with the semantic potential of the poem's visual properties—its line and word breaks as well as its punctuation. But such interpretations—however exciting—must remain conjectural, for there is as yet no solid evidence—in the shape of a book-length study of these features—of a consistent attempt on Dickinson's part to exploit these aspects of linguistic inscription.

In other words, the dividing of words between lines is not uncommon in Dickinson's writing (especially in the later years), and occurrences in her manuscript poems may not be deliberate. At least in the letters to Higginson, there does not appear to be a pattern of words being consciously split for artistic effect. If there is a tendency here, it is this: Generally speaking, the material inscription of the letters that formed words and the words that formed lines in Dickinson's correspondence with Higginson were not an important concern for the poet.

Among the many objections that might be raised against such a provisional conclusion, the most obvious is that Higginson (judging by his negative comments on formal aspects of Dickinson's poetry, as reflected in her replies to his letters) was profoundly conservative—even ignorant—when it came to literary innovation. But there is a sense in which this conservatism strengthens the conclusion I am proposing, for if Higginson was as conservative as he is made out to be, there would be no point in Dickinson experimenting with lineation and word division in her correspondence with him. And if one objects to this line of argument by saying that if such instances are not deliberate in the Higginson correspondence (as seems to be the case), why are they accidental only there and not everywhere else? For example, when Dickinson writes to Samuel Bowles (in November 1862) and splits "ar- / gument" between lines twelve and thirteen of the second page, "super- / sede" between the last line of page three and the first of page four, and "content- / tion" between lines five and six of the fourth page (*L*, 2:419–420; HL, bMS AM 1118.99c L277), does this mean that the split word "econom- / ical" in the version of "Victory comes late" she sent to him in 1862 is similarly accidental (*L*, 2:399–400; HL, bMS Am 1118.99c L257)? If the letters were crafted with care (as they were) and yet feature nonsignificant word splitting, what does this mean for the significance of split words in the poems?

It might be objected that Higginson and Bowles were men of the world, public figures who were not intimate enough with Dickinson for her to relax and reveal her truly innovative side. And there is some truth in this. The letters to Bowles, for instance, are more reserved than those to her sister-in-law and close friend Susan Dickinson, which are casually inscribed on an array of different papers—envelopes and scraps as well as more formal stationery. It has been argued that the scraps bespeak a "comfort-level" with Susan that Dickinson could never feel with Higginson or Bowles. The very materiality of these different texts, then, has a meaning. But precisely how this meaning can be formulated is difficult to say. For some critics, confidentiality enables Dickinson to be experimental. But perhaps it means the opposite. Familiarity may mean that normal epistolary and literary regulations can be suspended. Perhaps Dickinson relaxed with Susan because the appearance of the writing on the page had no significance for either of them—except occasionally as Dickinson played with some accidental detail of the paper or fragment on which she was writing. In other words, in this instance the relevance of Dickinson's scripts can arguably be limited to the historical relationship she had with her sister-in-law. It might be a function of their friendship and not have any importance for her poetry as a whole. With Bowles and Higginson, who offered the possibility of publication and access to the literary scene or some measure of institutional literary respectability and esteem, her circumspection or self-control might be taken as a sign that, had she published, she would have normalized her lines and accepted the conventions of print. She might even have given the poems titles. Another way of putting this would be to say that the "published" version of a poem like "Victory comes late" shows a willingness to compromise or negotiate her linguistic and scriptural forms.[15] Also, the fact that Dickinson complained to Higginson in 1866 that a line in "A narrow Fellow in the grass" had been "defeated" by the unsanctioned insertion of a comma in the third line of its printed version does not mean that she paid the same minute attention to details of punctuation in all other poems. Variant copies of the same poem demonstrate inconsistency on this point (from another perspective, they are restlessly inventive).[16]

* * *

Another claim made about the poems included in correspondence—and about the letters themselves—is that they break down the boundaries between poetry and prose. There are several ways in which this assertion might be understood, but for the purposes of this essay I want to concentrate on the poems included in the correspondence without any apparent attention being drawn to their existence *as poems*. The argument is that these poems are not lifted out of their context or separated from the matrix of personal connections that constitute the relationship between the letter reader and the writer, as they were by Dickinson's editors. Again, Thomas Johnson's edition is usually blamed for imposing standards derived from the conventions of print on Dickinson's handwritten letters, thus obscuring the extent of her experimentation. To indicate the presence of a poem or a stanza within a letter, Johnson indents and therefore separates the poem physically and generically from its prose context.[17] Ellen Hart, who is among the critics who suggest that Dickinson was experimenting with generic boundaries when she included a poem in a letter without indicating formally that it was different, makes two central points:

> First, Dickinson did not visually separate prose and poetry in her letters. Her prose lines and the lines of a poem are similar in length, she did not consistently divide poetry from prose through spacing, and she did not vary margins. A standard prose format for the letters results in visual inaccuracies, such as Johnson's paragraphing: Dickinson did not use indentation to indicate paragraphs. Second, the relationship between poetry and prose is so complex in Dickinson's writing that lineating poetry but not prose sets up artificial genre distinctions. There are no easily drawn periods in Dickinson's writing, no distinct point where it is possible to say, "Before this the genre of the letters is exclusively prose, and there is no need to lineate." Furthermore, when prose is not lineated, poetic devices that Dickinson uses in her prose may be deemphasized, muted, or obscured.[18]

Hart's arguments are cogent and bespeak a long familiarity with the manuscripts, though it is not absolutely clear to me (in the current era of the prose poem, the long line, and the letter/poem) that lineation is needed to detect the presence of the poetic in Dickinson's correspondence. But in the case of a draft letter written to Mrs. Edward Tuckerman in 1880, Hart's comments are not completely accurate:

> Dear friend,
>   I thought
> of you, although
> I never saw
> your friend.
> Brother of
> Ophir
> Bright adieu [page break]
> Honor, the
> shortest route
> To you—
>   Emily— (L, 3:682) [19]

The margins in this short note are relatively consistent for the prose part of the letter, but not for the poem. The first five lines feature empty spaces of approximately 1.3, 0.9, 2.3, 2.3, and 2.8 centimeters (unless otherwise stated, measurements are from the right edge of the paper), so that there is no graphic indication that the prose has ended and the poem has begun. Instead, prose and poetry run into each other, which may be an attempt on Dickinson's part to disguise the extra-epistolary origins of the poem by suggesting an organic continuity between the two—that "it is a poem that has grown up in a field of prose, like tares among the wheat."[20] But the sixth line ends 8.4 centimeters from the right-hand edge of the page, and there are spaces of 4.6 and 4.3 centimeters after the first and third lines on the second page. Contrary to Hart's view, at this point there does seem to be *some* visual indication of a generic shift—though this is only one small example. Hart would rightly argue that her generalization covers the majority of the poems in manuscript form (and even allows for such discrepancies). Nonetheless, the conclusion to be drawn from the Tuckerman note may be that Dickinson's prose lineation is caused by a combination of arbitrary factors: the size of the page, for example, and the length of Dickinson's words as they are written on the page. Within the poem, however, *some* aspects of the lineation are deliberate, and we need to set up guidelines for knowing which.

If we look again at the correspondence between Dickinson and Higginson, this time in search of what conclusions can be drawn about the visual marking of generic shifts, the results are interesting. There are some obvious instances when Dickinson enclosed poems on separate sheets of paper in the same envelope as a letter. Most famously, when she wrote to Higginson for the first time on 15 April 1862, asking if her verse was alive, she included four poems on separate pages. In February of 1863, however, she tried something slightly different. She enclosed "The Soul unto itself" (P683) on two pages detached from the main body of the letter but also included "Best Gains— must have the Losses'Test—" (P684) and "Not 'Revelation'—'tis—that waits" (P685) *within* the text of the letter itself (*L*, 2:423; GC, Ms. Am. 1093 [17]). Both 684 and 685 are two-line poems according to Johnson, who indented them and then assigned them numbers in his editions of the *Poems*, but Dickinson gives no indication in her letter that she intended the first to be read *as poetry* or independent of the prose that surrounds it (just as Hart leads us to expect). The second, which is written over four lines in the manuscript, is slightly different in that the space between the last word in the line before it ("disclosed—") and the right edge of the paper is appreciably greater than those after other end words on the same (fourth) page, and in that this space is then repeated in the second line of the poem as it is transcribed on the page, and again in the fourth line of the poem as it is transcribed on the fifth page of the letter (where it is the second line from the top). Listed consecutively, the distances measure approximately 6, 6, and 8.7 centimeters. Most of the other lines in the rest of the letter end within a centimeter or less of the right edge of the paper; thus the sequence of open spaces not dictated by necessity tends to make the poem stand out more on the page. These spaces function almost as a typographical convention that signals the presence of a generic shift. Whether this is deliberate is another question. For now, it is perhaps enough to record that a reader would have been aware of some kind of shift in register, even if the poet did not indent or attach quotation marks or otherwise announce the fact that she was changing genre.

In 1863 Dickinson reverted to earlier habits by writing a short (one-and-a-half-page) note to Higginson, signing it, and then writing immediately afterwards the second stanza of "That after Horror—that 'twas us" (P286) (GC, Ms. Am. 1093 [17]). But in L459 (L, 2:553–554; GC, Ms. Am 1093 [85]), sent to Higginson (it is conjectured) in spring 1876, Dickinson included within the text of the letter itself "The things we thought that we should do" (P1293); this letter is a useful example of those instances when she did not signal the inclusion in any obvious way but where the reader can nevertheless see that it is different. On the first page of the manuscript of this letter, the lines usually reach either very close to the right-hand edge of the paper or they stop about one centimeter short. On the second, third, and fourth pages, line length is more erratic; this excerpt begins at the top of the second page:

refreshed.
Labor might
fatigue, though
it is Action's
rest
The things
we thought
that we should do
We other
things have
done
But those
peculiar
industries
Have never [page break]
been begun.

The Lands
we thought

that we
should seek
When large
enough to
run
By speculation
ceded
To Speculation's
Son—

The Heaven,
in which we [page break]
hoped to pause
When Discipline
was done
Untenable to
Logic
But possibly
the One—
I am glad
you remember
the "Meadow
Grass."
That forestalls
Fiction.

After the word "rest" in the fifth line, there is a space of approximately 6.9 centimeters. Normally, such a space is dictated by necessity, by a long word, for example, that would not fit into the space left after the first word in the line, or by the need to indicate formally that a new paragraph follows. Hart is perfectly right in saying that Dickinson does not usually indent at the *beginning* of a paragraph, but this is only half the truth; new paragraphs are usually indicated at the *end* of the previous one by blank space in the last line.[21] There is no long word following "rest," so it seems likely that Dickinson is using the space to announce the beginning of a new sequence of ideas, which in this instance turns out to be a poem. The handwriting seems to me to become larger in the poem, especially on the third page, but what immediately interests me is the multiplication of instances where lines fall far short of the right-hand edge (as they do not in the first page). Lines eight, twelve, and thirteen are fairly clear examples of this on the second page, while lines eight (in particular), ten, and twelve are equally clear examples on the third. The distances between "run" (on line eight of the third page), and "Son" (on the twelfth line of the same page), and the right-hand edge of the paper are both roughly 8.5 centimeters, which is fairly substantial given that they do not precede new paragraphs. In addition, Dickinson skips a line between the stanzas of the poem. Normally, the gap between the bottom of one line and the top of the next is about five millimeters, but between the bottom of the last line of a stanza and the top of the next it is about a centimeter. In short, Higginson (or any other reader) would have been conscious of a change in layout that corresponded to a shift from prose to poetry. The new paragraph beginning with "Labor" and ending with "rest" provides a kind of bridge between the conventional courtesies of the first page and the poetic density of the second, in the sense that it marks a change in register or tone (the second is much more condensed) and breaks up the scriptural regularity of the page.

It is worth pointing out that Dickinson regularly used capitals to indicate the beginning of a poetic line, so that, for example, although "By speculation / ceded / To Speculation's / Son—" is arranged as four lines on the third page, these represent only two lines of poetry. Much has been made of the potential significance of Dickinson's line arrangements, but in this case the combination of upper-case letters, iambic meter, and rhyme makes it seems reasonable to believe that Johnson was not entirely misguided in assuming that here were three quatrains whose transcription as thirty-two lines was not intellectually, semantically, metrically, or generically significant. Another example, this time from a pencil draft to, it is conjectured, Professor Edward Tuckerman in 1883 or 1884, is numbered as P1622 by Johnson (I number the lines for ease of reference):

(1) A sloop of
(2) amber slips
(3) away
(4) upon an ether
(5) sea,
(6) and wrecks in
(7) peace a purple
(8) tar
(9) the son of
(10) ecstasy [22]

I have deliberately not indicated where Dickinson's capitals are because it is possible to reconstruct the poet's wishes with respect to the arrangement of lines from the alignment of words, margins, and spaces on the page. Although most lines come near the right-hand edge of the paper, lines 3, 5, 8, and 10 do not; they feature spaces of approximately 7.8, 8.7, 8.7, and 6 centimeters between the last vowel or consonant and the edge of the page. Clearly, in all of these cases the words are either written singly for the sake of emphasis or are extensions of the lines that precede them. If for the sake of argument we consider these words less as units of meaning on their own than as elements of the poetic line, it is fairly easy to argue that Johnson did not act unreasonably in arranging the lines as he did in the *Variorum* edition (the punctuation is another matter):

> A Sloop of Amber slips away
> Upon an Ether Sea,
> And wrecks in Peace a Purple Tar,
> The Son of Ecstasy— [23]

Does this mean that the line arrangements of the manuscripts can be ignored when transcribing poems onto the page of a book or the screen of a computer? This is a difficult question, and the answer may depend on the intended audience and the kind of edition being prepared. But respecting Dickinson's wishes involves more than the exact reproduction of her line arrangements. The spaces between end words and right-hand margins are also clearly significant, as are her capitals and the meter (not all of which are as predictable as the examples I have chosen). Future editorial decisions will have to be argued on an individual basis, which is perhaps one reason why the Dickinson Editing Collective, established to produce more reliable editions of the texts, may be able to improve on the efforts of its predecessors, since it will have the benefit of contributions from several scholars rather than one or two. It is also why, in my view, the editions produced by the Collective must always remain provisional, subject to the latest thinking about Dickinson's methods and conjectured intentions.

One final example, "The Sea said 'Come' to the Brook" (P1210), is worth examining because, again, there are several versions of the poem, which Johnson dates to 1872. The "he" in the second stanza of the second version/poem (if there is a second stanza) is interesting because there is no reason for it to be on a separate line. Dickinson could easily have fitted at least one, if not both words from the next line onto the same line if she had wanted to. Instead, the word's isolation indicates a pause that corresponds to the end of a poetic or metrical line:

> The Sea said
> "Come" to the Brook—
> The Brook said
> "Let me grow"—
> The Sea said

"Then you will
be a Sea"—
"I want a Brook—
Come now"—
The Sea said
"Go" to the Sea—
The Sea said
"I am he
You cherished"—
"Learned Waters—
Wisdom is stale
to Me" ____ [line drawn in manuscript] [24]

The Sea said
"Come" to the
Brook—
The Brook
said "Let me
grow"—
The Sea
said "Then
you will be
a Sea—
I want a
Brook—
Come now"! [page break]

The Sea
said "Go" to
the Sea—
The Sea
said "I am
he
You cherished"—
"Learned Waters—
Wisdom is
stale—to Me" (*L*, 2:500; GC, Ms. Am. 1093 [43])

Another of the claims about Dickinson—made most persuasively by Susan
Howe and Martha Nell Smith—is that she used letters visually. As Howe
memorably formulates it, "Letters are sounds we see."[25] One of the examples
used by both Howe and Smith is "The Sea said 'Come' to the Brook," where,

according to Smith, the *S*'s are shaped like waves and the *T*'s formed to resemble choppy seas. Taken in isolation from the rest of the letters and poems, the argument seems convincing, and it is often repeated in other contexts as though it were established fact. Of course, Smith's point here is part of a larger argument, as she describes a writer challenging the rigidities of conventional printing; in Howe's view, we miss this challenge by reading Dickinson's poems in ordinary type form.[26]

But in fact the letter *S* is shaped in exactly the same way in many other manuscript poems and letters, and one may legitimately wonder whether the effect described by Howe and Smith is only that—an effect, not an intention. In a letter to Higginson in November 1871, for instance, there are several examples of *S* (and even *s*) shapes which are exactly the same as those in P1210: "Shakespeare" on the third page of the manuscript is a very clear instance of this (GC, MS. Am. 1093 [37]). And in a poem enclosed within the letter, "Step lightly on this narrow spot" (P1183, written about 1871), the *S*'s in the words "Step," "Spot," "Seams," and "Step" are almost horizontal, while the *T*'s and *t*'s are slanted and crossed in such a way that they resemble *X*'s (or *x*'s). Interestingly, Dickinson sent a copy of P1210 to Higginson in late 1872, and there are no real differences between the *S* and *y* shapes in the poem and those in the letter (the *y* in the word "you" resembles an *s* shape in both, which is why I mention it) (*L*, 2:500; GC, Ms. Am. 1093 [43]).

* * *

Over the past decade, critics have increasingly come to view Dickinson's nonpublication as a choice made in the interest of preserving the textual integrity of her work. In particular, much has been made by Martha Nell Smith of a cluster of statements made separately by Dickinson and Susan as suggesting a common poetic manifesto.[27] "I had told you I did not print," Emily wrote to Higginson in early 1866, complaining that the published version of "A narrow Fellow in the Grass" had been altered in the 17 February edition of the *Springfield Daily Republican* (*L*, 2:450).[28] In another letter to Higginson, Susan wrote that the poems "will ever be to me marvellous in manuscript or type."[29] Finally, there is this passage from Susan's letter of 18 February 1891 to William Hayes Ward, editor of the *Independent*:

> Dear Sir.
> Thank you for spending so much time over my letter. I recognize fully all Miss Emily's lack of rhyme and rhythm, but have learned to accept it for the bold thought, and everything else so unusual about her.
> I think if you do not feel that your own literary taste is compromised by it, I would rather the three verses of the "Martyrs"

should be published if any. I shall not be annoyed if you decide not
to publish at all. I should have said *printed*.[30]

For Smith, the cumulative effect of these quotations is an expression of
skepticism about the medium of print itself, or about its technological limitations—its rigid typefaces and inflexible lines and margins. Kamilla Denman
is typical when she says that Dickinson's "reluctance to publish was based,
at least in part, on an aversion to the conditions of print."[31] I would alter the
emphasis somewhat and say that all these statements are about the *ideology*
of print—its inevitable tendency to regularize for the sake of a large audience
and to give priority to market criteria over personal or aesthetic ones. Like
the snow of "It sifts from Leaden Sieves" (P311), print buries the unique
characteristics of handwriting under a blank uniformity.[32] We can be fairly
certain that Emily and Susan were not comfortable with the *idea* of publication; Dickinson's letters and poems, and her nonpublication (however much
that changed from year to year), testify to that. And Susan goes on to say in
the 1891 letter to Ward that she had thought of "a vol. to be printed at my
own expense" and circulated privately. In choosing this route she could fore-
stall criticism as well as the advertising of "personal detail" and "peculiari-
ties." She also wrote, "I sometimes shudder when I think of the world reading
her thoughts minted in deep heartbroken convictions."[33] The emphasis here
is on privacy and propriety, not on the significance of scriptural details. And
there are unmistakable traces of class prejudice here, for Susan's shudder is
the reaction of a refined sensibility to the gaze of the unrefined.[34] Indeed,
the letter as a whole is deeply preoccupied with the rights of property, literary and otherwise. Susan is dazed by the announcement that "stranger hands
were preparing [Dickinson's poetry] for publication."[35] Issues of propriety are
also reflected in other letters by Susan to Ward: "I wish I could persuade my
daughter [Martha] to send you an Easter poem she has just written—but she
is immovable, *having a most feminine horror of print* [italics mine].[36] Emily's
and Susan's objections to print may be seen as part of an internalized ideology
of the feminine that insists that domestic privacy is an important aspect of
a woman's identity and integrity. As Susan wrote, "(after all the intoxicating
fascination of creation) she [Emily] as deeply realised that for her, as for all of
us women not fame but 'Love and home and certainty are best.'"[37] Publication
brings publicity, which threatens *personal* integrity. Exactly how much print
threatens the *aesthetic* integrity of the *poems* is an open question.[38]

At this point, perhaps more attention needs to be paid to Smith's claim
that Susan would have produced a very different edition of Emily's poems, one
which, in Susan's words, would have been "rather more full, and varied, than
[that of Higginson and Todd]," with excerpts from the letters and "quaint bits to
my children"[39]—though this presentation would have been influenced both by

its mode of publication and its projected readership, mainly friends and family who would have found the poems and excerpts from letters personally as well as aesthetically significant—like snapshots, of particular interest to those who knew or were related to her. Sue's description implies a desire to reflect the range of her sister-in-law's talents but not necessarily her mode of textual production. From this statement at least, there is no reason to suppose that she found the handwriting or layout of the poems and letters semantically significant.

Some idea of Susan Dickinson's editorial methods can be recovered from the fragments stored with the Dickinson family papers at the Houghton Library, Harvard University. Among these is Susan's manuscript for Emily's obituary, which was published in the *Springfield Daily Republican* on Thursday, 18 May 1886. This manuscript is potentially useful because at the end Susan quotes the first stanza of one of Dickinson's earliest poems (P27, thought by Johnson to have been written in 1858):

> Morns like these, we parted
> Noons like these, she rose,
> Fluttering first, then firmer,
> To her fair repose.[40]

Here is Dickinson's version, as I have transcribed it from its holograph form:

> Morns like these—we parted—
> Noons like these—she rose—
> Fluttering first—then firmer
> To her fair repose.[41]

And here is Mabel Loomis Todd's version, as it appeared in *Poems by Emily Dickinson,* Second Series (1891):

> Morns like these we parted;
> Noons like these she rose,
> Fluttering first, then firmer,
> To her fair repose.[42]

Alterations to the punctuation of this poem occur first in Susan Dickinson's manuscript copy of its opening stanza, and it says much about the strength of cultural norms for poetry that she and Todd independently arrived at similar presentations. Susan's version partly vindicates Todd's, in the sense that both appear to proceed from the assumption that Dickinson's manuscripts existed in a raw state and required editorial finishing before appearing in print. Given that Susan must have known of her sister-in-law's unhappiness about alterations to the punctuation of another poem, Susan's changes show either indifference, a sense that punctuation was not important in such an early poem, or an awareness that Dickinson's objections to changes in her punctuation were less generalized, less a manifesto, than we have supposed. Another possibility is that Susan was more conventional in her tastes than Emily and not fully conscious of the extent of her friend's innovations. Still other factors may come into play here. Susan may have been quoting from memory, or it may be that aesthetic considerations were secondary at this time of terrible loss—that what was important was that the sentiments expressed in the stanza were personally and generically appropriate. Having said that, it must be added that the obituary itself is a wonderfully controlled and careful piece of writing. Susan very consciously addresses and corrects many of the myths that had already sprung up about Dickinson (which reminds us again how public Dickinson's privacy actually was). Susan had several hundred of Dickinson's manuscript poems to choose from, and she selected one that simultaneously promotes her sister-in-law as a literary authority—someone to be quoted—and downplays her lack of religious orthodoxy (and all this in bird imagery that had private associations as well as links to the vocabulary of a wider feminine culture). Given this attention to detail, it seems surprising that Susan failed to reproduce Emily's punctuation—unless, of course, it had little or no significance, either for her or Dickinson (at least in this poem).

Interestingly, given current assertions that Dickinson did not distinguish between poetry and prose in her letters, Susan did not separate the stanza graphically from the prose that precedes it, but the typesetter for the *Republican* did. This practice prefigures the later treatment of Dickinson's letters by her editors. But Susan made no attempt to undo the typesetter's change in layout when she received a printed copy of the death notice for proofing, although she made several other alterations. The implication may well be that some nineteenth-century writers left the responsibility for the typographical arrangement of their work to the printer and objected to changes only when the aesthetic or semantic integrity of the text had been seriously compromised. In this instance, Susan clearly did not feel that her intentions had been significantly interfered with, and one wonders what significance this might have for Dickinson's epistolary practices. Was Dickinson playing with genre, as some commentators claim, or is the alleged erosion of generic differences in her correspondence a function of their informality, their status as personal documents?[43]

What is clear from the papers owned by Harvard University is that at some point after Dickinson's death Susan began to prepare a volume of her poems for publication (most of the texts are listed in the third volume of Thomas Johnson's *The Poems of Emily Dickinson*, where numbers 1649 to 1709 exist largely as transcripts made by Susan). The problem facing any

reader attempting to reconstruct Susan's editorial practices from the copies
that she made of Dickinson's originals is that in most cases only the copies
remain. But there are exceptions. Here is "Remembrance has a Rear and
Front" in two versions, the first approximating Dickinson's own, and the
second as Susan transcribed it:

Remembrance has
a Rear and Front
'Tis something
like a House—
It has a Garret
also
For Refuse and
the Mouse—

Besides the
deepest Cellar
That ever Mason
laid–
+ Leave me not
Ever there alone
Oh thou Almighty
God!
_____ [line drawn in manuscript]
    Fathoms
it's contents
Ourselves be not
pursued![44]
_____ [line drawn in manuscript]
                        front

Remembrance has a rear and
Tis something like a House
It has a Garret also
For Refuse and the Mouse
Besides the Deepest Cellar
That ever Mason laid
Look to it by the contents
Ourselves be not pursued

                                    —E [45]

It needs to be said immediately that the Dickinson version I print is from
Set 10 and may not be the same one Susan received. Nonetheless, several

points can be ventured from a comparison. Familiarity with other manuscripts allows us to be fairly sure that Susan dispensed with Dickinson's
own lineation, even though we cannot be certain exactly what changes she
made. The broken lines characteristic of the handwritten poems from the
eighth fascicle onwards have been replaced by one neat eight-line stanza.
The punctuation has also been omitted, though Susan elongates the last
letters of certain words in a way that might be taken as indicating dashes.
However one reads the handwriting, it seems possible that these transcriptions were not final but part of a process by which the poems were prepared
for eventual publication. From the evidence at Harvard, it seems that Susan
did not work completely on her own. Both her adult children, Ned and
Mattie, seem to have had specific tasks. Although we cannot know that
this is so, it would appear that Susan compiled and then copied Emily's
poems to her, tidied the lineation and some of the punctuation, and then
gave them to Ned or Martha to type. When typing was complete, Sue
proofread the typescript against her copy, added punctuation if and when
she saw fit, and sometimes supplied a title. In the following poem, for
instance, most of the punctuation has been added to the typescript by hand,
as has the title, and in the twelfth line "merry" has been written above a
crossed-out "many":

Afterward
Beside the autumn, poets sing,
A few prosaic days,
A little this side of the snow,
And that side of the Haze.

A few incisive mornings,
A few ascetic eves,
Gone Mr. Bryant's Golden Rod,
And Mr. Thomson's sheaves.

Still is the bustle in the brook,
Sealed are the spicy valves,
Mesmeric fingers softly touch
The eyes of merry elves.

Perhaps a squirrel may remain
My sentiments to share—
Grant me Oh Lord a sunny mind
Thy windy will to bear.

—Emily Dickinson

Susan Dickinson was a poet herself, of course, and given her intimate and continuous familiarity with Dickinson's writing, one wonders if it might be possible to gain a clearer view of the significance of details in Dickinson's manuscripts through Susan's own poetic practices. For instance, there are two extant versions of a poem by Sue that begins "What offering have I, dear Lord." One is handwritten, the other typed. Here are the first two stanzas of the autograph copy (I have indicated words that appear to be canceled with strikeout marks):

<blockquote>
have I <del>oh</del> dear Lord
What offering <del>can I bring</del>
                thee Lord
To show I am thy child
What service shorn of
                selfishness
And not with sin defiled!
—— —— ——

The day is past for turtle doves
For incense burnt in clouds
Or even spikenard costly
                rare
That bro't thy loving words.
—— —— —— —— —— ——
</blockquote>

Here is the typewritten version of the same poem, which I quote in full:

<blockquote>
What offering have I, dear Lord,
To show I am thy child!
What service shorn of selfishness
And not with sin defiled?

The day is past for turtle doves,
For incense burnt in clouds—
Or even spikenard costly rare
That bro't thy loving words.

Thou art not poor as we of earth,—
All space and time are thine
Save one unyielded wealth I hold,—
The will that should be thine!
</blockquote>

The point to be made here is that the twelve lines of the first two stanzas in the autograph version have been tidied up in the typewritten version, where they are neatly compressed to eight. Contemporary editorial procedure would suggest that had this been a Dickinson poem we would have retained the twelve lines. One hesitates to push the point too far, but the possibility I offer for consideration is that Dickinson would not have intended us to take similar phenomena in her own manuscripts as seriously as we do now. Like Susan's split lines, hers may simply be a function of their unpublished state (rather than features that prevented publication because she would not relinquish the right to use them in print). In the two versions of a poem by Susan entitled "Irony" (both clearly works in progress), the handwritten copy often contains divided lines that are made single in the printed copy. One might be tempted to say that if Susan ignored her own line arrangements when her poems were typed, perhaps Emily would have done the same. But, it might be argued, Susan was a very different writer, and reading Dickinson through her habits is a questionable procedure.

Nevertheless, what I hope to have established is that Susan's editorial methods (to the extent that they are recoverable from the Harvard collections, which are not extensive) provide us with insights that can be used in different ways. If one champions Susan as Dickinson's literary confidant, then it has to be admitted that one or both might have been more conventional than present-day scholarship would have us believe. It may be that Susan misjudged the extent of Dickinson's textual innovations, or perhaps she understood her well enough to feel certain that various graphic properties of the manuscripts had no significance. Still a third possibility is that she (like Higginson and Todd) felt that compromise was necessary to get Dickinson published.

* * *

Jerome McGann has made what is in many ways the definitive statement of contemporary critical consensus about the Dickinson texts, namely, that they need to be read in their original form to be truly appreciated and understood: "Emily Dickinson's poetry was not written *for* a print medium, even though it was written *in* an age of print. When we come to edit her work for bookish presentation, therefore, we must accommodate our typographical conventions to her work, not the other way around."[46] McGann's assertion that the poetry was not written for print is different from saying it was not printed. The first presupposes an intention; the other reports a fact. McGann assumes something not all critics are agreed upon. Indeed, the 'existence of the fascicles may suggest that the poems *were* prepared for some form of publication, though of course publication need not be synonymous with print. We need to modify McGann's claim, for although the majority of Dickinson's poems did not appear in print during her lifetime, it does not follow that they were not meant to be printed. The fascicles were not sent to any of Dickinson's closest friends in the way that individual poems were. This fact suggests that their intended audience may not have been intimate, local, or even contemporaneous. There is no evidence, for instance, that Susan knew about them. McGann's desire to avoid imposing twentieth-century typographical conventions onto Dickinson's texts is admirable, powerful, and often persuasive, but it does not obviate the possibility that his own perspective derives from modernist experiments with the medium of print, which he then inscribes onto a premodernist body of writing.

In "The Poet as Cartoonist" Martha Nell Smith compares aspects of Dickinson's "hand-made mode of production" and what she terms her cartoons (doodles or graphic appendages); she supports McGann's view when she writes (correctly, one acknowledges), "our study moves her comic text into the public sphere and demands shifts in thinking about what can count as a cartoon"[47]—and, by implication, what counts as a poem. Nevertheless, we cannot be certain that Dickinson herself would have approved of either shift. In other words, it is possible that what we identify as significant when we look closely at the physical or material details of her manuscripts are the consequences of our own editorial choices and interpretative conventions. It may well be that the informality and playfulness manifested by some of her texts is a function of their status as private, unpublished texts. Giving them a wider set of implications may be imposing on them a significance they were never meant to have. Another way of putting this would be to say that Emily Dickinson may not have been fully conscious of the potential her unpublished manuscripts possessed—or would acquire—as published documents. It may be later scholars who invent or reconstruct that potential. This is not the same as saying that critics misrepresent Dickinson. It is not even saying that Dickinson was ignorant of this potential. But it does mean that when we give privately produced papers a public significance, we should be aware that we are doing something that Dickinson herself did not do.

At stake, too, is Dickinson's place in the literary canon. If she is demonstrably not in control of, or not directing, the implications of her own textual practices, then she takes a step backwards into the nineteenth century; if she is visibly (and visually) in control, she takes a step forward into (and perhaps beyond) the mixed and postmodernist media of the twentieth century. (One might wonder, though, if what is ultimately at stake is the belief that all artists are fully and always in control of their own meanings.) The contemporary preoccupation with Dickinson's manuscripts may be seen as an attempt to lift her texts out of history, to say here was a poet who made eminently modern collages using visual forms and using form visually. Claims made on Dickinson's behalf certainly put more distance between her and the century she inhabited. In a sense, they establish her claim to what Northrop Frye called the "doodle" aspect of poetic discourse, which Jonathan Culler (quoting Frye) defines as the "'elaboration of verbal design,' as in shapes, stanzas, and conventional forms that create patterns for the eye" (and, one might add, for the mind).[48]

Are we further misrepresenting Dickinson's poems by presenting them in manuscript form as though the manuscripts were constructed with the aim of public consumption and/or aesthetic experimentation? There are a number of ways in which the theorization of Dickinson's scriptural practices can be understood and formulated: as nineteenth-century graphic initiatives whose significance has been fully recovered by textual scholars only in the twentieth century; as the accidental by-products of a nineteenth-century home-based literary production not oriented towards publication and impossible to transpose into print at that time (because of technological and editorial limitations) but with implications for twentieth-century poetics and/or aesthetics; and as formal deviations interpreted as significant by twentieth-century readers and then imposed upon the nineteenth century as fully deliberate graphic experiments. Are we reconstructing Dickinson's intentions, drawing our own conclusions for our own purposes, or behaving as if our conclusions were hers? The first possibility, it seems to me, has not yet been proved statistically, while the second and third are impossible either to prove or disprove. They are suspicions and doubts we must carry with us whenever we approach a Dickinson text, whether our primary interest is in attending to its status as a text or to its significance as poetry. In the end, perhaps such questions can never be finally answered. Perhaps we can only proceed in the hope that our reconstructions of Dickinson's texts approximate the range of choices she offered herself, and that we do not mar their integrity too much. The truth is that the visual characteristics of Dickinson's handwriting are not determinate, and it is impossible to recover their meaning with any degree of certainty. One feels that it will be always so with Emily Dickinson, who left no explicit statements about which methods of poetic presentation, assemblage, and transmission she desired. To borrow the image of the bee who avoids the chasing schoolboy in P319, she continues to mystify and to elude us. Long may she run.

NOTES

Transcribed letters and poems from the Thomas Wentworth Higginson collection are reproduced by courtesy of the Trustees of Boston Public Library. Quotations from Emily Dickinson's manuscripts are used by permission of The Houghton Library, Harvard University, Copyright © The President and Fellows of Harvard College. Letters are reprinted by permission of the publishers from *The Letters of Emily Dickinson*, ed. Thomas H. Johnson, Cambridge: The Belknap Press of Harvard University Press, Copyright © 1958,

1986 by the President and Fellows of Harvard College. Poems reprinted by permission of the publishers and the Trustees of Amherst College from *The Poems of Emily Dickinson,* ed. Thomas H. Johnson, Cambridge: The Belknap Press of Harvard University Press, Copyright © 1951,1955,1979,1983 by the President and Fellows of Harvard College, and from *The Complete Poems of Emily Dickinson,* ed. Thomas H. Johnson, Copyright © 1929, 1935 by Martha Dickinson Bianchi, Copyright © renewed 1957,1963 by Mary L. Hampson: Little, Brown and Company, Boston. I acknowledge the assistance of the following during the course of researching this article: Leslie Morris, Curator of Manuscripts, and the staff of the Houghton Reading Room at Harvard University; Giuseppe Bisaccia, Eugene Zepp and Roberta Zonghi and the staff at the Galatea Room of the Boston Public Library, Rare Books & Manuscripts Division; the staff of the Special Collections Room at Amherst College Library; David Porter; Alfred Habegger; Jeremy Hawthorn of the Norwegian University of Science and Technology; Daniel Lombardo and Jessica Teters of the Jones Library, Amherst; Cristanne Miller; Tim Morris; Jonathan Morse; and Lise Utne.

1. Martha Nell Smith, quoted in Elinor Heginbotham, "Plenary Session: Editing Dickinson," *Emily Dickinson International Bulletin* 7 (November/ December 1995): p. 5.

2. Ralph Franklin, *The Editing of Emily Dickinson: A Reconsideration,* 2 vols. (Madison: University of Wisconsin Press, 1967); *The Manuscript Books of Emily Dickinson* (Cambridge: Belknap Press of Harvard University Press, 1981).

3. See Mary Carney, "Dickinson's Poetic Revelations: Variants as Process," *The Emily Dickinson Journal* 5 (1996): pp. 134–135, for a fairly typical appropriation of Franklin's findings for purposes he clearly would not approve.

4. Susan Howe, *The Birth-Mark: Unsettling the Wilderness in American Literary History* (Hanover, N.H.: University Press of New England for Wesleyan University Press, 1993): p. 134.

5. Jerome McGann, *Black Riders: The Visible Language of Modernism* (Princeton: Princeton University Press, 1993): p. 38.

6. David Porter, Review Essay, *Emily Dickinson Journal* 4 (November 1995): p. 127.

7. Howe, *The Birth-Mark,* p. 148.

8. Houghton Library, Harvard University, MS Am 1118.3 (52). Subsequent references to manuscripts in the Houghton Library will be noted in the text with the abbreviation HL.

9. McGann, *Black Riders,* p. 28.

10. Peter Campbell, "Character Building," *London Review of Books,* 9 June 1994, pp. 21–22. Campbell emphatically denies that "someone who has read the poetry of . . . Emily Dickinson only in a printed format which bears little relationship to the original manuscripts [has] a necessarily imperfect understanding of [her] art."

11. Franklin, *The Editing of Emily Dickinson,* p. 120.

12. *Letters of Emily Dickinson,* ed. Johnson, 2:542–543; Manuscript (photostat), Gallatea Collection, Ms. Am. 1093 (57), Boston Public Library. The Boston Public Library and Thomas Johnson assign different numbers to the manuscripts; in the *Letters,* the manuscript is BPL (Higg 72). When referring to the photostat of a manuscript, I will identify the letter by the number assigned to it by Johnson and in parentheses give the volume and page number(s) in the *Letters* and the manuscript number of the item in the Gallatea Collection. Subsequent references will be cited in the text, where the *Letters* will be abbreviated as *L* and the Gallatea Collection as GC.

13. I list here the years in which the letters were written, the number of letters for that year, and the number with word separation (I do not count word separation more than once in any given letter): 1875: 2,2; 1876: 12, 6; 1877: 8, 5; 1878: 5, 0; 1879: 3, 1; 1880: 6, 1; 1881: 2, 1; 1882: 2, 0; 1883: 1, 1; 1884: 2, 0; 1885: 2, 2; and 1886: 3, 2. There are three years in which no division takes place—1878, 1882, and 1884—as well as one— 1880—when there is only one letter containing division. In the early years of the correspondence, from 1862 through 1874, there are five letters with word divisions out of a possible twenty-one. (Two manuscripts were not available to me, so the figure is approximate, but fairly reliable.) Separation is therefore slightly less frequent than in later years: one in four letters rather than one in three. The letter numbers (as they occur in Johnson's edition) are 261 (seventh page, fourth and fifth lines of the manuscript: "chap- / ters"); 280 (fourth page, lines seven and eight: "pro- / spective"); 319 (fourth page, ninth and tenth line: "enchant- / ment"); 368 (fourth page, lines two, three and four: "congrat- / ulation superflu- / ous"); 405 (first page, lines eight and nine, eleven and twelve: "per- / mission"; "per- / haps").

14. Needless to say, I am not claiming that Dickinson was somehow *incapable* of such an intention.

15. The difference between "public" and "private" variants of P690 is established more extensively by Carney in "Dickinson's Poetic Revelations," 136. Carney asserts—rightly—that the existence of these variants "suggests Dickinson's resistance and simultaneous acquiescence to the poetic conventions of her time."

16. Johnson is similarly undecided. He claims that the irregular line and stanza divisions clearly suggest "a conscious experimentation" at times, while at other times they reflect "indifference" (*Poems of Emily Dickinson*, lxiii). When Margret Sands quotes (and italicizes) only the "indifference" part of Johnson's comment, she seriously, and unfairly, misrepresents Johnson's view. See her otherwise excellent "Re-reading the Poems: Editing Opportunities in Variant Versions," *Emily Dickinson Journal* 5 (November 1996): p. 141.

17. In doing so Johnson was guided by his duty as an editor to alert the reader to the presence of these poems, and his reasons are scholarly and impeccable. And even when editing the correspondence, the poetry was still his primary interest. The conventions of his day also insisted on such a presentation, and to expect Johnson to have behaved differently is unrealistic.

18. Ellen Louise Hart, "The Elizabeth Whitney Putnam Manuscripts and New Strategies for Editing Emily Dickinson's Letters," *Emily Dickinson Journal* 4 (April 1995): p. 49.

19. The manuscript facsimile is no. 41 at the Frost Library of Amherst College, Special Collections.

20. The phrase is Jerome McGann's, from his "Emily Dickinson's Visible Language," *Emily Dickinson Journal* 2 (November 1993): p. 50. McGann's example is a letter to Samuel Bowles (L229) that includes "Would you like summer? Taste of ours." (P691). As he says, "the poem slips into the prose without any marginal signals that the textual rhythms are about to undergo a drastic shift." This is true, but it is also true that by the seventh line of the facsimile, gaps have begun to appear in the lines, corresponding (perhaps) to the end of metrical lines. The blurring of generic distinctions is accompanied by what might be construed as their continuing formal demarcation.

21. Johnson imposes typographic conventions that Dickinson did not, of course, but, I would argue, his usage is prompted by hers.

22. Manuscript no. MS D56 (836) at Amherst College, Special Collections.

23. Johnson, *Poems of Emily Dickinson*, 3: p. 1113.

24. Franklin, *The Manuscript Books of Emily Dickinson*, 2: p. 1342.

25. Howe, *The Birth-Mark*, p. 139.

26. Ibid., p. 150.

27. See Martha Nell Smith, *Rowing in Eden: Rereading Emily Dickinson* (Austin: University of Texas Press, 1992), especially chaps. 5 and 6, where Smith discusses many of the same statements and issues I list here. For a more recent and fuller presentation of Susan's work (including the poems by her under discussion) and the extent of her collaboration with Emily, see Smith et al., *Writing by Susan Dickinson* at http://jefferson.village.virginia.edu/dickinson.

28. In fact, Dickinson is concerned that Higginson will believe her to have been economical with the truth in claiming that she was not interested in mass-publication.

29. Susan Huntington Dickinson, in Millicent Todd Bingham, *Ancestors' Brocades: The Literary Debut of Emily Dickinson* (New York: Harper and Brothers, 1945), p. 86.

30. Ibid., p. 115. Some of the same nervousness about the impropriety of publication is seen on the title page of the 1883 *Hymns, Home, Harvard* by Mary Silsbee, which states "printed, not published"; see Edwin Haviland Miller, *Salem is My Dwelling Place: A Life of Nathaniel Hawthorne* (Iowa City: University of Iowa Press, 1991): p. 148.

31. Kamilla Denman, "Emily Dickinson's Volcanic Punctuation," in *Emily Dickinson: A Collection of Critical Essays,* ed. Judith Farr (Englewood Cliffs, N.J.: Prentice Hall, 1996): p. 191. Denman discusses the publishing history of "A narrow Fellow" and the altered punctuation of "You may have met Him—did you not / His notice sudden is" to the *Republican*'s "You may have met him—did you not? / His notice sudden is." In 1872, Emily sent these lines to Susan: "You may have met him? Did you not / His notice sudden is." Denman sees this as showing "that the convention of print had no impact on her choice of punctuation, except to reinforce her original intentions." It seems equally clear to me, however, that the opposite is also the case: the inclusion of the question-mark is a direct response to the printed version, which demonstrated an ambiguity in the meaning that Dickinson was unhappy about and tried to tighten up.

32. Since character can mean both individual personality and handwriting, print can be seen as removing the personality from script.

33. Susan Dickinson, in Bingham, *Ancestors' Brocades*, p. 86.

34. Susan may not be thinking just of the public. The penultimate line about "missing many favorites among the collection *[Poems: First Series]* which knowing your taste I wonder over" is a clear criticism of Higginson's co-editor, Mabel Loomis Todd.

35. Susan Dickinson, in Bingham, *Ancestors' Brocades*, p. 86. The "conflict of possession" soon resulted in the flurry of letters between William Hayes Ward, editor of *The Independent,* and Susan, Lavinia, and Mabel over Susan's attempted placement of "Through the strait pass of suffering" (P792) in that magazine, and later in the court case over Mabel's claim to have been assigned Dickinson land as a gift by Austin; see Bingham, pp. 111–120. The letters should be read for themselves, and Bingham's (highly partisan) commentary either ignored or treated with caution.

36. Ibid., p. 118.

37. Ibid., p. 86. Susan herself had written that the reason for her delay in preparing the poems for publication was her dread of "publicity for us all" (*Ancestors' Brocades*, p. 115). In another letter, she refers to her long-term ownership of some of Dickinson's manuscript poems, many of which were "too personal and adulatory ever to be printed" (Bingham, *Ancestors' Brocades*, 116). Clearly, Susan was made extremely uncomfortable by the prospect of some of the more private poems addressed to her finding their way into the public domain.

38. This should not be taken as signifying that the publishing history of these texts has not included serious and consistent misrepresentation of various kinds. It means that in the present cycle of Dickinson's reception, we are still not clear about the extent and significance of textual misrepresentation—or indeed whether we are perpetuating it in a new way.

39. Susan Dickinson, in Bingham, *Ancestors' Brocades*, 86; see Smith, *Rowing in Eden*, p. 218.

40. Susan Huntington Gilbert Dickinson, "Manuscript obituary notice of Emily Dickinson," at the Houghton Reading Room, Harvard University, bMs. Am. 1118.95 (Box 9), 12.

41. Franklin, *The Manuscript Books of Emily Dickinson*, 1:13.

42. *Poems by Emily Dickinson:* Second Series, ed. T. W. Higginson and Mabel Loomis Todd (Boston: Roberts Brothers, 1891), p. 186.

43. One of the objections that might be justifiably raised at this point is that Dickinson's letters and notes were almost never casual. They went through several drafts and were carefully crafted. But that does not mean that their appearance on the page mattered in any consistent way. The shift from the neat print of the early years to the very different inscriptions of the later years might argue indifference as much as experimentation.

44. Franklin, *The Manuscript Books of Emily Dickinson*, 2:1323. The reader will doubtless be aware that I am comparing *my* versions of Dickinson's poems and Susan's transcription, and that there may therefore be some inaccuracies. I hope the larger point I am trying to make remains acceptable, however.

45. Susan Huntington Gilbert Dickinson, "Transcripts of Emily Dickinson's Poems," at the Houghton Reading Room, Harvard University, bMs. Am. 1118.95 (Box 12).

46. McGann, *Black Riders*, p. 38.

47. Martha Nell Smith, "The Poet as Cartoonist," in *Comic Power in Emily Dickinson*, ed. Suzanne Juhasz, Cristanne Miller, and Martha Nell Smith (Austin: University of Texas Press, 1993): p. 66.

48. Jonathan Culler, "Changes in the Study of the Lyric," in *Lyric Poetry: Beyond New Criticism*, ed. Chaviva Hosek and Patricia Parker (Ithaca, N.Y.: Cornell University Press, 1985): p. 28.

G. THOMAS TANSELLE

Emily Dickinson as an Editorial Problem

For nearly half a century, since Thomas H. Johnson published his three-volume edition (1955) of Emily Dickinson, most readers have encountered her poetry in the texts he provided, punctuated most noticeably with short dashes, although the usual array of commas, periods, and exclamation points is not entirely absent. Readers have therefore come to think of Dickinson as one of those poets (another is E. E. Cummings) whose work is immediately recognizable on the printed page by its idiosyncratic visual characteristics. But before 1955, readers had access only to conventionally punctuated (and often reworded) texts, as prepared by the various editors (family members, friends, and descendants of friends) who gradually brought out her poems in ten volumes between 1890 and 1945. Johnson's texts were therefore startling to Dickinson's audience in the 1950s; and many of those readers, while acknowledging that Johnson had been right to try in other respects to bring the poems closer to their manuscript forms, were troubled by the dashes. As the years went by, however, and the initial shock subsided, many readers (if not quite all) came to regard the dashes as inevitable and immutable. (Readers are remarkably docile in responding to the makeup and presentation of texts, even while they argue passionately over interpretations, as if reading did not involve questioning what is actually there on paper as well as what it means.) Both attitudes—wishing to rid the text of dashes and treat-

Raritan, Vol. 19, Issue 4 (Spring 2000): p. 64–79.

ing them as an unalterable part of the work—have often been put forward in so thoughtless a way that neither seems a tenable position. Indeed, neither one by itself is satisfactory if it is offered as the only justifiable approach.

The dashes are by no means the only editorial issue that Dickinson's manuscripts raise, but they form such a dominant visual feature that they serve as a focal point for the whole series of questions that any editor of her work—and therefore any reader, for editors are just one class of readers—must face. If readers are generally oblivious to such matters, they are likely not to be entirely so in the case of Dickinson, for the editorial problems posed by her work have achieved an unusual degree of fame, and the importunate dashes constitute a ubiquitous reminder of them. Many teachers of American literature even seem to think that Dickinson's texts offer a unique editorial situation. If Dickinson was firmly resolved not to publish her work (a question not settled in some scholars' minds), one could at least call that situation uncommon; but the issues that editors have to deal with in assessing her manuscripts, far from being unique, are the same ones they must always confront in editing any writer's work.

This point can be illustrated by examining the standard reasons given for printing Dickinson's work with dashes and for printing it with conventional punctuation. Those favoring dashes say simply, "That is what she wrote, and we have no choice." Those preferring conventional punctuation say, "She would have expected her poems to be given traditional punctuation if they were printed." These sentiments are often uttered as if they were self-evident and required no further justification. But in fact neither of them, in these overly simple formulations, is self-evident; they both conceal a tangle of difficult issues. When the issues are thought through, it becomes clear that both these clichès spring ultimately from valid approaches, and there is no way to call one of them the only right way.

The idea that dashes are the proper punctuation because they are *there*, in the documentary evidence, begs two basic questions. First, it assumes that the marks are in fact dashes. They do generally look like short dashes, though naturally they are not all precisely the same length nor precisely horizontal. But did Dickinson think of them as dashes when she inscribed them? Or were some of them meant to be commas and periods, which became elongated through an idiosyncracy of her handling of her pen and pencil? These questions reflect the ineluctable role of interpretation in all acts of transcription. (Photographic reproductions involve less interpretation, but even they are not fully adequate substitutes for the originals, since they may conceal evidence crucial for reading, such as the means for distinguishing different inks representing different stages, determining the order of inscription of letters written on top of other letters, or recognizing which marks are actually show-through from the writing on the other side of the paper.) Any attempt to "copy" the verbal content of one handwritten document into another document by a new act of handwriting, or by keyboarding or typesetting it into typographic letterforms, entails constant judgment as to what is *there* in the original. Whether certain letters are supposed to be capital or lowercase is often unclear, for example; and there is hardly a writer who does not sometimes inscribe a word so carelessly that its identity can only be approached through the context—which not infrequently will support the candidacy of more than one similarly shaped word.

The goal of reporting what is present in a manuscript sounds straightforward and objective, but it always entails interpretation and judgment. Different transcribers may make different decisions as to which letters are capitals or what word is represented by an unclear squiggle, but in each case they are reporting what they believe is present in the manuscript. Other, more clearcut, cases similarly require one to translate manuscript marks into conventional forms, as when a wavy line at the end of a word, obviously intended to stand for "ing," is therefore transcribed as "ing." In the same way, anyone arguing that some of Dickinson's dashlike marks were really sloppy formations of commas and periods (Johnson granted this possibility) could transcribe them as such and still be transcribing what is *there.* Let me make clear that I am not talking about editorial alterations (I shall get to that in a moment). An editor who *alters* dashes to commas is doing something very different from the editor who believes that some of the marks actually are commas and that they must necessarily be reported as commas.

It is not easy to know what is present in any manuscript, but let us suppose that an editor, after careful examination of all of Dickinson's manuscripts, concludes that the marks are indeed dashes. At this point the other question I alluded to earlier comes up: does it necessarily follow that this editor must retain the dashes in an edition? If one answers yes to this question, one is in fact declaring that the focus must be on the text of the manuscript rather than the text of the intended work. For manuscripts, even those in the handwriting of the authors of the texts, frequently contain letters, words, and punctuation that were not intended. Such "slips of the pen" occur in almost everyone's writing. One common class is caused by anticipating the next word, as when one writes "verg" instead of "very" because the next word is "great." Dickinson in fact did this (in "The life we have is very great"). She also wrote "beyoned" for "beyond" (in "The lonesome for they know not what"), illustrating in the process another category of miswriting—the automatic formation of a standard combination of letters (in this case the suffix "ed") at an inappropriate point. There is no question that the texts of the manuscripts read "verg" and "beyoned"; but the texts of the verbal works intended by Dickinson read "very" and "beyond," even though those words are not physically present. Since language is an intangible medium and may be misrepresented in any physical rendition, there is no way in many instances for an editor to be faithful simultaneously to the manuscript and to the intended work.

To say that the dashes must be printed in the texts of Dickinson's poems because they are present in the manuscripts, therefore, is to bypass the question of what kind of edition is being aimed for. If the goal is the accurate transcription of the manuscript texts, then one would of course have to print the dashes (having already decided that the marks are in fact dashes), just as one would print "verg" and "beyoned." And there is always reason to be interested in whatever is in a manuscript (Dickinson's or anyone else's), since it all conveys hints as to the psychology of the writer in the act of writing. But if the goal is to offer the intended texts of Dickinson's poems as literary works, then everything in the manuscript texts must be approached critically; at every point a judgment must be made as to whether what is there represents accurately what was intended. I am not suggesting that all the dashes are slips of the pen (they might all be something other than dashes; but if it is decided that they *are* dashes, then it is perhaps not credible to claim that every one is a slip of the pen and that another mark was always intended). Nor am I attempting at present to make the case that *some* of them are slips of the pen, though some of them certainly could be, just as "verg" is. All I am trying to establish is that deciding *what* is in a manuscript text does not automatically determine what was intended by the inscriber of that text.

This point leads directly to the second of the two great clichés about the editing of Dickinson: that she would have expected her poems to be punctuated conventionally if they appeared in print. Possibly she would, but that expectation would not necessarily convey approval, for expectation and intention are very different things. Over the centuries, authors have repeatedly disliked some, if not all, of the changes publishers have made in their works (many of which they expected the publishers to make), but they have often felt powerless to protest, or not had the energy to fight, or fought and lost. (They could of course have refused to let their work be published; but the fact that the drive to appear in print regularly produces acquiescence does not mean that the resulting text is sanctioned by the author in any other than a technical sense.) There is only one known instance of Dickinson commenting on the editorial treatment of her poems in print: in mid-March 1866 she wrote to Thomas Wentworth Higginson complaining about the question mark that had been inserted at the end of the third line of "A narrow fellow in the grass" when it was published in the *Springfield Daily Republican* a month earlier (she said that it was "defeated ... of the third line by the punctuation" and that the "third and fourth were one"). But her disapproval here cannot be used either to claim that she approved of everything else or to suggest that she wished to have unconventional punctuation in print—for the inserted question mark does not make the punctuation more conventional but substantially changes the meaning (and thus results from an editorial misinterpretation).

Dickinson's comment, therefore, is of no help in the effort to determine what she may have expected editors to do to her poems or—had she considered publication—whether her preference (that is, her artistic intention as opposed to her expectation) would have been to have her poems remain exactly as she wrote them (except for slips of the pen). Because she avoided publication and because the published form of the few poems of hers that did appear in print during her lifetime cannot be assumed to reflect her intention, it is sometimes claimed that her work presents an unusually difficult editorial situation, in which an editor has no authorial guidance as to what should be presented to readers. Even if we exclude the vast body of ancient and medieval literature and limit ourselves to the past five centuries (or the past two, for that matter), this claim is absurd. Dickinson may have been unusual in the apparent strength of her aversion to publication, but the editorial issues posed by her work are precisely the same as those presented by every other writer. In the more common cases where authors' works appear in print with their approval during their lifetimes, it cannot be assumed that those published forms reflect accurately what the authors preferred, for writers (like everyone else) have all kinds of reasons for acquiescing to things they do not really agree with. A great deal of the time, I believe, what is published is not what was intended by the author. To give only one example (though it is almost pointless to cite one example out of such vast multitudes): George Orwell obediently made the revisions that his publisher Victor Gollancz asked him to make in *Keep the Aspidistra Flying,* but he wrote to his agent that he had "utterly ruined the book." Of course, there is also the question whether this comment tells the whole truth. But that is the essential point: one must approach all evidence critically, recognizing that not only what appears in print but also what an author says cannot automatically be taken at face value. The essence of an editor's duty—as of any other historian's—is to bring an educated judgment to bear on every piece of evidence.

In truth, Dickinson's writings are easier to edit than many authors' for the very reason that there is a much smaller quantity of problematical evidence to deal with—easier, that is, if the goal is to offer texts that conform to the author's intention. If Dickinson had published her poetry, there would still be the problem of deciding the extent to which the published versions represented what she desired. If the manuscripts also survived, one could not automatically prefer them, or the published texts, at points where they differed: one would have to decide which (if any) of the differences in print resulted from the author's alterations subsequent to the surviving manuscripts and which were introduced by the publisher. (Similarly, when manuscripts have alternative uncanceled wordings, as Dickinson's often do, the presence of one of those wordings in print does not in itself mean that the choice was the author's.) And even if

the corrected proofs survived (as such proofs do for a great many nineteenth-
and twentieth-century authors), one would still have to think about the places
where the proofs do not agree with the manuscripts and yet were not altered by
the author: did the author positively prefer those changes, or simply overlook
them, or accede to them out of fatigue because there were so many other revisions required? Such questions abound in editing writers who published their
works, and the survival of documents from many stages of the publication
process is likely to complicate, rather than clarify, the editor's task.

In Dickinson's case, the fact that many poems survive in a single manuscript text that she had copied out as a final version means that an editor has
a better chance of printing authorially intended texts than the editors of most
authors do. Authorial intention is of course not the only interest that a reader
may legitimately have: in recent years there has been much more interest
than ever before in literature as a social product rather than as the creation
of individuals. For this approach, the relevant texts are those that appeared in
print, since they are the products of the publication process (a social activity)
and are what people read. Obviously this approach cannot readily be applied
to Dickinson. But a variation of it has indeed been tried: the manuscripts she
copied out for various recipients become the "publications," and the exact
forms of the poems in them, including their physical arrangements, are what
the audience for these manuscripts had in front of them to respond to.

The mistake that is not always avoided in such analyses is equating the
features that affect readers with the features that the author intended. It is
sometimes claimed, for example, that the way Dickinson broke her run-over
lines is the way she wanted those lines always to appear. There is no question that the manuscript lineation (like all other features of the manuscripts)
could have affected the responses of those who read the manuscripts (just as
every characteristic of a printed text may influence audience interpretation).
But it does not follow that Dickinson necessarily thought of her manuscript
spacings as integral parts of her poems. Anyone taking the "social" approach
to editing would retain the manuscript line-breaks simply because they were
elements in the texts that were read by Susan Dickinson and some forty other people that constituted Dickinson's contemporary audience. But anyone
hoping to produce a text that reflects as much as possible what Dickinson
intended has to judge which features of the physical documents should be
eliminated as nontextual—which, that is, are utilitarian aspects of particular
acts of physical transmission and are not parts of the literary works and therefore not features that need be included in other efforts to transmit the texts of
those works. Since documents (manuscript or printed) are social instruments,
enabling texts to be transmitted between people, documentary texts—often
with nonauthorial elements that authors expected rather than intended—
must be the focus of a social approach to literary editing; but the essence of

intentionalist editing is to be open to the possibility of altering documentary texts when necessary in order to construct texts that conform to the author's intention more closely than those documentary texts do.

• • •

These thoughts about editing Dickinson (which I believe are applicable to the editing of all writers) are occasioned by the appearance of R. W. Franklin's two new editions, both entitled *The Poems of Emily Dickinson* but carrying different subtitles: a three-volume *Variorum Edition* (1998) and a one-volume *Reading Edition* (1999). These volumes result from the only manuscript-based reconsideration of the whole Dickinson corpus since Johnson's (and thus only the second that has ever taken place). Franklin's *Variorum* is a superb achievement, the outgrowth of his thirty-five years of studying the manuscripts. (He first raised questions about Johnson's edition only ten years after its publication, in his 1965 dissertation that became the 1967 book *The Editing of Emily Dickinson: A Reconsideration.*) The differences between Franklin's and Johnson's texts are not likely to have a significant effect on the reading and interpretation of most of the poems; but it is important to have texts that are as accurate as possible, and Johnson did make a number of errors owing to the fact that he was forced to use photostats for the manuscripts that had descended in the Todd/Bingham family.

Furthermore, Franklin's intensive study of the physical evidence has enabled him not only to revise the dating of some poems but also to discover that in certain instances Johnson printed as a single poem what should be more than one, or printed as separate poems what should be combined. One of the most famous poems affected by this situation is "Further in summer than the birds," the earliest version of which is now printed with two additional stanzas that Johnson had treated as a separate poem. Many of Franklin's decisions of this kind seem unquestionable, but others will strike some readers as less conclusive. That fact is no criticism of the edition, however, for some uncertainty is the price inevitably paid for the benefits of a critical edition—and having the results of Franklin's prolonged thinking on these matters is a great benefit indeed. As a result of these combinations and separations, along with Franklin's differing judgment as to which poetrylike lines in Dickinson's letters deserve to be treated as poems and which do not (Franklin recognizes that "there is no definitive boundary between prose and poetry in Dickinson's letters"), Franklin's edition presents a total of 1,789 poems, as compared with 1,775 in Johnson's. These changes and the altered dating of some poems have caused Franklin to renumber all the poems—a decision that some find awkward but one that is not worth arguing about.

What is more important to examine is the basic conception of Dickinson's work that underlies Franklin's editing. One of his immensely valuable earlier contributions to Dickinson study was his two-volume 1981 edition of *The Manuscript Books of Emily Dickinson,* which records in photographic facsimile his reconstruction of the forty fascicles into which Dickinson gathered her poems, along with fifteen "sets" of manuscripts containing poems copied out as if for fascicles—amounting in all to about two-thirds of her poetry. (The reconstitution of the fascicles, based on the evidence of evolving handwriting, paper stocks, sewing holes, stain offsets, and the like, helps to date her poetry but does not support the idea that she assembled the poems in any kind of thematic order. Thus the *Variorum* is arranged chronologically according to the earliest version of each poem, not by fascicle groupings; readers who wish to know the fascicle order are provided with this information in one of the fourteen helpful appendixes.) Because the *Manuscript Books* came out at a time when many textual theorists and literary critics (two groups that should not be distinct but unfortunately have often been so) were favoring a social approach to literature and thus preferring documentary texts to editors' critical reconstructions of authorially intended texts, some people felt that no further editing of Dickinson was needed. This conclusion seemed to be reinforced by the fact that Dickinson's fascicle "publications" were under her control, and therefore the manuscripts could be thought to accommodate the intentionalist and the social approaches simultaneously. There in the facsimiles, as some members of the Dickinson Editorial Collective argue, are the texts exactly as she copied them out for an audience (however small), and every detail of spatial arrangement (such as line-breaks and the formation of letters) and every uncanceled alternative wording are part of the reading experience that all who wish to read Dickinson should have, an experience that is destroyed by the conventions of printing. It is a noteworthy aspect of Franklin's accomplishment that, having provided grist for this particular mill, he takes a firm stand in asserting that Dickinson's intention did not encompass everything in the fascicle manuscripts.

In regard to the manuscript line-breaks, for example, his answer to such critics as Martha Nell Smith (*Rowing in Eden,* 1992) is unambiguous and welcome:

> Available space ordinarily determined the physical line-breaks in Dickinson's poems. . . . The shapes of her materials—odds and ends of wrapping paper, advertising flyers, notebook leaves, discarded stationery—gave physical contour to her poems as they went onto paper. . . . There are many examples in which two or more copies of the same poem appear on papers of different shapes, yielding different line-breaks for each. . . . Once line-breaks began, it is not easy to find a manuscript of any poem in Dickinson's hand that exactly matches the physical lineation of the same poem in other copies.

It should be clear to anyone who examines the manuscripts that he is right: even the turnovers where there is considerable space left at the right edge of the paper conform to a margin that Dickinson set for herself. The fundamental distinction between document and work should be kept in mind here: to take the position (justified, I believe) that the manuscript lineation is not an intended part of the work is not to rob it of biographical significance. Every aspect of a manuscript is obviously of interest in helping to establish the frame of mind of the writer; but that point is not diminished by saying that some features of a manuscript text were not intended to be a part of the literary work, and any edition focusing on works rather than documents must recognize that certain characteristics of manuscripts may have to be eliminated in favor of authorial intentions. The same line of reasoning supports the need for making choices among uncanceled alternative wordings in Dickinson's manuscripts, a procedure that does not deny (as some people seem to think) the value of observing the fluidity of her texts.

If Franklin had not understood these points, he would not have undertaken his *Variorum Edition* at all. That he is interested in presenting the texts of works rather than the texts of documents is indicated by his affirmation that his edition "is based on the assumption that a literary work is separable from its artifact" and by his incorporation of his own "emendations" into the texts—wording, punctuation, and indentation that he regards as intended but that were not present in that form in the manuscripts. In the light of this approach, the reader may experience some momentary confusion upon learning that Franklin's aim is "to present a separate text for each known manuscript" because "nearly every text differs in some respect from all others." One naturally asks why individual manuscript texts of a poem are given separate treatment (as in a documentary edition) if the emphasis is on the work rather than its artifactual manifestations. The difficult answer is that "Dickinson invested individual manuscripts with identities of their own, even if, for all their variance, she thought of them as representing a single poem." If multiple manuscripts represent a single poem, and if the edition is presenting poems and not documents, why should the text of each manuscript (that is, the intended text, incorporating emendations) be offered separately?

What Franklin means but does not make entirely clear is that each manuscript, having been produced for an individual occasion, contains a work that stands on its own, worthy of being studied independently; and yet there are enough links between some of these works that they ought to be thought of as related versions rather than as totally independent works. In editing any author whose revisions are extant, one must decide which revisions are relatively minor adjustments, aimed at perfecting the work as previously conceived, and which push the work, in one way or another, toward a conception not previously envisaged. Henry James's revisions for his New York Edition provide a classic illustration: the revised *Portrait of a Lady*, for example, has enough connections with the first edition carrying that title that one would hesitate to call the two totally independent works (as independent as *The Portrait of a Lady* is from *The Wings of the Dove*); yet they are sufficiently independent that one could not imagine how a single text could do justice to them both. Presumably this is the kind of relationship that Franklin is postulating among the variant manuscripts of a single "poem." He speaks, for example, of the extensively revised "Two butterflies went out at noon" as "one poem having two variant manuscripts." The texts in his edition are not manuscript transcriptions, since they include editorial emendations; what they consist of are editorial reconstructions of the texts intended by the author on each of the occasions represented by the surviving manuscripts.

That every manuscript text deserves this independent treatment (resulting in nearly 2,500 texts of the 1,789 "poems") is not unimaginable, but such consistency may lead the reader to question whether the distinction between works and documents has been fully carried through. Furthermore, some manuscripts preserve the record of more than one occasion. Manuscript C of "There came a day at summer's full," for example, contains an 1862 text plus some "much later" revisions; the two versions that thus occupy the same physical space are set out by Franklin in full texts, but both have to be referred to as "C," since the organization is by document, and as a result the later version of C is from a later date than D. And if such revisions on a single document produce independent versions, then it might be asked whether the many instances of manuscripts with uncanceled alternatives could be thought of as containing versions that are just as separate as those that happen to be located on different manuscripts.

Although I do not regard these points as insignificant, I nevertheless think of them in this instance as a mere quibble, considering what the edition very thoughtfully accomplishes. Whether or not one wishes to regard all these variant texts as Jamesian versions, the edition gives all the information one needs: the text of each manuscript with notes on its line-division, revisions, and uncanceled alternative readings; an indication of editorial emendations and choices among alternative readings; an account of the manuscript, noting the date now assigned to it; and a history of each poem's publication, including the variants in those published texts. I cannot praise enough the way all this is laid out on the printed page, with varying margins and type sizes to keep the different categories of information distinct and to prevent their overshadowing the texts. Perhaps the most significant typographic decision—a basic editorial one as well—was to represent the "dashes" as spaced hyphens (that is, very short dashes). Franklin says nothing about them in his concisely informative introduction; he clearly regards some form of dash as intended (otherwise he would have altered them, as he did Dickinson's slips of the pen), and his choice of a hyphen-length mark better reflects Dickinson's manuscript practice than the somewhat longer dash that Johnson used. It is also apparent that some kind of dash does often seem appropriate for Dickinson's fractured syntax.

Franklin's *Variorum Edition* will become—and rightly so—the source from which Dickinson's texts will henceforth be drawn or reconstructed. One example of how it can be used as the basis for other editions is provided by Franklin himself in his *Reading Edition*. (I do not know whether this term was the editor's or the publisher's, but such phrases as "Reading Edition" or "Reader's Edition" should be abolished, implying as they do that an edition with fuller documentation is not intended for readers, or is unreadable. The apparatus that scholarly editions offer is a basic and rewarding part of the reading experience, and editions that eliminate some of this information are correspondingly impoverished. In Dickinson's case, the sense of fluidity conveyed by the multiple alternative readings is significant for understanding the nature of her work.) What Franklin has done in his *Reading Edition* is to present a single text of each poem— "as Dickinson did," he says, "when sending poems to others." His principle of selection, for those poems (about a fourth of the total) that exist in variant manuscripts, is normally to choose the latest version—though various circumstances, explained in the introduction, rightly cause him sometimes to select an earlier manuscript. Indeed, it is too bad that, at least in some instances, both an earlier and a later version could not be included: "As imperceptibly as grief," for example, is present only in the last of its sixteen-line versions, and the additional sixteen lines that were in its earliest version are thus not available; and the two stanzas added to the Johnson text of "Further in summer than the birds" are again taken away, since they are not part of Dickinson's final version.

When a manuscript version that he has chosen for inclusion contains alternative readings, he makes choices among them. It is not clear to me, however, why he wishes to assure readers (if he does) that "the resulting texts are not composite, derived as they have been from readings on a single document." He may have felt that he had no choice but to take this position, having in the *Variorum* defined the text of each manuscript as an independent version. But as long as one grants that a manuscript may at any point fail to reflect its author's intention (and the incorporation of emendations does grant this point), then drawing readings from different documents does not in itself constitute a mixing of versions. It can instead be an instance of using all relevant evidence for the purpose of producing a version that was intended but never accurately written out. (Franklin does draw on evidence from documents other than the one supplying the main text when one or more of those documents show Dickinson's definite choice between the same two words that exist as undifferentiated alternatives in the manuscript he is following.) A policy that disallows any combining of readings from different manuscripts has greater consequences for the *Reading Edition*, which is selective, than for the *Variorum*, where all the textual evidence is present in any case. This is not to say that the actual texts would necessarily be very different: my point may in this instance be largely of theoretical significance.

Otherwise I find nothing to question in the *Reading Edition*. Within the guidelines Franklin has set himself, his choices of versions and of alternatives within versions are extremely sensible—and they are efficiently recorded at the end of the volume, making this the first time any volume of Dickinson's poems aimed at a general audience has offered information about the derivation of its texts. (Incidentally, readers should be aware that three errors in the *Variorum,* including one omitted line, are here corrected.) And his decision to retain what he can confidently regard as Dickinson's spelling, punctuation, capitalization, and usage is fully justified for an edition that aims "to follow her private intentions and characteristics." But the fact remains that the *Reading Edition* represents only one act of many possible acts of selection from the evidence, and additional selections are bound to appear. Johnson wrote in his 1955 edition that future editors might wish to alter the spelling, capitalization, and punctuation of his texts, but he did little of that when he produced his own one-volume edition in 1960. Similarly, Franklin's one-volume edition contains texts that depart only rarely from the corresponding ones in his three-volume edition; but he recognizes that "there can be various kinds of reading editions, with different technological bases or with greater intervention in the interests of editorial taste or recognized convention."

In a recent *New York Times* review of a Dickinson exhibition at Harvard, timed to celebrate Franklin's achievement, Holland Cotter wrote that "Dickinson has always been to some extent a creation of her editors." This statement is misleading if it is meant to suggest that Dickinson is unusual in this regard: the judgment of editors mediates our approach to all authors. And if we wish to think of degrees of mediation, I would say that less of it has been practiced on Dickinson than on many other writers. Dickinson has been fortunate in her two scholarly editors, and with Franklin's *Variorum* we can have confidence that she is being responsibly presented to us. However the future rates her poetry (a matter less certain than her secure historical position as a nineteenth-century phenomenon, anticipating modernism by several decades), there will be a demand for further one-volume editions, in which various approaches—including, perhaps, a different interpretation of the dashes—can be worked out. But underlying them all will be the firm foundation of Franklin's *Variorum.* Its arrival is a literary event, and its presence will be a cause for continuing celebration.

The Poems of Emily Dickinson: Variorum Edition and *The Poems of Emily Dickinson: Reading Edition,* edited by R. W. Franklin, Belknap Press of Harvard University Press.

DAVID S. REYNOLDS

Emily Dickinson and Popular Culture

Although the myth of Dickinson's alienation from her society is slowly dissolving, it has not been sufficiently recognized just how open she was to forces within her surrounding culture. In some ways, of course, Dickinson was the quintessentially *private* poet. It is also important to note, however, that she had a keen eye on American popular culture and drew poetic sustenance from it.

Indeed, there is evidence that she had a deep, frustrated desire for popularity. As a family acquaintance, Mrs. Ford, wrote to Mabel Todd, "I think in spite of her seclusion, she was longing for poetic sympathy and renown, and that some of her later habit of life originated in this suppressed and ungratified desire for distinction." Dickinson herself did at times express this desire for fame, as when she remarked to her sister-in-law Sue, "Could I make you and Austin – proud – sometime – a great way off – 'twould give me taller feet – '" (*LED*, p. 378). She once recalled that she and her cousin Louise Norcross had "in the dining-room decided to be distinguished. It's a great thing to be great, 'Loo,'" she remarked. Although she could adopt a pose of literary shyness before the *Atlantic Monthly* editor Thomas Wentworth Higginson, writing to him that publication was as "foreign to my thought, as "Firmament to Fin," the fact remains that she sent this leading man if letters six poems in response to his call for pieces from "new or obscure contributors" (*LED*, pp. 378, 539). Her

The Cambridge Companion to Emily Dickinson, edited by Wendy Martin (Cambridge: Cambridge University Press, 2002): pp. 176–190.

thirst for fame and popularity sometimes surfaces in her poems, as when she writes that her "Holiday" will be "That They remember me," and her "Paradise" will be "the fame – / That They – pronounce my name –" (J 431).

If fame was the "Paradise" she fantasized about, then she was destined for paradise. Time would prove that her poetry could have strong appeal for the mass audience. When her *Poems* were posthumously published in 1890, the first edition went through six printings in as many months and eleven editions in the first two years, a remarkable sale for a poetry volume, then or now. While it is true that this volume's strong sale is partly explained by the editors' careful tailoring of her poetry for the masses – by regularizing its punctuation and so forth – the later rediscovery and reprinting of the original fascicles, in all their awkward glory, in no way diminished Dickinson's popularity, among critics as well as general readers.

A major reason for her enduring popularity is that she was extraordinarily receptive to the popular literature and culture of her own time. She was thoroughly familiar not only with classic literary sources – especially the Bible, Shakespeare, Keats, the Brontë sisters, Elizabeth Barrett Browning, Emerson, and Thoreau – but also with many popular contemporaries that have since fallen from view. Her poems and letters reveal that she was a highly receptive witness of many phenomena in nineteenth-century popular culture, including imaginative sermons, reform movements, penny newspapers, best-selling novels, and women's literature. She was unique among American women of her day in the breadth of her awareness of the most experimental tendencies in contemporary American culture. Much of her poetry can be viewed as an individualistic adaptation of popular literary strategies.

For example, she felt the impact of the widespread shift in popular religious discourse from the doctrinal to the imaginative. Between 1800 and 1860, popular sermon style, which had in Puritan times been characterized primarily by theological rigor and restraint of the imagination, came to be dominated by diverting narrative, extensive illustrations, and even colloquial humor.

Many of the central tensions in Dickinson's poetry result from the collision between the old and the new sermon styles. She was well positioned to feel every tremor produced by the collision. Her father, Edward Dickinson, was an avowed devotee of the old-style doctrinal preaching: he typically called a well-reasoned sermon by the conservative David Aiken "an intellectual feast," while he branded an imaginative sermon by the more liberal Martin Leland as "Unclean-unclean!" (*YH* 1, p. *53;* L 11:251–252). Edward Dickinson also had a puritanical distaste for light literature. Emily recalled that her father read "lonely & rigorous books" and advised his children to read only the Bible (L 11: 475).

She had a particularly vivid memory of her brother Austin coming home one day with Longfellow's novel *Kavanagh,* hiding it under the piano cover, and making hand signs to Emily about the book. When the children later read the novel, their father was incensed. While it may seem strange that so apparently innocent a novel as *Kavanagh* should provoke such a storm, we should recognize how revolutionary the novel was, given the strict doctrinal standards of Edward Dickinson. Longfellow's novel dramatizes the collapse of theological preaching, represented by the departing Rev. Pendexter, and the ascendancy of imaginative religion, embodied in the handsome young preacher Arthur Kavanagh. Kavanagh's piquant pulpit illustrations and stories lead one character to exclaim, "Such sermons! So beautifully written, so different from old Mr. Pendexter's."[1] Emily Dickinson mentioned the novel often in her letters and felt a special kinship with the novel's heroine, Alice Archer, a gloomy, dreamy girl who sublimates her hopeless infatuation for Kavanagh in poetic visions – in much the same way that Emily herself may have been driven to a kind of poetic frenzy by her unrequited passion for a real-life Kavanagh, the Rev. Charles Wadsworth.

Critics have long pondered the Wadsworth-Dickinson relationship, hard evidence of which is frustratingly slim. It is known that while visiting Philadelphia in 1855, during her only trip outside of Massachusetts, Emily most likely was taken to hear Wadsworth preach at Arch Street Presbyterian Church. It is also known that Wadsworth later visited her at least twice in Amherst, that two volumes of his sermons were given to her, that she probably read many of his other sermons in newspaper reprintings, and that she developed strong feelings toward him. Some believe that Emily's great "terror" in 1862 and her incredible poetic productivity that year was a response to Wadsworth's removal to Calvary Church in San Francisco (hence the double pun involved in Emily's description of herself as "the Empress of Calvary"). Intriguing as the relationship is, the much-debated issue of Emily's feelings for Wadsworth is perhaps less relevant than the fact that in the mid-1850s, just at the moment when she was beginning to write serious poetry, she was deeply moved by a preacher who must be regarded as one of the antebellum period's foremost innovators in American sermon style.

Her response to Wadsworth had been prepared for by her increasing preference for imaginative preaching, often against her father's wishes. In 1851 she probably went to hear the popular Henry Ward Beecher, who was visiting Amherst giving a lecture, significantly, on "Imagination." By 1853 she could go into raptures over a notably anecdotal sermon on Judas and Jesus given by the visiting preacher Edwards A. Park, a sermon whose secular emphasis she later described: "It was like a mortal story of intimate young men" (*YH* i, p.287). The Martin Leland sermon that her father dismissed as "unclean" was imaginatively liberating for her, as she mimicked Leland's theatrical manner and repeated sections of the sermon aloud. Also in the early 1850s, she befriended the popular author and editor Josiah G. Holland, whose liberal religious views were criticized by one conservative paper as "creedless, churchless, ministerless Christianity" (*YH* i, p. 296). By aligning herself with several of the most progressive religious stylists of the day, Emily Dickinson was launching a silent but major rebellion against the doctrinal tradition valued by her father.

Her excitement about Wadsworth, therefore, can be viewed as a natural outgrowth of her increasing attraction to the new religious style. One newspaper compared Wadsworth to an earlier pulpit innovator, John Summerfield, but stressed that "Wadsworth's style . . . is vastly bolder, his fancy more vivid, and his action more violent. . . [His topics are] peculiar, and quite out of the usual line"; he is typically "rapid, unique and original, often startling his audience . . . with a seeming paradox."[2] Mark Twain would also be struck by the uniqueness of Wadsworth's pulpit manner, noting that he would often "get off a first-rate joke" (*YH* ii, p. 112) and then frown when people started laughing. In short, Wadsworth's style was adventurous, anecdotal, and very imaginative, with a tendency to the startling and paradoxical. Emily Dickinson once praised his "inscrutable roguery" and seemed to copy his impish style in many poems and in her message to J. G. Holland: "Unless we become as Rogues, we cannot enter the Kingdom of Heaven" (L ii: 901, 703). The jocular familiarity with which she generally treats divine and biblical images doubtless owes much to the new sermon style that Wadsworth perfected.

It is helpful to know that such imaginative revisions of religion were going on around Dickinson and that she was extraordinarily responsive to them. By her own confession, she came to detest theological preaching ("I hate doctrines!" she declared after one old-fashioned sermon), and she devoured every example of the new religious style that came within her rather limited purview. She once commented that the only way to tell if a poem is good is to ask whether, after reading it, you feel like the top of your head has been taken off. She seemed to apply the same rule to the sermons she attended and the books she read. A religious work, in her eyes, must possess both striking imagery and a sense of ultimacy; theology or moralizing is secondary to the work's *effect* upon the imagination. For instance, she disdained three Baptist tracts about "pure little lives, loving God, and their parents, and obeying the laws of the land" – purely secular pious stories that, in her words, "dont *bewitch* me any" (L i: 144). In contrast, even though she was skeptical about Christian doctrines, she could revel in the Rev. Aaron Colton's "enlivening preaching, . . . his earnest look and gesture, his calls of *now today*" (L i:120). Similarly, she could be totally captivated by "a splendid sermon" from Edwards A. Park, which left the congregation "so still, the buzzing of a fly would have boomed out like a cannon. And when it was all over, and that wonderful man sat down, people stared at each other, and looked as wan and wild, as if they had seen a spirit, and wondered they had not died" (L i: 272).

The combined imagery here of the fly, death, and religion seems to anticipate Dickinson's famous poem "I heard a Fly buzz – when I died." At any rate, we should note that in both the poem and her letter describing Park's sermon, it is not theology or Christianity that counts but rather the existential impact of a momentous situation.

What new religious stylists like Wadsworth and Park had finally taught Emily Dickinson is that religion could be freely applied to many secular situations and expressed through startling imagery. Because of Dickinson's extensive use of witty conceits, many critics have likened her to the metaphysical poets of the Renaissance or to the American Puritan poet Edward Taylor. There is, however, a crucial difference between the metaphysicals and Dickinson: all their creative flights are finally confined by Christian doctrine, whereas she soars adventurously beyond doctrine by mixing the sacred and the secular, the Christian and the pagan. And she had been taught how to achieve this mixture by her popular religious culture.

One of her poetic responses to the new religious style was the redefinition of church, sermons, and worship along totally secular lines. Witness the reduction of religious images to the world in the following stanzas:

> Some keep the Sabbath going to Church –
> I keep it, staying at Home –
> With a Bobolink for a Chorister –
> And an Orchard, for a Dome –
>
> . . .
>
> God preaches, a noted Clergyman –
> And the sermon is never long
> So instead of getting to Heaven, at last –
> I'm going, all along. (J 324)

This poem may be regarded as a clever adaptation of the antebellum religious style: not only does it shift worship from the church to nature and sing praise to short sermons, but it actually converts God into an entertaining preacher obviously trained in the new sermon style. A similar fusion of the sacred and the secular is visible in the poem that begins "To hear an Oriole sing / May be a common thing – / Or only a divine" (J 526), in which the last phrase arrests the reader with its offhandedly casual treatment of the holy. Sometimes this casualness is taken to playful extremes, as when she refers to God as "Papa above!" watching down upon a "mouse," who asks for the privilege of living forever "Snug in seraphic Cupboards" (J 61). Among the many other Dickinson poems that daringly reapply sacred imagery are: "These are the days when Birds come back –" (J 130), "There's a certain Slant of light" (J 258), and "Mine – by the Right of the White Election!"

(J 528). In these poems such images as Holy Communion, sacrament, hymns, and the doctrine of election are detached totally from their sacred referents and fused with either nature or the human psyche. In still other poems she displays a jaunty freedom with the Bible, as in "The Bible is an antique Volume" (J 1545), which includes a series of secular re-enactments of sacred imagery, such as calling Eden "the ancient Homestead," Satan "the Brigadier," and sin "a distinguished Precipice/Others must resist."

Another fertile seedbed of imagery for Dickinson was temperance literature, which also stimulated many other writers of the American Renaissance, including Whitman, Melville, Thoreau, and Poe. No reform movement had as widespread an influence in antebellum America as temperance. To combat America's extraordinarily high alcohol consumption, which by 1830 reached the staggering amount of around ten gallons of absolute alcohol per adult citizen annually, waves of temperance orators and writers swept the country between 1835 and 1860.

Although much temperance literature was didactic in a straightforward way, an increasing proportion of it, capitalizing on the popularity of sensational fiction, was lurid and violent in its renderings of alcohol's ravages. With the rise of the Washingtonians, an organization of reformed drunkards who thrilled the public with their graphic anecdotes about battles with the bottle, the temperance movement became riddled with contradictions and ambiguities. Notorious instances of backsliding – particularly that of the Washingtonian leader John Bartholomew Gough, who in 1845 disappeared for a week and then was found in a whorehouse recovering from an alcoholic binge – gave rise to the oxymoronic character of the "intemperate temperance advocate," a staple figure of ridicule in subversive popular fiction. George Lippard in his best-selling reform novel *The Quaker City* sneered at "intemperate Temperance lecturers," caricaturing them in his portrait of the Rev. F. A. T. Pyne, who snickers, "We temperance folks must have some little excitement after we have forsworn intemperance. When we leave off alcohol, we indulge our systems with a little Opium."[3] Likewise, George Thompson in *Life in Boston and New York* presents the hypocritical temperance reformer Bob Towline, who boasts that "for over a year I lectured in public, and got drunk in private – glorious times!"[4] In fiction, the intemperate temperance stereotype eventually produced Mark Twain's Dauphin, the bald-pated con artist who runs temperance revivals in order to raise funds to buy whiskey.

In verse, this popular character was creatively reworked in the persona of one of Dickinson's most famous poems, J 214 ("I taste a liquor never brewed –"), which shows the poet adopting and transforming images and themes of popular temperance reform. This transforming process is visible in the opening verse, where she presents an "I" who is a wonderfully fresh avatar of the intemperate temperance advocate. The speaker is both completely drunk and completely temperate. She can exult in her drunkenness because hers is a liquor "never brewed," filling tankards "scooped in Pearl," an image suggesting the pearl-like whiteness o f the air she loves and the extreme preciousness of her love of nature.

Having immediately revised the ironic trope of the intemperate temperance advocate, in the next two verses Dickinson gambols with it, revising several other popular images in the process:

> Inebriate of Air – am I –
> And Debauchee of Dew –
> Reeling – thro endless summer days –
> From inns of Molten Blue –

> When "Landlords" turn the drunken Bee
> Out of Foxglove's door –
> When Butterflies – renounce their "drams" –
> I shall but drink the more!

This speaker is not the hypocritical intemperate temperance advocate, publicly sober but privately debauched, but the exultantly open one, proclaiming a debauchery that is allied with the highest form of temperance. Dickinson, who was fully aware of antebellum popular culture in all its dimensions, seems to be intentionally playing on well-known temperance images. A central sequence in Timothy Shay Arthur's 1854 temperance best-seller *Ten Nights in a Bar-room* involves a landlord, Simon Slade, who kicks out of his saloon the drunken Joe Morgan, who later renounces alcohol due to the ministrations of his dying daughter. Dickinson uses similar imagery in her references to "'Landlords'" who turn drunks out their doors and to alcoholics who "renounce their 'drams.'" Her use of quotation marks underscores the fact that she is "quoting," or borrowing, images from others – specifically, from temperance writers like Arthur. But she uses these images only to transform them. The drunkard being dismissed here is a bee that has extracted nectar from a flower. The renouncers of drams are butterflies that are leaving their resting places and fluttering through the air. And the "I" watching this beautiful spectacle only gets more and more drunk for having enjoyed it.

Dickinson has carried popular temperance images to a truly new, transcendent space, a fact she enforces in the poem's closing conceit of seraphs and saints celebrating the "little Tippler" for her intoxication over nature's bounty emphasizes the poem's metaphysical dimension. The playful oddity of the hat-swinging angels, the gaping saints, and the girl leaning against the sun gives the poem a metaphorical energy that leaves the reader intoxicated, as it were, with the poet's imaginativeness.

Dickinson's creative toying with temperance images continues in poem J 230 ("We – Bee and I – live by the quaffing – "). Once again, the "I" is the transformed intemperate temperance advocate, who can openly say that she lives "by quaffing" since her drinking companion is the bee and her "ale" and "burgundy" are beautiful things of nature. When Dickinson writes, "Tisn't *all Hock* – with us – /Life has its *Ale* – ," she is again adopting a popular trope: the italicized "*all Hock*" was a common phrase used at temperance meetings to urge all present to pledge ("hock") themselves to sobriety. When the "I" says that she and the bee don't use the "*all Hock*" prompt, she is saying that pledges against alcohol are unnecessary for those who understand that life itself "has its *Ale*."

Dickinson's adaptation of popular sources continues to the end of the poem:

> Do we "get drunk"?
> Ask the jolly Clovers!
> Do we "beat" our "Wife"?
> I – never wed –
> Bee – pledges *his* – in minute flagons –
> Dainty – as the tress –on her deft Head –
>
> While runs the Rhine –
> He and I – revel –
> First – at the vat – and latest at the Vine –
> Noon – our last Cup –
> "Found dead" – "of Nectar" –
> By a humming Coroner –
> In a By–Thyme!

The quotation marks used around several phrases are strategic, for Dickinson is quoting extensively from popular culture. The common temperance trope of the drunken husband who brutalizes his wife is cited in the rhetorical questions "Do we 'get drunk'?" and "Do we 'beat' our 'Wife'?" The sensationalists' association of alcohol with death is repeated in the reference to the drunkard "'Found dead'" by a coroner. The taking of the temperance pledge is recalled in the phrase about one who "pledges *his*."

But all of these standard temperance images are couched in paeans to ordinary natural phenomena – bees, clover, nectar, and noontime – that redirect temperance rhetoric toward an affirmation of life itself. The bee and the persona get drunk in their mutual enjoyment of clovers. They revel in "the Rhine," a pun that associates drinking famous German wine with a love of beautiful landscapes like that of the River Rhine. The standard image in temperance literature of destructive all-day binges is recreated in the persona's boast of being "First – at the vat – and latest at the Vine – ," while another popular theme, the deadly effects of alcohol, is redirected in the images of drinking the "last Cup" of noon, being killed by "Nectar," and being found by a "humming Coroner," the bee. By manipulating popular temperance imagery, Dickinson joyously expresses her sense of the intoxicating nature of common experience.

Another popular genre that influenced Dickinson was popular sensational literature, ranging from the crime-filled penny newspapers that arose in the 1830s to the sensational pamphlet fiction that flooded America in the 1840s and 1850s. The antebellum public was fed on an increasingly spicy diet of horror, gore, and perversity in both mass newspapers and the closely allied genres of trial pamphlets and paper-covered adventure novels. Emerson complained that his countrymen spent their time "reading all day murders & railroad accidents" in newspapers.[5] Thoreau, similarly, spoke of the "startling and monstrous events as fill the daily papers."[6] Although sensational literature was not uniquely indigenous, American sensationalists gained a worldwide reputation for special nastiness and grossness. Whitman noted, "Scurrility – the truth may as well be told – is a sin of the American newspaper press."[7] In 1842 a British journalist wrote, "*Our* press is bad enough ... But its violence is meekness and even its atrocities are virtues, compared with the system of *brutal and ferocious outrage* which distinguished the press of America," a sentiment echoed by the British traveler Emily Faithfull, who declared that "the American newspaper very often startles its more cultured readers with extraordinary sensational headings and the prominence it gives to horrors of all kinds – murders, elopements, divorces, and wickednesses in general."[8]

Competing with the penny newspapers were sensational pamphlet novels (often called "romances") featuring rollicking adventure and outcasts such as pirates, freebooters, and all kinds of criminals. Frequently published in garish yellow covers emblazoned with melodramatic woodcuts and eye-catching black lettering, this action-filled pamphlet fiction, priced cheaply and hawked in street book stalls, caused increasing alarm among conservative commentators. Surveying the sudden popularity of "Yellow Jacket Literature," one author complained in 1855 that "the popular press is teeming with works of vapid or unhallowed fiction, or grossly immoral books and prints," noting that in this fiction "the murderer, robber, pirate, swindler, the grog-shop tippler, the lady of fashion, the accomplished rake and libertine, are meritorious characters, held up in a spirit of pride and levity, and surrounded by a 'halo of emulation.'"[9]

Dickinson was profoundly aware of these darker dimensions of the American popular mind. It is notable that when she wrote poetry about popular culture, she was inevitably preoccupied with its violent, disorienting elements, as in poem J 1226 ("The Popular Heart is a Cannon first"). Dickinson recognizes that the "Popular Heart" can be best described in violent images pertaining to war, weapons, drinking, ditches, and prison. The popular culture she perceives is fluid and ever changing, having been torn from both the future ("Not a Tomorrow to know it's name") and from historical memory ("Nor a Past to stare"). It is associated with the muddy realm of ditches, and it thrives on diverting crime ("Ditches for Realm and a Trip to Jail /For a Souvenir").

Her letters of the 1850–1853 period show that she was fascinated by sensational literature. The increasing space given in American newspapers to crimes and tragedies was a great source of amused interest to her. In an 1853 letter to Josiah Holland of the *Springfield Republican,* she declared that the lurid contents of his paper had changed her into a quirky disturber of the peace. "One glimpse of *The Republican,*" she wrote, "makes me break things again – I read in it every night. Who writes those funny accidents, where railroads meet each other unexpectedly and gentlemen in factories get their heads cut off quite informally? The author, too, relates them in such a sprightly way, that they are quite attractive" (L 1264). Always hungry for sensational news, she elsewhere thanked her brother Austin for a juicy news clipping about a manslaughter and asked him to send "anything else that's *startling* which you may chance to know – I dont think deaths or murders can ever come amiss in a young woman's journal" (L 1:114). Her tone in these letters captures precisely the combined grossness and offhand levity of sensational newspaper reporting.

The open admission into her consciousness of several popular sensational elements prepared the way for the haunted themes and broken style of her poetry. In a poem written around 1858 (J 8), she creates a horrific atmosphere by describing a wooded road haunted by banditti, a wolf, an owl, a serpent, screaming vultures, and beckoning "satyrs fingers." A similarly straightforward, monovocal use of sensational images occurs in these verses:

> I never hear the word "escape"
> Without a quicker blood. (J 77)

or,

> Had I a mighty gun
> I think I'd shoot the human race
> And then to glory run! (J 118)

or,

> We like a Hairbreadth 'scape
> It tingles in the Mind . . .
> Like paragraphs of Wind (J 1175)

Such poems barely rise above the pedestrian sensationalism of penny papers and pamphlet novels. They are full of standard sensational images, including hairbreadth escapes, war, guns, murder, and accidents. Although they bear witness to Dickinson's fertile imagination, as when she compares the tingling effect of an escape to that of "paragraphs of Wind," they resemble popular pamphlet fiction in that they revel in action and adventure without pretending to probe deeper meanings.

More characteristically, Dickinson does with sensational literature what she did with religious and temperance rhetoric: she radically personalizes it by redirecting it toward quotidian experience and private emotion. Innovatively, she points out that all of us carry within ourselves narratives more exciting than the most sensational popular romances:

No romance sold unto
Could so enthrall a Man
As perusal of
His Individual One – (J 669)

She regularly uses the sensational to freshly illuminate themes related to nature, human psychology, and the poetic process. For instance, poem J 11 is a kind of "yellow novel in verse," featuring sensational images of pirates, buried treasure, and murder threats. Dickinson utilizes these common images not to concoct some adventurous plot but to sing praise to the beauty of a sunset:

I never told the buried gold
Upon the hill – that lies –
I saw the sun – his plunder done
Crouch low to guard his prize.

In this poem the sun is presented as a pirate who leaves on a hill plundered treasure enjoyed by the first person speaker, who assumes the persona of a hidden onlooker. To sustain the mood of excitement, Dickinson develops the pirate conceit over five verses. After shaking off a momentary fear of being killed by the pirate-sun, the onlooker marvels over the pirate's "wondrous booty" (the sunlight on the hill), consisting of "the fairest ingots / That ever kissed the spade!" Playfully, the onlooker wonders whether to "keep the secret" of the pirate treasure or reveal it, worrying that, as she tries to decide, "Kidd will sudden sail" (the sun will depart). She ended by trying to come up with a suitable division of the spoils between herself and Kidd, the more famous pirate:

Could a shrewd advise me
We might e'en divide –
Should a shrewd betray me –
Atropos decide!

If here her persona is that of a pirate's co-conspirator, elsewhere it is that
of a criminal. In poem J 23, she poses as a thief:

I robbed the Woods –
The trusting Woods. . . .
I scanned their trinkets curious –
I grasped – I bore away!

Through such pointed redirection of sensational images, Dickinson suggests
that criminality is exciting not for its own sake, as a source of mere diversion
or fantasy, but for its usefulness as a vehicle for wresting beauty and meaning
from everyday experience. If here she "robs" nature, elsewhere she poses as
the victim, rather than the perpetrator, of crime. In poem J 42, for instance,
nature is the invasive criminal threatening the speaker, who cries, "A Day!
Help! Help! Another Day!"

Dickinson's most successful applications of sensational images occur
where she directs such images inward, using them as metaphors for the recesses of the psyche. If popular novelists terrified readers with vividly described horrific settings, she took the new step of reminding readers that the
scariest rooms lay within. "One need not be a Chamber – to be Haunted – ,"
she writes. "The Brain has Corridors – surpassing / Material place" (J 670).
It's far safer, she continues, to meet at midnight an "External Ghost" or to be
chased galloping through an abbey by some would-be assassin than to confront "That Cooler Host, . . . one's a'self." The most appalling terrors spring
from the fantasies and aggressions lurking within:

Ourself behind ourself, concealed –
Should startle most –
Assassin hid in our Apartment
Be Horror's least.

This theme of the horror within the mind is echoed in several other Dickinson
poems, as when she describes "The Loneliness whose worst alarm / Is lest itself
shall see" (J 777). Internalizing adventure imagery, she writes elsewhere,

Adventure most unto itself
The Soul condemned to be –

Attended by a single Hound
It's own identity. (J 822)

By finding psychological equivalents of sensationalism, Dickinson fashions vistas more horrifying than anything in popular fiction. This becomes clear when we compare a gory image in sensational fiction with a similar one in Dickinson's poetry. In the quintessential sensation novel, George Lippard's 1845 best-seller *The Quaker City,* the villainous protagonist, Devil-Bug, gleefully dashes out the brains of an old woman by swinging her body like a hammer on a brass andiron. The scene is described in typically graphic fashion. "The brains of the old woman," Lippard writes, "lay scattered over the hearth, and the body which Devil-Bug raised in the air, was a headless trunk, with the bleeding fragments of a face and skull, clinging to the quivering neck" (p. 241). As ghastly as this scene is, it lacks the resonant painfulness of Dickinson's poem "I felt a Cleaving in my Mind" (J 937).

In Lippard's handling, the dashing out of brains is external to the reader's consciousness, because it results from the perverse criminality of a murderous character. Dickinson converts the dashing out of brains into a metaphor for losing one's mind. Recalling a bewildering psychological episode, the speaker describes a "Cleaving" in her mind, "As if my Brain had split." The unclear referent of "I tried to match it – Seam by Seam –," where "it" could refer both to the mind and the brain, casts ambiguity over the remaining lines, in which the mind's unraveling, "Like Balls – upon a floor," has gory overtones of a brain being splattered. But the image of the splattered brain is far more excruciating in Dickinson than in Lippard, since it connotes severe mental trauma, not just aberrant criminal activity.

A similar psychological reinterpretation of sensational images occurs in the famous poem that begins, "I felt a Funeral, in my Brain" (J 280). Again, a comparison with Lippard's *The Quaker City* reveals Dickinson's improvements on the sensational mode. Lippard had taken sensationalism to new extremes of irrationalism, going beyond even his friend Poe in his exploration of the distortions of time and space caused by the excited fancy. For example, his description of Devil-Bug's dystopic dream of the future of Philadelphia begins with a nightmarish vision of "a hazy atmosphere, with coffins floating slowly past, and the stars shining through the eyes of skulls, and the sun pouring his livid light straight downward into a wilderness of new-made graves which extended yawning and dismal over the surface of a boundless plain." Next Devil-Bug sees the sun assume the shape of a skeleton-head, surrounded by stars, "each star gleaming through the orbless socket of a skull, and the blood-red moon went sailing by, her crescent face, rising above a huge coffin which floated through the livid air like a barque from hell" (p. 370). Pre-surrealistic in its oddness, Lippard's novel resembles its main setting, Monk Hall, a labyrinthine structure riddled with trap doors that are always opening beneath the reader's feet, sending him tumbling "down, down, down" (in Devil-Bug's oft-repeated words) into another dimension.

Dickinson experiments with a similar range of imagery, involving death, coffins, time/space distortion, and headlong plunges into other dimensions. But by gathering all these Lippardian phenomena into the consciousness of a first-person speaker, she gives them entirely fresh connotations. The fact that the speaker "*felt* a Funeral, in my *Brain*" [my italics] points the poem in two directions simultaneously: first, toward a delineation of an actual funeral service, followed by passage into the after-life; and second, toward a description of a descent into madness, followed by the collapse of reason. The "I" of the poem, like the personae of several other Dickinson poems, could be recalling her own funeral, with mourners "treading – treading –," sitting down at a service, and finally carrying out the coffin, at which point the speaker's soul passes alone into the silent, infinite other world described in the last two verses. At the same time, the "I" could be reliving a terrifying time when it felt as though she were losing her mind. This psychological interpretation is reinforced by a succession of phrases – "in my Brain," "My Mind was going numb –," "creak across my Soul" – that point to the possibility that the "Funeral" here signifies the death of the speaker's rationality and normalcy. In this light, the last two verses, in which the speaker feels "Wrecked, solitary" as "a Plank in Reason, broke," point to the utter alienation and confusion of the insane person.

The last three lines,

And I dropped down, and down –
And hit a World, at every plunge,
And Finished knowing – then –

bring the poem's two major themes to apt culmination. As a conclusion to a death poem, these lines portray the soul, cast into the unknowable after-life, hurtling into infinite space and time. As an end to a psychological poem, they suggest the mind plunging without direction toward chaos, until the speaker has "Finished knowing" – i.e., lost the ability to understand anything. On both levels of meaning, the image of dropping "down, and down" and hitting "a World, at every plunge" has far more resonance than does Lippard's account of people falling "down, down, down" through the trap doors of the multilayered Monk Hall. For Lippard, the arch-sensationalist, the downward plunge of the murder victim is one more bloody plot twist designed to amuse thrillseekers. For Dickinson, the explorer of death and the human mind, the downward plunge of the speaker is a frightening tumble into ineffable mysteries.

Having surveyed a number of the cultural elements that fed into Dickinson's poetry, it is fitting to conclude by considering her in light of other American women writers, whose best works constituted a real literary flowering between 1858 and 1866, the very years that were by far her most productive as a poet. These years saw, on the one hand, the temporary diminution of the organized women's rights activity that had begun at Seneca Falls, New York in 1848 and, simultaneously, a search for more literary ways of expressing women's rage and fantasies. It was a period of extreme self-consciousness about the proliferation of varied women's roles in American culture. Mary Louise Hankins's *Women of New York* (1860) described no fewer than thirty-two kinds of American women – including, significantly, the confidence woman, who could playfully act out all the other women's roles with devilish ease. The variability Hankins perceived was enacted by women writers who took pride in literary acts of self-transformation and manipulation. In characterization, this pride was projected in characters like Medora Fielding in Lillie Devereux Blake's *Southwold* (1859) or Jean Muir of Louisa May Alcott's *Behind a Mask* (1866), canny heroines who avenge women's wrongs by feigning virtue. In plot, it produced broken narrative patterns. In theme, it was evidenced by a growing preoccupation with doubt and negativity. In style, it gave rise to minimalism, ellipsis, and compaction. Intrinsic to this women's literature was a belief in the tormented but dauntless core self of the woman artist, lying below all gender roles and regulating them at will, asserting its power through waspish imagery and daring to tackle universal themes that lay beyond myth or gender. Given the extreme fertility of this historical moment in American women's culture, it is perhaps understandable that fully sixty-two percent of the almost 1,800 poems Dickinson was to write in her lifetime were produced in the 1858–1866 period.

Dickinson had special affinities with the authors of the so-called "literature of misery," the genre named and described by Samuel Bowles, the energetic editor she knew well.[10] If the women authors of the literature of misery sought to establish an artistic middle ground between the effetely conventional and the openly feminist, so Emily Dickinson explicitly rejected the "Dimity Convictions" of traditionalists and the public methods of women's rights activists, while she made the era's boldest quest for specifically artistic exhibitions of woman's power. If other women writers typically hid behind shifting literary masks, Dickinson played so many roles, from the childlike "Daisy" to the regal "Empress," that it becomes difficult to identify her actual, biographical self. If they often shifted tone and perspective in successive sketches or chapters, Dickinson regularly did so in successive verses, lines, and even words. If their experimental style was attacked as crude and formless, so was Dickinson's, as is most famously evidenced by Thomas Wentworth Higginson's complaint about her "spasmodic" style. If their work grew principally from the severe inward pain that gave the literature of misery its name, some of Dickinson's best poetry had a similar source, as suggested by verses in which she describes grief or pain as exhilarating: one thinks especially of the poem "I can wade Grief – / Whole pools of it –" (J 252). If along with this pain went a heady confidence in the creative act as the American woman's surest means of self-assertion, Dickinson too was nourished by this confidence, inherited partly from her father (an advocate of women's education and an outspoken admirer of the pioneering woman writer Catharine Sedgwick) and manifested continually by Dickinson's unparalleled poetic innovations. If they had redirected radical-democrat energies toward a search for a gender-free literary reality, Dickinson consummated this search in poetry that strains always toward the universal, poetry that reflects her great radical-democrat declaration: "My Country is Truth . . . It is a very free Democracy."[11]

In addition to these overall affinities between Emily Dickinson and other American women writers, there are more specific connections in the area of imagery and themes. Her repeated use of volcano imagery, for instance, is very much in the vein of the literature of misery. A basic assumption of this literature is that since women's energies were allowed no viable outlet, they gathered in upon themselves and lay burning inwardly, always threatening to erupt through a placid exterior. The heroines of the literature of misery often looked like sweet moral exemplars but raged inwardly with the ferocity of women victims bent on revenge. This fusion of docile and fiery qualities is summed up by a character in Sara Parton's *Ruth Hall* (1856), who generalizes, "Whenever – you – see – a – blue-eyed – soft-voiced – gentle – woman, – look – out – for a hurricane. I tell you that placid Ruth is a smouldering volcano."[12] In Blake's *Southwold*, the author describes Medora Fielding in a typical moment: "No one could have guessed that the calm indifference of her manner concealed a volcano of rage and scorn."[13] The heroine of another novel, *L'eoline*, declares, "A woman made reckless by wrongs, is without compassion," since beneath her gentle exterior lies "a spirit fearless and relentless as the untamed tigress."[14] Even the style of the literature of misery was a kind of dormant volcano, frequently muted and quietly imagistic but always with explosive implications.

Dickinson brought a full self-consciousness to the use of volcano imagery, recognizing that it applied both to women's lives and to women's literary style. Her sensitivity to these interrelated levels of meaning is powerfully captured in the first lines of the successive verses of poem J 601:

A still – Volcano – Life –

. . .

A quiet – Earthquake Style –

. . .

The Solemn – Torrid – Symbol –

These lines are a highly compressed, self-reflexive enactment of the thematic and stylistic polarities of American women's literature. Dickinson's irregular prosody, with its ubiquitous dashes and caesurae, shows rhythm and structure being shattered by the pressure of vehement emotion brought under severe restraint, a stylistic feature common in the literature of misery (witness, for example, the pre-Dickinsonian pauses in the above-quoted passage from *Ruth Hall* on "a – blue–eyed – soft–voiced – gentle – woman, –"). In Dickinson's case, there is evidence that confirms the connection between volcano imagery and women's issues. At a key moment in the longest of her three "Master" letters she communicates the extreme tensions created by her buried feelings as follows: "Vesuvius dont talk – Etna – don't –" (L ii:374). Although most generalizations about her character and personal life are tentative at best, the one that certainly holds true is that her extraordinary passional and intellectual powers were inevitably repressed and deflected, gaining full expression only in cryptic, loaded metaphors. It appears, therefore, that there is personal and gender-specific import in such famous Dickinson images as "Vesuvius at Home" (J 1705) , "the reticent volcano" (J 1748), and "On my volcano grows the grass" (J 1677). We might be tempted to look for specific biographical sources for Dickinson's volcano imagery (such as the much discussed issue of a possible homoerotic attraction to her sister-in-law Susan Gilbert Dickinson), but more significant than such psychoanalytic guesswork is the realization that, whatever the personal motivations behind individual poems, Dickinson frequently discovered new applications for the volcano, one of the most common images in American women's writings.

Those who focus narrowly on a few Dickinson poems that seem directly feminist or on particular personality quirks that make Dickinson appear to be a nineteenth-century madwoman do not truly account for her stature as a paradigmatic American woman writer. Her real representativeness lies in her incomparable flexibility, her ability to be, by turns, coy, fierce, domestic, romantic, protofeminist, antifeminist, prudish, and erotic. She militantly asserted her creativity through ingenious metaphorical play and through brash imaginings of a gender-free literary reality. In this sense, of course, she was much like other authors of the American Women's Renaissance who evaded simple gender categories by freely combining the stereotypes generated by their culture, just as she shared their philosophical adventurousness and devotion to technique. But in Dickinson these common principles are so greatly exaggerated and intensified that they produce a wholly new kind of literature. Other women writers' manipulations of female stereotypes pale beside her endless adaptations and truly innovative fusions of these stereotypes. Their questions about religion and philosophy seem timid next to her leaps into an indefinite realm beyond all religion and philosophy. Their affirmations of women's creativity through stylistic experimentation are tentative when compared with her unremitting quest for the startling metaphor, the unusual rhyme, the odd caesura.

Even when she deals directly with gender issues, clear statement on these issues is abrogated on behalf of jaunty stylistic gamesmanship, signaled by tonal fusions and shocking images. Take the poem "I'm 'wife' – I've finished that" (J 199; c. 1860). Some critics have interpreted this as a wry, anti-marriage poem extremely unusual in a day when marriage was extolled as the highest good. The fact is that American women's wrongs literature had long portrayed the suffering of wives. Indeed, the year before Dickinson wrote the above poem there had appeared a dark women's novel, *The Autobiography of a Married Woman*, whose heroine becomes so disillusioned with marriage that she exclaims, "O, mothers! Train your daughters to self-reliance, and not to feel that they are to marry simply because everybody does marry. . . .There are very few happy marriages; there can be but few, where interest and self-love form the tie."[15]

Dickinson's poem stands out not for any new statement about marriage it might contain but for its playful fusion of the opposing views on marriage that were circulating in American culture. One view, related to the conventional ethos of domestic fiction, was that marriage was a state of heavenly bliss and of remarkable power for women. In Dickinson's own life, this idealization of domesticity was reflected in her well-known enjoyment of housekeeping activities and in certain statements in her letters, such as her 1851 message to Susan Gilbert: "Home is a holy thing – nothing of doubt or distrust can enter it's blessed portals" (L 1:150). In the poem, this view is enforced by the images of the home as heaven and the wife as "Czar" and "Woman" – images that invest the marriage relation with both bliss and power for women. The contrasting view, related to the outlook on marriage held by many suffregists and women's wrongs authors, saw marriage as an unequal state in which women suffered a range of ills, from economic deprivation to loss of independence. In Dickinson's life, this hostility to marriage was reflected in her indomitable spinsterhood and in direct cries of protest in letters, such as her exclamatory note to Abiah Root, "God keep me from what they call *households*," or her early comment to Susan Gilbert that their unmarried state must seem enviable to "the *wife*, . . . sometimes the *wife forgotten*" (L 1:99, 210). In the poem above, the anti-marriage view is crystallized in subtle images, such as "soft Eclipse" and "Stop there!" suggesting the termination of a woman's independence in marriage.

Dickinson was not the first American writer to incorporate both positive and negative views of marriage. Sara Parton, the author whose "spicey passages" Dickinson had read to her father,[16] had done this in successive sketches in *Fern Leaves,* and many women writers of the 1850s had studied tensions between womanly independence and heterosexual love. Dickinson was perhaps the first, however, to fuse contrasting views in a single text and in individual metaphors. The literary fusion enables her to achieve a far more complete view of marriage than was advanced by either the pro-marriage or anti-marriage groups. The message, if any can be gleaned, is that marriage is a heavenly state of power in which women gain safety and comfort but, at the same time, lose the painful but exhilarating self-sufficiency of maidenhood. More important than the poem's message, however, is its stylistic power. How concisely Dickinson communicates the treatment of wife as the husband's objective possession through the quotation marks around "wife" and "Woman"! How subtle are the tonal shifts in the poem, as the persona wavers between enthusiasm and skepticism about marriage! How potently does the phrase "soft Eclipse" communicate that cushioned banality she envisages in marriage! As always in Dickinson's poetry, the greatest triumphs here are stylistic.

Given Dickinson's literary aims, it is not surprising that she directly rejected women's rights and was notably inconsistent on women's issues. In the course of her close relationship with Thomas Wentworth Higginson she never showed interest in one of his favorite reforms, women's rights, and when the progressive popular novelist Elizabeth Stuart Phelps wrote to her in 1872 asking for her aid in the women's cause, she burned Phelps's letter and mailed her a flat refusal. This indifference to political feminism was part and parcel of serious authorship during the American Women's Renaissance. It is no accident that Dickinson's most productive literary period was in the early 1860s, for this was the moment when all women's rights activity was suspended. As early as 1858, outside opposition and internal dissension had created a notable diminution of suffrage activity, and the Civil War brought a complete cessation of women's conventions between February 1861 and May 1866. Dickinson's earliest (and many of her best) poems were written between 1858 and 1866, precisely the years that produced some of the finest works of Lillie Devereux Blake, Elizabeth Stoddard, Rebecca Harding Davis, Louisa May Alcott, Alice and Phoebe Cary, and Harriet Prescott Spofford. Was Dickinson conscious that she was a member of this pioneering literary sisterhood? Little evidence survives to give us a sure answer, but her comments about one of these authors – Harriet Prescott Spofford – show that she was more moved by contemporary American women's writing than by any other favorite classic authors, even Shakespeare. After she finished the last installment of Spofford's story "The Amber Gods" (in the February 1860 issue of the *Atlantic*) she begged her sister-in-law to send her everything Spofford wrote. "The Amber Gods," an imaginative tale involving mysterious amber beads and frustrated love, elicited this high compliment from Dickinson: "It is the only thing I ever read in my life that I didn't think I could have imagined myself" *(YH* II, p. 6) She was even more affected by Spofford's "Circumstance" (1860), a story about a woman alone in the Maine woods who fends off a half-human "Indian beast" by singing to him. Dickinson was so haunted by the story that she wrote to Higginson in 1862: "I read Miss Prescott's 'Circumstance,' but it followed me, in the Dark – so I avoided her –" (L II:404). Coming from a woman who believed that literature should be bewitching and devastating, this was high praise.

Whatever cross-influences between Dickinson and the other women writers may have existed, it is certain that she absorbed their overall goal of depoliticizing women's discourse and shifting creative energy away from monolithic expression toward flexible impersonation. She took to a new extreme the liberating manipulation of female stereotypes. In successive poems she assumed with ease an array of shifting personae: the abandoned woman ("Heart! We will forget him!" J 47); the loving wife ("Forever at His side to walk –" J 246); the fantasist of erotic ecstasy ("Wild Nights – Wild Nights!" J 49); the acerbic satirist of conventional women ("What Soft – Cherubic Creatures – / These Gentlewomen are – ," J 401); the expectant bride on the eve of her wedding ("A Wife – at Daybreak I shall be –," J 461); the sullen rejecter of a lover ("I cannot live with You," J 40).

This is, of course, only a small sampling of other countless poses. We should not be concerned that these poses frequently contradict each other and that several of them seem far more conservative or obsequious to males than might be expected from the strongest woman poet in the English language. Instead, we should recognize her elusiveness as the major ingredient of her artistry and of her representativeness as a writer of the American Women's Renaissance. If Sara Parton's "Floy" showed her power by sending impossibly mixed signals to baffled male reviewers, if Blake's Medora Fielding and Alcott's Jean Muir took vindictive pride in never showing a true face to men, if the "confidence woman" in Hankins's *Women of New York* proudly impersonated every female stereotype, Dickinson outdid them all by donning an unparalleled variety of masks behind which the core self lay as an ever-present but always invisible manipulator. Even in letters to confidants, Dickinson was quick to hide behind personae and to point up the totally fictive nature of other poetic poses. As she wrote to Higginson in 1862, "When I state myself, as the Representative of the Verse – it does not mean me –" (L II:412). For Dickinson, all women's stereotypes become matters of literary theater and metaphorical play.

A result of this endless capacity for manipulation was her unusual fusion of female stereotypes, which is particularly visible in "My Life had stood – a Loaded Gun –" (J 754). A common stereotype in popular fiction was the adventure feminist, the tough woman who could survive extreme physical peril and outbrave men in battle. We have seen that another image associated with women, the volcano, was commonly used in the literature of misery to represent the quiet but inwardly explosive woman who was denied a viable outlet for her energies. The first stereotype enacted fantasies of power; the second reflected the realities of repression and powerlessness. In her poem Dickinson takes the wholly original step of fusing these contrary images. On the one hand, the "I" of the poem is the ultimate adventure feminist, the omnipotent aggressor who does all the hunting and speaking for her master and always guards him from danger. On the other hand, she has a "Vesuvian face" that signals the total repression of her aggressions in deference to him. Whether or not the man here referred to as "Owner" is the intended recipient of Dickinson's pained "Master" letters, the poem makes it clear that Dickinson is conjuring up an adventure-feminist fantasy and, simultaneously, suggesting the suspicion that this imagined power is an illusion. A loaded gun is not useful until it is fired, just as the "I" of the poem gains power only when carried off by her master. The fantasies and frustrations the "I" embodies, however, are secondary to the potency of the poem itself. This ingenious fusion of contradictory female stereotypes sets off a string of lively metaphorical associations that themselves constitute the aggressiveness of the woman writer.

Dickinson's most sophisticated poems are those in which she permits imagery from radically different cultural arenas to come together in an explosive metaphorical center. In some other women's writings of the 1850s, such as Parton's *Ruth Hall* and Cary's *Married, Not Mated*,[17] disparate cultural images are *juxtaposed* in single texts, creating a certain density and stylistic innovativeness. In Dickinson's poetry, such contrasting images are consistently *fused* in single stanzas, even in single words, so that they radiate with fresh suggestions – and create intriguing puzzles for would-be interpreters. Notice the poetic fusions in the famously cryptic poem "Mine – by the Right of the White Election!" (J 528). In this poem, negative images reminiscent of sensational literature ("Scarlet prison," "Bars," "Veto," "Grave's Repeal") are fused with affirmative, ecstatic religious imagery ("White Election," "Vision," "Confirmed," "Delirious Charter!"). The lack of a clear referent for "Mine" points up the radical open-endedness of meaning that results from the creative fusion of opposing cultural elements. Dickinson had profited immensely from her earlier awareness of different progressive phenomena in popular culture: on the one hand, the sensational writings that had featured prisons, death, and blood; on the other hand, relaxed religious discourse, which suddenly became available for creative recombination with secular imagery. Dickinson grafts together the two kinds of imagery and retains the ultimacy of vision that had long governed her ponderings of large issues. Dickinson's wholly original fusion of contrasting types of images in dense poetry truly distinguishes her. If, as many critics believe, "Mine" refers to the poetic gift, it may be said that Dickinson is fully justified for the boasting, assertive tone of this poem. Through reconstructive fusion, she had managed to create a poem that salvages both the sensational and the religious by bringing them together and infusing them with a new emotional intensity and metaphysical resonance.

A similar intensification through poetic fusion occurs in one of her most famous love poems, "Wild Nights – Wild Nights!" (J 249). It is not known whether Dickinson had read any of the erotic literature of the day or if she knew of the stereotype of the sensual woman.[18] Given her fascination with sensational journalism and with popular literature in general, it is hard to believe she would not have had at least some exposure to erotic literature. At any rate, her treatment of the daring theme of woman's sexual fantasy in this deservedly famous poem bears comparison with erotic themes as they appeared in popular sensational writings. The first stanza of the poem provides an uplifting or purification of sexual fantasy not distant from the effect of Walt Whitman's cleansing rhetoric, which was consciously designed to counteract the prurience of what he called the "love plot" of much popular fiction. Dickinson's repeated phrase "Wild Nights" is a simple but dazzling metaphor that communicates wild passion – even lust – but simultaneously lifts sexual desire out of the scabrous by fusing it with the natural image of the night. The second verse introduces a second nature image, the turbulent sea and the contrasting quiet port, which at once universalizes the passion and purifies it further through abstract metaphor. Also, the second verse makes clear that this is not a poem of sexual consummation but rather of pure fantasy and sexual impossibility. Unlike popular erotic literature, the poem portrays neither a consummated seduction nor the heartless deception that it involves. There is instead a pure, fervent fantasy whose frustration is figured forth in the contrasting images of the ocean (the longed-for-but-never-achieved consummation) and the port (the reality of the poet's isolation). The third verse begins with an image, "Rowing in Eden," that further uplifts sexual passion by yoking it with a religious archetype. Here, as elsewhere, Dickinson capitalizes nicely on the new religious style, which made possible such fusions of the divine and the earthly. The persona's concluding wish to "moor" in the sea expresses the sustained intense sexual longing and the simultaneous frustration of that longing. In the course of the poem, Dickinson has communicated great erotic passion, and yet, by effectively projecting this passion through unusual images of nature and religion, has rid it of even the tiniest residue of sensationalism.

It is fair to generalize from these and other letters that Dickinson was unique among American women of her day in the breadth of her awareness of the most experimental tendencies in contemporary American culture. Her excitement over press reports of tragedies, her attraction to the new religious style, and her interest in women's writing all reveal a sensibility that was absorbing various kinds of popular images. Dickinson recognized the need for an artistic form that would serve to control and fuse these often contradictory elements. She appropriated the iambic rhythms and simple verse patterns of English hymnody, which had been famously utilized in the Isaac Watts hymns she knew from childhood, as controlling devices to lend structure and resonance to these disparate themes.

In her poetry, therefore, Dickinson was both inscribing her culture and personalizing it. She was that rare oxymoronic being, a *private-public* poet.

NOTES

1. Kavanagh (1849; rpt., *Hyperron and Kavanagh* [Boston: Houghton Mifflin, 1886]): pp. 325–326.

2. *Springfield Republican*, October 22, 1850; reprinted from the *New York Evening Post.*

3 Lippard, *The Quaker City; or, The Monks of Monk Hall*, ed. David S. Reynolds (1845; rpt., Amherst: University of Massachusetts Press, 1995): pp. 201, 291.

4. Thompson, *City Crimes; or, Life in Boston and New York* (New York: William Berry, 1849): p. 121.

5. *Emerson in His Journals*, ed. Joel Porte (Cambridge, MA.: Harvard University Press, 1982): p. 433.

6. *The Journal of Henry Davrd Thoreau*, ed. Bradford Torrey and Francis II. Allen (New York: Dover, 1962), vol. IV, p. 267.

7. *Brooklyn Daily Eagle*, 26 February 1847.

8. *Foreign Quarterly Review* (London), October 1842, and E. Faithfull, *Three Visits to America* (Edinburgh: David Douglas, 1884), p. 336.

9. Anonymous, *Confessions and Experience of a Novel Reader* (Chicago: William Stacy, 1855), p. 73.

10. *Springfield Republican*, 7 July 1860.

11. Quoted in Rochard B. Sewall, *The Lyman Letters: New Light on Emily Dickingson and her Poetry* (Amherst: University of Massachusetts Press, 1965), p. 71.

12. Sara Parton, *Ruth Hall: A Domestic Tale of the Present Time* (New York: Mason Brothers, 1855), p. 133.

13. L. D. Blake, *Southwold: A Novel* (New York: Rudd & Carleton, 1859), p. 47.

14. *The Una*, June 1855.

15. Anonymous, *The Autobiography of a Married Woman. No Girlhood* (New York: S. A. Rollo & Co., 1859), p. 155.

16. Millicent Todd Bingham (ed.), *Emily Dickinson's Home: Letters of Edward Dickinson and his Family* (New York: Harper & Brothers, 1955), pp. 312–313.

17. Phoebe Cary, *Married, Not Married, or, How They Lived at Woodside and Throckmorton Hall* (New York, 1856).

18. See David S. Reynolds, *Beneath the American Renaissance: The Subversive Imagination in the Age of Emerson and Melville* (New York: Knopf, 1988), ch. 7.

WORKS CITED

Bingham, Millicent Todd. (ed.), *Emily Dickinson's Home: Letters of Edward Dickinson and his Family.* New York: Harper & Brothers, 1955.

Reynolds, David S. *Beneath the American Renaissance: The Subversive Imagination in the Age of Emerson and Melville.* New York: Knopf, 1988.

Sewall, Richard B. *The Lyman Letters: New Light on Emily Dickinson and her Poetry.* Amherst: University of Massachusetts Press, 1965.

CAROLYN LINDLEY COOLEY

Musical Qualities of Dickinson's Poetry: Nineteenth-Century Views

The discovery of Emily Dickinson's poems shortly after her death in 1886 remains one of the major events in American literary history. When her sister Lavinia found almost eighteen hundred poems in Emily's dresser drawers, she realized that she had discovered a veritable treasure, but she could never have dreamed of the world-wide and enduring ramifications of her incredible find. Her immediate desire was to have them published in a limited number of copies to share with special friends, and the urgency with which she pursued this project was perhaps generated from the fact that she had already destroyed numerous manuscripts and letters which had been sent to Emily, many of them from nationally recognized people. Lavinia's appeals for help with the publication of the poems began with her sister-in-law Susan Dickinson, with whom Emily had shared many lofty thoughts and poetic aspirations. Susan's literary influence on Emily had been extensive, as Emily's letter of 1882 to Susan reveals: "With the exception of Shakespeare, you have told me of more knowledge than any one living —" (L 757). Susan's early enthusiasm for the project turned to indifference and finally to discouragement of publication at all. Lavinia then approached Thomas Wentworth Higginson, prominent man of letters and the "Preceptor" from whom Emily Dickinson sought literary advice over a period of twenty years, sending him 102 poems enclosed in seventy-

Carlyn Lindley Cooley, *The Music of Emily Dickinson's Poems and Letters: A Study of Imagery and Form,* (Jefferson, NC: McFarland & Company, 2003): pp. 59–69.

one letters. Higginson, who had admired Emily's dazzling thoughts while deploring her lack of form, declined Lavinia's offer, protesting that his busy schedule and the near-cryptic status of the poems presented insuperable obstacles for his participation in such an undertaking. He did, however, agree to source go over the poems if they could be put into careful shape for consideration. Lavinia's last alternative, Mabel Loomis Todd, a friend of the family who had artistic gifts in the fields of art, music, and literature, proved to be her best choice, for Todd was "technically the best equipped person in town to edit the poems,"[1] and the importance of her acceptance of the formidable tasks of transcribing Dickinson's poems and of finding publishers for them cannot be overstated. Without Todd's vision, her tenacity, her intuitive insight into Dickinson's genius, and, perhaps most importantly, her *faith* in the poems, there is a distinct possibility that Dickinson's creative efforts might have been lost to the literary world completely.

Instead, Todd devoted much of the next ten years of her life to preparing the poems for publication, to acting as co-editor with Thomas Wentworth Higginson of the first two series of *Poems by Emily Dickinson*, and to becoming sole editor of the third series and of the two-volume *Letters of Emily Dickinson*. Also, Todd made a significant contribution to the study of nineteenth-century literary criticism by collecting and preserving hundreds of original magazine and newspaper reviews about Dickinson's poems and letters in separate scrapbooks for each of the three volumes of poems and a single scrapbook for the two-volume edition of letters. She obviously comprehended the importance of saving these documents for posterity because she took the same thoughtful care in compiling these clippings as she had taken in editing the poems and the letters. She saved brief notices as well as lengthy ones, and she hired a professional service to obtain all known comments and reviews from areas beyond her purview.

In 1989, Willis J. Buckingham almost doubled Mabel Todd's collection of 325 reviews when he edited his *Emily Dickinson's Reception in the 1890s:A Documentary History*, yet he acknowledges that it is "to Todd's vision and effort that credit for his book's comprehensiveness must largely fall."[2] The six hundred entries in Buckingham's volume include all known commentary on Dickinson published in the eighteen-nineties, thus providing a rare and exceptionally broad perspective for assessing American verse criticism and book publishing during last decade of the nineteenth century. Because these primary sources have been virtually unavailable until the publication of Buckingham's book, the tendency has been toward generalization of information rather than specific focus on specialized topics. Therefore, Buckingham says, "the fullest promise of these reviews will finally lie in the capacity of new generations of readers to discover in them—and to compose out of them—yet another valued constituent of their own patient questioning of Dickinson's words."[3] In the light of that promise, these reviews have been scrutinized for what they might yield to this study of Emily Dickinson and music, and the search has provided surprising and deeply satisfying results.

The diverse reactions found in the nineteenth-century reviews prompts contemporary scholars to ask two major questions: "Why was Emily Dickinson liked so well?" and "Why was she liked so little?"[4] Out of a number of potential answers to these questions, two distinct possibilities prevail consistently throughout the criticism. First, Dickinson was "liked so well" because of the musical qualities of her verse, and, second, she was "liked so little" because of the seeming lack of form in her poetry. Examination of some key nineteenth-century reviews illustrates these reactions and provides insight into the acceptance and the rejection of Dickinson's verse by her contemporary, or near-contemporary, readers and reviewers.

Many of the earliest literary critics and reviewers recognized the musical quality of Dickinson's verse, and nineteenth-century criticism is replete with analogies connecting Emily Dickinson and music. Dickinson often compared herself to a bird and her poetry to song, and critics of the last decade of the nineteenth century appear to have agreed with that analogy. One critic wrote of Dickinson's poetry, "Surely there were never such 'wood-notes' warbled in lovelier and more silvery trebles,"[5] and another, writing for *Truth*, the New York weekly of high society and social satire, called Dickinson "the strangely gifted, recluse singer," finding that she has "a native impulse to harmony often attaining the melody akin to a wild-bird's song."[6] One article in the "Books and Authors" section of the *Boston Sunday Courier* addresses Dickinson's great intellectual activity and its incomparable results, the accomplishment of verse, in these terms:

> As a caged thrush sings, so sang she, for the sake of singing and of making beautiful her place in the world, while she might. . . . It is true, we liken this singer to the thrush in the cage, because of the calm environment with which she chose to surround her movements. It is equally true that her song is as untutored, as wild, free and lovely as the thrush's song, with clear, sure notes, bearing messages ever.[7]

A similar thought, written for the *Boston Daily Traveller*, supports the "freedom and fullness" of Dickinson's verse as "the expression of the inward thought," without concern for either criticism or praise, claiming that it "has a charm as indefinable as the song of a wild bird that sings out of the fullness of its heart. There is no fear of discord."[8] And, in the first discussion of Emily Dickinson in a language other than English, the German critic "A. Von E."

wrote an appreciative essay comparing Dickinson to a German woman poet, Annette von Droste-Hulshoff. Acknowledging their differences in regard to publication, the article states that the German poet thought of publishing her poems as early as her youth, while "the American poet, bird-like, sang spontaneously for herself alone."[9] Rupert Hughes, speaking of the startling originality and the captivating individuality of Dickinson's ideas in an 1896 article for *Godey's Magazine,* placed her above all other female poets. Though recognizing that Dickinson is a grievous sinner against rhyme and metre, he finds "such a rush and fire to her measures" that he likens it to "the gushing outburst of an improvisatory bird, careless of Richterian theories of eight measures to the period, careless of everything but of voicing itself just as it feels."[10]

The vast majority of comparisons between Dickinson's verse and bird song were positive ones, but Dickinson's severest critic, the Englishman Andrew Lang, took every occasion to make negative comments on this American poet whom he could not understand. In one column for *Illustrated London News,* Lang wrote that "one might as well seek for an air in the notes of a bird as for articulate and sustained poetry here."[11] In another, he attacked William Dean Howells for the article he wrote for *Harper's New Monthly Magazine* in praise of Dickinson's poem, "New feet within my garden go." In his review, Howells wrote such accolades as "there is a still, solemn, rapt movement of the thought and music together that is of exquisite charm" and "This is a song that sings itself."[12] Lang, who failed to catch the music of the poem which Howells so clearly heard, retaliates with the following observations on the same poem: "What in the world has a troubadour to do in New England? And why did he climb a tree? Or was he a bird? And how can solitude be betrayed by a troubadour, somewhere near Boston, in the foliage of an elm?" In fact, Lang fails to find anything of value in the poem at all, saying, "There are no words that can say how bad poetry may be when it is divorced from meaning, from music, from grammar, from rhyme; in brief, from articulate and intelligible speech."[13] Though Lang's evaluation seems almost an embarrassment to present-day critics of Dickinson's poetry, it is nevertheless important because of the light it sheds on the varying attitudes regarding the musical qualities of Dickinson's poetry during the nineteenth century.

The majority of critics and readers who commented on music in their articles found it to be one of the most attractive qualities of Dickinson's verse. Many of the reviewers praised Dickinson and her poems through the medium of musical terminology. Possibly the most extravagant example of applying musical terms to describe Dickinson and her poetry is in this article which Samuel J. Barrows wrote for the *Christian Register:*

> Miss Dickinson was a recluse. She communed very little with
> society, but much with nature and with her own mind. She was not

made to play a part in the world's great orchestra. She was more like an Aeolian harp through which the wind swept over a delicately attuned nature, sometimes awaking the minor, sometimes the major chord, and now and then striking a dissonant note which only seemed to give more richness and piquancy to the harmony. Her poetry was never made of sustained notes or flowing strains. It was made of little gusts of song, snatches of melody, broken chords, and arpeggios.[14]

Though not all the reviews used musical terminology so profusely, a great many of them found that music provided an extremely appropriate figurative language by which Dickinson and her poetry could be described. One anonymous reviewer, writing for the *Fall River* [Massachusetts] *Monitor,* commented on the large sale of the second series of Emily Dickinson's poems and on the most cordial commendation from press reviews of the poems, in spite of the fact that Dickinson was a comparatively unknown writer. This reviewer found that "her verses are not merely those bits of exquisite melody that catch the fancy and haunt the memory with their sweetness. Melodious as is much of Miss Dickinson's versification, it is not the chief or the most marked characteristic of her writing," which the author believed to be her deep thought and strong originality.[15] Robert Bridges, in an article for *Life,* one of the most elegant and cultivated magazines in America during the eighteen-nineties, asserted that those who like philosophy in verse will easily find it in Dickinson's poetry, but he suggests that they will probably overlook what is a finer thing—"the original fancy which compresses striking images into a few words, or catches a strange melody in most irregular measures."[16]

One reviewer of "Books and Bookmen" in *Light,* the society and entertainment weekly for Worcester, Massachusetts, commented on the incredible interest and admiration that the first series of Dickinson's poems evoked and mentions that the preface in the second series acquaints the readers, to a limited extent, with the writer herself. It reveals "what a remarkable being she was, unquestionably, divinely touched by the spirit of song."[17] An article in the *Boston Home Journal* section, "Books and Authors," praises the first volume of *Poems by Emily Dickinson,* predicting that it will become a cherished companion to thousands of lovers of poetry who never even heard of Emily Dickinson's name, but who will at once recognize "the richness of the mind of her who was wont to sing from a heart overflowing with love for nature and humanity."[18] Another musical comment on this first book of poems, found in the "New Books" section of the Boston independent review and opinion weekly *Commonwealth,* states that Dickinson had no wish for publicity, no desire for fame, and "no ambition to sing in accord with other poets."[19] In a review for the *Springfield Republican* addressing Dickinson's unique style, Charles Goodrich Whiting avers that literary form, as used by others, she regarded little. Instead, she was determined to express herself just as she did, "having her own standard of rhythm, or perhaps we should say music, and her own choice of words."[20]

Thomas Wentworth Higginson himself, Dickinson's preceptor and a highly respected literary critic, in a review for "Recent Poetry" in *Nation*, possibly the country's leading weekly periodical commenting on politics and letters, promoted Dickinson's work in these musical terms:

> Emily Dickinson resolutely refused to publish her verses, showing them only to a very few friends. As a consequence, she had almost no criticism, and was absolutely untrammelled; so that the verses are sometimes almost formless, while at other times they show great capacity for delicate and sweet melody, suggesting the chance strains of an Aeolian harp. But in compass of thought, grasp of feeling, and vigor of epithet, they are simply extraordinary, and strike notes, very often, like those of some deep-toned organ."[21]

Poet and critic Bliss Carmen, in a review for the *Chicago Post,* made a similar observation when he claimed that "Emily Dickinson's peculiar scheme of rhyme was handled with such mastery, with such an exquisite ear for cadence, as to become in her hands a new and original stop in the great organ of English verification."[22]

Edward J. Harding began his review in "Today's Literature" for the *Chicago Tribune* in 1891 by quoting Dickinson's "And the noise in the pool at noon excels my piano," lines she once sent to Thomas Wentworth Higginson. Harding, literary editor for the *Tribune,* perceived that Dickinson was "groping after a music more spiritual than is made on the piano." This was a mood he claimed to be seeking for himself "in the shadowy recesses of his inner consciousness," which, he claimed, "gives a premonitory quiver when it encounters a rhythmical nature such as Emily Dickinson, who had a delicacy of expression like Chopin's—she was a New England Chopin—a Chopin living in the bleak-soul-unfavorable conditions of the Yankee atmosphere."[23] This somewhat startling comparison is nonetheless appropriate, for Chopin's great appreciation for the effects the piano could produce matched Dickinson's respect for the effects induced by poetry, and his finest works, like those of Dickinson's, were in forms that he himself worked out or perfected. The astounding musicality of Dickinson's verse coupled with the American quality of the New England landscape and atmosphere make Harding's analogy of these two artists both pertinent and viable.

The instant popularity of the first series of Emily Dickinson's poetry and of the two series which followed "is something unique in literature, being wholly posthumous and achieved without puffing or special effort, and indeed, quite contrary to the expectation of both editors and publishers," according to Higginson in his 1896 review for "Recent Poetry" in *Nation*. He added the following comment, which can only be viewed as extraordinary in light of his early and persistent discouragement to Emily Dickinson herself about publication: "No volumes of American poetry, not even the most popular of Longfellow's, have had so wide or so steady a sale."[24]

Mabel Loomis Todd, in her comments on public reaction to Dickinson's poetry, claimed that the critics hardly knew where to place Emily Dickinson's "strangely compelling poems" when they were first published. Todd, by reading and comparing the many notices about Dickinson's poetry, found that the reviewers agreed in allowing her the possession of undoubted genius, while at the same time they deplored the fact that Dickinson seemed to care so slightly for the form in which her "startling little poetic bombs were cast."[25] In an 1895 "tea talk" in Worcester, Massachusetts, Todd acknowledged the general agreement of critics about Dickinson's lack of form, but she expressed her deeper understanding of Dickinson's poems by saying, "Yet there is a strange cadence of hidden music underlying her verse, which is like an orchid growing among the ordinary flowers of the field."[26] A writer for "Poems Fresh From the Press" in the *Cleveland Sunday Plain Dealer* picked up on Todd's observation that Dickinson's verses all show a strange cadence of inner rhythmical music, adding that, "Charmed by that music and seized by the thought the reader does not discover until upon closer investigation that her lines are daringly constructed and frequently defy all accepted rules of versification."[27]

The controversy between form and substance in Dickinson's poetry was a consistent one during the last decade of the nineteenth century, with critics somewhat divided in their attitudes. Many of them, accustomed to the conventional poetic patterns of the day, found Dickinson's departure from accepted forms highly distasteful, while others applauded her rare ability to achieve a sense of rhythm while disregarding the form of it. And, surprisingly, quite a number of critics combined these attitudes, acknowledging that their blending demonstrated Dickinson's capacity to achieve poetic thought in her own, quite original way. Critics in the last two groups almost invariably recognized the musicality of Dickinson's verse as the ingredient which most clearly qualified her works as poetry.

Arlo Bates, well known in the New England area as a poet, novelist, critic, and literary editor, provided an example of the combined attitude toward Dickinson's poetry in his "Books and Authors" review for the *Boston Sunday Courier* in 1890. In the first place, he found that "there is hardly a line in the entire volume, and certainly not a stanza, which cannot be objected to upon the score of technical imperfection," and he claimed that Dickinson was "as unlearned in the technical side of art as if she had written when the forms of verse had not yet been invented. . . . Her ear had certainly not been susceptible of training to the appreciation of form and melody, or it is inconceivable that she should have written as she did." Having said that, Bates nonetheless acknowledged that there is hardly a line of her work "which fails to throw out some gleam of genuine original power, of imagination, and of real emotional thought," and he declared that it was "the muse herself and no other who inspired Miss Dickinson's songs."[28] A year later, Mary D. Cutting acknowledged in her review for "Literature" in the *Christian Inquirer* that the charge to be brought against Dickinson's poems is their lack of rhyme and their want of finished form, yet she contended that they are not wanting in metrical movement. That, she claimed, is usually original and sustained, so that, "borne along by the poetic thought and musical movement, the absence of rhymes is at times almost lost sight of." Cutting believed that Dickinson's poems do not always violate poetical techniques, and occasionally there appears "a strain of musical rhythm and flow, suggesting the conclusion that its common absence is from choice or perhaps the necessity to sing after unconventional methods. She is not lyric; she will not charm the fancy by the cadence of her verse, but she will stir the heart by its melodic note."[29]

One writer for the *Concord People and Patriot* found that Dickinson excluded everything that could interfere with her thought, generally sacrificing rhyme and rhetoric. However, this writer conceded that "whatever Dickinson's lines may neglect in form, they accord with the inner soul of harmony."[30] An anonymous critic writing on Dickinson's poems for *Housekeeper's Weekly* in 1892 found her verses so running over with the spirit of poetry that one was hardly conscious of any lack in their outward form. This critic claimed to be often surprised on studying the construction of a verse to find that it contained no rhyme at all, yet, he said, "I had not missed it, so beautiful was the thought, so expressive the diction, and so musical the inward rhythm, though the outward might be faulty."[31] Another critic, writing for *Queen, The Lady's Newspaper* in London, experienced a similar response to the poetry, calling Dickinson's *Poems, First Series* "one of the most remarkable books of verse that has fallen into my hands. It is full of thought of the rarest kind, and of subtlest music, too, although her verse obeys no law. It seems as if Miss Dickinson was satisfied to have a song in her heart, and cared little into what words it fell."[32]

As might be expected, explicit negative commentary about Dickinson's lack of form was led by Andrew Lang, the previously cited London critic who vilified Dickinson at every opportunity. In an 1891 article he wrote for the

London Daily News entitled "An American Sappho," Lang berates Dickinson's verse for its lack of form: "It is really next to impossible to see the merit of poetry like Miss Dickinson's. She had thought a great deal, she did little but think, yet the expression of her thought is immeasurably obscure, unmelodious, and recklessly willful."[33] An anonymous American critic concurred with Lang in this piece written for the *New York Commercial Advertiser,* which considers Dickinson's poetry to be without form, having "every mark of haste, incomplete knowledge of the language, lack of rhythm, and sown thick with impossible, distressing rhymes." In fact, the writer continued:

> Miss Dickinson never learned the fingering of her instrument, as pianists say. She was mastered by words and sounds. She did not know the technique of verse. She never realized that poetry is an art, which must be satisfied. She is like one who says, 'I will compose a symphony,' and does not know the elements of music. Miss Dickinson had no ear for verse. Words made no music for her.[34]

Though countless other examples could be given of the ambiguity concerning form and substance in Dickinson's verse, the assessment of this ambiguity is expressed quite well in the *Concord* [N.H.] *People and Patriot.* In this article, Dickinson's poems are recognized as being so out of the common that they must be judged by their own rules, since the poet had no regard for the conventional concordance of rhymes nor did she observe rhythm in the ordinary sense. Yet, the article states, "the reader must feel that she somehow satisfied the inner soul of harmony. To her ear these poems must have been melodious, and that is the impression they leave on the sensitive mind, despite their deviation from common critical standards."[35]

Clearly, a significantly high number of the critical reviews written during the eighteen-nineties expressed sensitivity to the musical qualities of Dickinson's poetry. However, it is one of the ironies of literature that Dickinson's poetry should be viewed as so obviously lacking in poetic form by readers and reviewers during the last decade of the nineteenth century, while contemporary criticism finds Dickinson's form to be one of the most distinctive aspects of her poetry and one of the most constant standards by which her poetry can be gauged. The form in which Dickinson's "startling little poetic bombs were cast" was a musical one, and the following chapter elaborates on that theory.

NOTES

1. Richard B. Sewall, *The Life Of Emily Dickinson* (New York: Farrar, Straus & Giroux, 1980): p. 170.

2. Willis J. Buckingham, ed., *Emily Dickinson's Reception in the 1890s: A Documentary History* (Pittsburgh: University of Pittsburgh Press, 1989): p. xi. Unless

otherwise noted, the remaining notes for this chapter indicate the entry numbers corresponding to those which Buckingham has assigned to each document in this documentary work.

3. Buckingham xx.

4. Buckingham xiv.

5. #318. Unlocated clipping, December 20, 1891.

6. #287. *Truth*, ca. December 1891.

7. #515. "Books and Authors." *Boston Sunday Courier* 102 (September 6, 1896) [3].

8. #17. A. T. "An Edition of the Poems of Emily Dickinson." *Boston Daily Traveller*, November 22, 1890, p. 11.

9. #581. A. von E. "For the Women's Section: Emily Dickinson, Part II." *Der Westen*, June 19, 1898, sect. 3, p. 1.

10. #553. [Rupert Hughes.] Chelifer (pseud.). "The Ideas of Emily Dickinson." *Godey's Magazine*, 133 (November 1896): pp. 541–543.

11. #126. Andrew Lang. "Some American Poets." *Illustrated London News*, 98 (March 7, 1891): p. 307.

12. #64. (William Dean Howells.) "Editor's Study." *Harper's New Monthly Magazine*, 82 (January 1891): pp. 318–321.

13. #72. [Andrew Lang.] "The Newest Poet." *Daily News* [London], January 2, 1891, p. 5.

14. #145. [Samuel J. Barrows.] "Emily Dickinson's Poems." *Christian Register*, 70 (April 30, 1891): p. 274.

15. #283. *Fall River* [Mass.] *Monitor*, ca. December 1891.

16. #27. [Robert Bridges.] Droch (pseud.). "Bookishness." *Life*, 16 (November 27, 1890): p. 304.

17. #300. "Books and Bookmen." *Light*, 4 (December 5, 1891): p. 322.

18. #16. "Books and Authors." *Boston Home Journal*, n.s. 4 (November 22, 1890): p. 10.

19. #83. "New Books." *Commonwealth*, 30 (January 10, 1891), p. 8.

20. #13. [Charles Goodrich Whiting.] "The Literary Wayside." *Springfield Republican*, November 16, 1890, p. 4.

21. #28. [Thomas Wentworth Higginson.] "Recent Poetry." *Nation*, 51 (November 27, 1890): pp. 422–423.

22. #587. Bliss Carman. "Bliss Carman's Marginal Notes." *Chicago Post*, July 15, 1899, p. 7.

23. #310. "Today's Literature." *Chicago Tribune*, December 12, 1891, p. 12.

24. #543. [Thomas Wentworth Higginson.] "Recent Poetry." *Nation*, 63 (October 8, 1896), p. 275.

25. #491. Mabel Loomis Todd. "Emily Dickinson's Letters." *Bachelor of Arts*, I (May 1895): pp. 39–66.

26. #480. "Out and About." *Worcester* [Mass.] *Spy*, January 24, 1895, p. 4.

27. #301. "Poems Fresh From the Press." *Cleveland Sunday Plain Dealer*, December 6, 1891, p. 4.

28. #21. [Arlo Bates.] "Books and Authors." *Boston Sunday Courier*, 96 (November 23, 1890): p. 2.

29. #135. Mary D. Cutting. "Literature." *Christian Inquirer*, 4 (April 9, 1891).

30. #343. *Concord* [N. H.] *People and Patriot*, February 1892.

31. #359. W. M. "Emily Dickinson's Poems." *Housekeeper's Weekly*, 3 (April 9, 1892): p. 4.

32. #194. E. R. "Talk About Books." *Queen, The Lady's Newspaper* [London], 90 (August 15, 1891): p. 253.

33. #232. [Andrew Lang.] "An American Sappho." *London Daily News*, October 3, 1891, pp. 4–5.

34. #545. "Emily Dickinson's Poems." *New York Commercial Advertiser*, October 10, 1896, p. 14.

35. #71. *Concord* [N. H.] *People and Patriot*, January 2, 1891.

LOGAN ESDALE

Dickinson's Epistolary "Naturalness"

It is certain that no works have done more service to mankind, than those which have appeared in this shape, upon familiar subjects, and which perhaps never intended to be published; and it is this makes them so valuable; for I confess for my own part, that letters which are very elaborately written, and originally intended for the press, are generally the most insignificant, and very little worth any person's reading.

—Lord Chancellor Hardwicke, verdict in *Pope v. Curll* (1741)[1]

It was the Distance –
Was Savory

—Emily Dickinson, Fr626 (1863)

In George Saintsbury's "The History and Art of Letter Writing," his introduction to *A Letter Book* (1922), he states what had long been repeated: "Perhaps the greatest negative caution of all is that a letter should not be *obviously* 'written for publication'" (35). Letter writers should, in other words, think only of their addressee and suit their words to that person, and to the occasion of the address; they should write according to the impulse of the moment, authentically and without punctiliousness. Saintsbury says that all of the letter writers he has selected for the book heeded the great negative caution, and wrote with a perfect "naturalness." Lapses that occur

Emily Dickinson Journal, 14.1; (Spring 2005): pp. 1–23. © The Johns Hopkins University Press.

are natural lapses because the letter writers would sometimes have worked in haste; as well, their aim to please friends rather than a general audience gives some liberty from the standard forms. Alexander Pope's letters were excluded, notes Saintsbury, for their artificial naturalness: their "imperfections" (my quotes) were too polished.[2] In contrast, "valuable" letters, to quote Hardwicke above, display a natural naturalness, and are intended for private circulation only.

When Emily Dickinson began writing in the mid nineteenth century, letters in print were a common sight for American readers: there were letter books (like Saintsbury's) for students and secretaries, reprints of eighteenth-century epistolary novels, collections of personal letters, and, above all, life-and-letters biographies.[3] By that time, letters were seen so often in published books that the restriction on letters (not for publication) would have seemed almost quaint. Such an injunction would have made, I think, almost as much sense as arguing that poems should not be written for publication. Certainly, successful authors in the mid to late 1800s would have been well aware that their personal letters might one day be edited and published. So how should we interpret the case of Dickinson, someone who apparently did not write her poems for publication? Did she apply the caution against writing letters for publication to her poems? I believe that she did: she realized that in transferring her privilege as a letter writer to write as she wished (for private circulation only) to her work as a poet, she could insist that her readers accept the poems "as is." If her poems were like letters, she could justify her "lapses" and insist that the poems did not aspire to be more polished or in print. As a letter writer, the poet wrote for herself, her correspondents, and for poetry.

Dickinson critics have, in the last twenty years especially, persuaded readers of the necessity of knowing her work "as is." Since access to facsimiles of the manuscripts is now regarded by many as essential to scholarship, the issue has become the means by which to distribute the facsimiles accurately and cost-effectively. Whether Dickinson wanted her work to be published "as is" is not my subject here as much as her culture's attitude toward the publication of private forms of writing—letters in particular. I situate my approach alongside that of Janet Altman, who, in an essay on late Renaissance epistolarity, explains her decision "to focus on the discursive contexts surrounding those moments when letters are actually turned into published books, as a more coherent way of investigating the conditions determining the constitution of the letter as literature" (50). My primary aim is to elucidate the "discursive contexts surrounding" the moments when Dickinson sent her work through the post, and when it was published. In doing this, I want to show how much a participant in her culture she was.

In the decade after Dickinson's death in 1886, her sister Lavinia, brother Austin, and friends Mabel Todd and Thomas Higginson conspired to publish three volumes of her poems and an edition of her letters. In the late nineteenth century, the notion that authenticity and privacy were under threat put these editors in a bind: they had to invade the privacies of her life and work in order to prove them authentic. Unequivocally linked at the time were authenticity and privacy, and both were seen as in short supply. The editing of the early volumes did compromise the truly "authentic" nature of Dickinson's work by ignoring the variants (even when used), smoothing her lines, titling her poems, and organizing them into four thematic sections (Life, Love, Nature, Time and Eternity); even so, in their prefaces Higginson and Todd played up the remaining elements that orthodox literary culture would have seen as imperfections.[4] What convinced readers of the work's authenticity as much as the uneven poems themselves was all the emphasis on Dickinson's reclusive lifestyle. Her acquaintances, editors and critics all helped to construct the idea that this writing revealed a woman who had hidden from society. Wishing for something authentic, the public found what they needed in the writing of an utterly private person. To a large extent, I think, these circumstances explain Dickinson's immediate popularity in the 1890s. In life and in writing, Dickinson was marketed as having, in other words, a natural naturalness.

But did she? Instead, I put Dickinson's work in a group with Pope's familiar letters and the letters in epistolary novels—all three displaying an artificial naturalness.[5] Though she resisted having her work printed, she carefully drafted and revised everything she wrote. In this essay, I argue that reading her work is not transgressive, though it was designed to seem so; I demonstrate Dickinson's playful participation in the culture that wanted to look into private lives; I note how the letter was used as a primary example by those who addressed the right to privacy, and examine the culture's skepticism that privacy actually exists, even in letters; I connect a "natural" or "imperfect" style with copyright issues; I assert that Dickinson was actively publishing through the post; and I cite many of the early letters to provide a reassessment of them as a sophisticated part of her epistolary project. The fact that her letters and poems would travel (from writer to addressee) to be read had its effect on the writer during composition—writing was a form of travel. And if everything she wrote had the "natural" qualities appropriate to epistolary texts, she could be proprietary as far as authorship was concerned; she was, though, more open-handed on the ownership issue.

Not for Publication

Higginson's preface to the first (1890) volume of Dickinson's poems begins as if he were introducing a collection of *letters*. He claims that the poems were "produced absolutely without the thought of publication, and solely by way of expression of the writer's own mind" (iii). As a result, the poems have an "uneven vigor" and are "set in a seemingly whimsical or even rugged frame" (vi, v). But, he notes, "when a thought takes one's breath away, a lesson on grammar seems an impertinence" (vi). Higginson dwells on the manuscript's reluctance to become a book partly to enhance the value of a debut effort; eager manuscripts, the preface implies, we can ignore.

Prefaces as a genre are from the first a form of advertisement. In *The Imprint of Gender*, Wendy Wall has discussed the origin of the preface in the Renaissance as "a pervasive cultural phenomenon in which writers and publishers ushered printed texts into the public eye by naming that entrance as a titillating and transgressive act" (172). The preface was an effect of print technology, developed both to draw attention to the spectacle of the manuscript "body" beneath its print "clothes," and to shield that body from the rough grasp of the public hand. To adjust the metaphor: an editor's apparatus both erects masculine walls around a feminine body inside—the manuscript in its private chamber—and invites readers to the keyhole. A preface functions as a door or an envelope; a preface both sympathizes with the manuscript's reluctance to accede to full disclosure, and constructs the charming idea of resistance for a market audience. Reading is thus figured as a transgressive act, an invasion of privacy.[6]

Higginson's method of introducing an unknown writer to a public audience follows that of Ralph Waldo Emerson, whom Higginson refers to both in the preface and in an essay published a month earlier: "Emerson said, many years since, in the 'Dial,' that the most interesting department of poetry would hereafter be found in what might be called 'The Poetry of the Portfolio'" ("Open" 3). Higginson refers here to Emerson's 1840 essay "New Poetry," which is structured in two parts: in the first part (the part that Higginson mimics, to some extent) Emerson theorizes on the importance of what he calls "Verses of the Portfolio" in new American literature; in the second part (the part that corresponds with the volume of Dickinson poems) he prints twelve manuscript poems by an unknown writer (likely himself), anonymously.[7]

In "New Poetry" Emerson argues that American readers need to turn their attention from the poets who have been educated in Latin and Greek to the untutored poets. The latter are largely unknown, he says, because poets "of genius in general are, more than others, incapable of any perfect exhibition," and "however agreeable it may be to them to act on the public, it is always a secondary aim" (139). They write "portfolio" poems, which are often unfinished since their existence owes all to the necessity of vivid expression and nothing to a desire for public attention. They express the spirit of the time and place, and should be published in their imperfect state, as are studies on canvas and blocked statues. Emerson points out that recent changes in the postal system—a lowering of postage rates and improvements in reliability—have made letter writing widely practiced. The publishing industry should follow suit and enable a more generous circulation of poems.

Emerson's argument involves a paradox that Dickinson's editors would face: the work should be published because it is genuine, and it is genuine because it was never intended for publication. That Emerson defines "port-folio" poetry in precisely the terms used to define "natural" letters leads me to believe that he borrowed his argument from prefaces to letter collections. For instance, in Pope's preface to a collection of his own (1737), he argued that genuine work will be known by its roughness: "But if an Author's hand, like a Painter's, be more distinguishable in a slight sketch than in a finish'd picture, this very carelessness will make them the better known from such Counterfeits" (xxxix). Employing such rhetoric himself, Emerson thus tacitly supports the publishing of private letters. And since he applies to poems what had long been said of letters, he basically announces the invention of a new hybrid genre, the letter-poem—written with lyric precision, but not for publication. For both letter writers and (epistolary) poets of genius, then, publishing in a book must be a "secondary" or undisclosed aim.

In his 1845 article "Anastatic Printing," Poe takes Emerson further, describing a technology that would allow writers to self-publish by producing copies of handwritten books at home. "Anastatic printing" involves a process of soaking a manuscript page in an acidic solution; a zinc plate is then applied and receives a negative impression; and facsimile printing proceeds from this zinc plate. With this technology at work the public will receive manuscript books "which are most valuable, but least in circulation on account of unsaleability"—unsaleable, I assume, because he has in mind something along the "portfolio" poems line (156). Not responsible to the conventions of the print medium, which generally demands "finish," this new method of publishing will encourage a revolution in style: writers can focus, he says, entirely on "precision of thought, and luminous arrangement of matter" (157).

And in 1855, Harriet Martineau began work on her autobiography. In her introduction to it later, Martineau explains that the book was the result of deciding "to interdict the publication of my private letters" (1). Since biographies at the time were largely composed of letters and she wanted to keep hers private, Martineau had to offer a non-epistolary substitute. She moves from this justification for her book to comment on the culture of "traitors" who publish not only what people have written in familiar letters but said to intimate friends in conversation. By the mid nineteenth century, in fact, letters were so often being published that people had been "deprived of epistolary liberty" (4). Even in a letter one must withhold for the sake of privacy. "Nobody will question," she says, "the hardship and mischief of a practice which acts upon epistolary correspondence as the spy system under a despotism acts upon speech" (3–4). Of course Martineau had herself enjoyed having access to private words in published form; at one point, for instance, she quotes Samuel Johnson on the problem of self-censorship in letters—a comment that he made to James Boswell in conversation! But she wants to make a show of support here for the commonly-held theory that when letter writers become overly conscious that they risk publicity, they will limit the naturalness of their epistles.

Dickinson's editors would market her poems and letters to a culture of readers that believed in that theory. She was an exception, they suggested, someone whose private life gave her "epistolary liberty"; unlike Martineau, she was free from the threat of publicity in her lifetime and thus could write with naturalness. It's this assumption that because of her private lifestyle she felt free to reject a finished quality that I question. Private though she was, Dickinson still wrote with an audience in mind, one for whom she performed; her wayward, unfinished style was deliberate. Contrary to what her early editors and critics implied, therefore, reading Dickinson is *not* a transgressive act. She certainly designed her work so that it matches the descriptions offered by Emerson and Poe for new American writing, but she did so because she wrote first for poetry itself, as Emerson had recommended, then for her correspondents. If she did know Emerson's "New Poetry," she would have keenly noted the paradoxical nature of the essay as a whole, the one part discussing writing not for publication and the other publishing some of this "new poetry." Emerson's essay for her would have been about an *aesthetics* of naturalness at least as much as the necessity of private writing.

Pickpocket

Dickinson's editors found on an envelope fragment something that must have given them pause: "As there are Apartments in our own Minds that – (which) we never enter without Apology – we should respect the seals of others" (PF21). I want to point out, though, that there are two ways of reading "we should respect the seals of others." Dickinson could be asking that people respect her privacy, or she could be reminding herself to respect the privacy of others. This first reading satisfies a habit of seeing Dickinson as reclusive. But with her appetite for life-and-letters biographies in mind, the second reading seems equally if not more valid: she was warning herself.

I turn now to an 1863 poem that has often been read as an instance of Dickinson sincerely expressing her desire for privacy. Marietta Messmer, for example, in *A Vice for Voices: Reading Emily Dickinson's Correspondence*, sees this poem as Dickinson's attempt to convey her "ideal form of reception": reading a letter is a "reverential, private act" (186). And because Dickinson is one of the "most private of authors," Messmer reads Dickinson as herself a letter (2). In other words, Messmer conflates the convention that a letter is a private document with Dickinson's reputation as a private person. I read the poem instead as a description of the poet not only acting out a violation of another's privacy, but inviting the reader to share in the moment. The poem is, moreover, a conventional preface: she offers a version of what Higginson will write when he describes his relationship to her work and the act of making it available to the public.

> The Way I read a Letter's – this –   [this: so]
> 'Tis first - I lock the Door –
> And push it with my fingers - next –
> For transport it be sure –
>
> And then I go the furthest off
> To counteract a knock –
> Then draw my little Letter forth
> And slowly pick the lock –   [slowly: slily / softly]
>
> Then – glancing narrow, at the Wall –
> And narrow at the floor   [floor: door]
> For firm Conviction of a Mouse
> Not exorcised before –
>
> Peruse how infinite I am
> To no one that You – know –
> And sigh for lack of Heaven – but not
> The Heaven God bestow –
>
>   (Fr700)

The poem ostensibly documents the thrill of receiving mail. The deliberate measures taken by the poet to counteract a violation of privacy in her room mirror those taken by the letter writer, who had sealed the envelope with a "lock" of wax or glue to prevent premature disclosure of the letter's contents in the hands of post office employees or nosy family members. In a way this is Messmer's argument: like the letter in its envelope Dickinson is in her room, and both have their seals. As the poet guards against disclosure, so too does the letter. The act of opening mail thus compares with forcing entrance to a private room. Even though the letter bears her name, we assume ("my little Letter"), its original owner's lock cannot discriminate; it will protect against all potential intruders.

This poem is about transgression, I think. The two variants for "slowly pick the lock" are "slily" and "softly," both of which suggest the stealth of someone quietly opening another's property; they figure the poet not only in a room, but outside a room in a hallway, the letter as a room. The poet is careful that no one witnesses her transgression—no one, that is, except the reader. Something given to her by the post has thus almost been transformed into something stolen. She says "my little Letter," but there exists a consciousness that the letter is also *not* hers, that it remains the property of the sender. After all, while she as the addressee is free to open and store the letter, the writer has the legal right to recall it. A letter is therefore an ambiguous object, claimed by two people. The addressee becomes a temporary and limited owner: although she can destroy the letter, she cannot publish the letter without the writer's consent.

In the final stanza the poet refers to "You," who *could* be the letter writer: "Peruse how infinite I am / To no one that You - know." In a sense, then, the poet is responding to the letter with this poem. As the poet moves to scan "her" letter, she asks that the letter writer notice the "infinite" precautions taken to ensure the privacy of the reading experience. "Your letter is safe with me," in other words. Yet those precautions are rather superficial: what would "glancing narrow, at the Wall - / And narrow at the floor" accomplish security-wise? What if "You" refers to the reader of the poem, as I think it does? (The letter writer would then be "no one.") Then the poet has invited the reader to participate in the opening of the letter. The poet pretends to be jealously guarding the privacy of the letter; and, at the same time, she threatens to violate that privacy by inviting others to join with her in reading its contents.

The injunction "sigh for lack of Heaven" suggests that the reader should ultimately feel shut out. The poem ends just as the poet removes the letter from its protective envelope; neither the name of the sender nor the contents of the letter is disclosed. This game was one that Dickinson loved to play in her own letters. Often in them she muses on what she would see if she were transported at that very moment into the room of her addressee. For instance, Dickinson begins a letter to Otis Lord in 1882: "What if you are writing! Oh, for the power to look, yet were I there, I would not, except you invited me – reverence for each other being the sweet aim" (L790). Like her culture, Dickinson was herself sorely tempted by "the power to look." Thus Dickinson's fascination with inaccessible places—though she knew that she could not make such places accessible without at the same time destroying them. Publishers were indeed doing well for themselves when they transformed a bundle of letters into a book, feeding off their readers' desire for the "power to look."

Becoming Private

The epigraph to the first edition of Dickinson's poems was her poem that begins: "This is my letter to the World / That never wrote to Me -" (Fr519). There has never been a saucier poem that has so often been read as sincere. Of course many people did write to Dickinson; she was a prolific *correspondent,* not a diarist. After her death, however, Lavinia burned all of the letters that had been sent to her. This act thus removed the evidence of her letters having been sent in exchange, and contributed to the misperception of Dickinson as someone to whom "the World never wrote."

Ralph Franklin once explained how Dickinson's poems survived: "at her death in 1886 she left a large group of manuscript poems in various states of completion. Her sister, Lavinia, destroyed the correspondence that she found, as was the custom, but the poems she decided were Emily's letter to the world. These, to our permanent literary debt, she did not burn" (xv). The customary burning of letters allowed the dead to take their secrets to the grave. Poems, on the other hand, were *not* usually burned. By referring to the poems as "Emily's letter to the world," however, Franklin adds to the fiction about Dickinson's poems being "saved." I repeat: only if the poems were in fact letters would they have been in danger of being burned. The poems were of course not burned, but published; and Lavinia and Todd were soon writing Dickinson's correspondents and requesting that her letters be returned so that they too could be published.

The first edition of Dickinson's letters went on sale in 1894.[8] Passages from many of the letters had been excised so that the book conformed to the culture's ambiguous attitude towards privacy. In Henry James's review of *The Letters of Robert Louis Stevenson to his Family and Friends*, published five years after Stevenson's death in 1894, he notes that "Nothing more belongs to our day than this question of the inviolable, of the rights of privacy and the justice of our claim to aid from editors and other retailers in getting behind certain eminent or defiant appearances" (1257). (Dickinson was certainly one with a "defiant appearance.") "There is no absolute privacy," James goes on, "save of course when the exposed subject may have wished or endeavoured positively to constitute it" (1257). He concludes that artists in particular "are well advised to cover their tracks" (1257). To "constitute" "absolute privacy" one stoked the fire. Twice near the end of his life, in 1909 and in 1915, James burnt piles of letters and notebooks.

Not surprisingly, then, Samuel Warren and Louis Brandeis's well known *Harvard Law Review* article "The Right to Privacy" (1890) uses letters and handwritten texts in general as the most obvious, material instances of our private lives—such lives becoming even more essential as the "intensity and complexity of life, attendant upon advancing civilization," increase (196). They point out that even if the case were as banal as a man writing to his son that "he did not dine with his wife on a certain day," that letter would be protected by law from being published without the man's consent (201). The aspect being protected, they note, "is not the intellectual product, but the domestic occurrence" (201). In other words, regardless of its state of literary "finish," a letter is safe from uninvited publication because it is a personal document. Letters already have a right to privacy that their writers need in their daily lives; put another way, people should be treated as if they were letters.

Edith Wharton's story "Copy" (1901) also uses letters to signify private life. The famous novelist Helen Dale and the famous poet Paul Ventnor meet again after twenty some years to ensure that their old love letters remain private by burning them. Dale was twenty and Ventnor almost ten years older when they had their affair, and both were beginning their commercially successful writing careers; they agree that now "we're public property" (278). When they reread the letters they discover that they had "plagiarized" them "word for word" in the books that would secure their fame and fortune (281). Beyond this somewhat amusing realization that letters are, in fact, often published indirectly, there is a keen sense of loss: instead of privacy, they now have only copyright. As they consider the difference between the urgent need to communicate then, and the dull option of preserving the letters for their memoirs now, they recall an old private garden that they were in the habit of visiting, which has since become a public park. Their letters are still private, and *their* "garden" still exists in their imagination—as constituted by those letters. But: "Shall we burn the key to our garden?" asks Ventnor. Dale answers: "Ah, then it will indeed be boundless!" (286). Into the fire go their letters.

Wharton's story proves James's point: absolute privacy does not exist unless the exposed person has "endeavoured positively to constitute it" (1257). As long as letters exist, their privacy is vulnerable. In fact, only in their destruction do letters *become* private; no actual evidence of privacy exists for show.[9] Likewise, only in death does someone become truly inaccessible. In this way, I think, Dickinson's utter inaccessibility after 1886 was confused with Dickinson's behavior in life. A public eager to know more about the notorious Amherst recluse encountered barriers, and as a result they projected backwards and attributed to Dickinson alive a similar distance from the world. Those people may not have understood how insightful they were: Dickinson, like Helen Dale, knew that annihilation was the only means to privacy (or as Dale said: a "boundless" state), so in her writing she experimented with crossing that line. For instance: "Peruse how infinite I am," she wrote in "The Way I read," just before the poem ends for the unrequited reader. The letter in her hand is then *gone* — it becomes private.

Nineteenth-century people did, in general, read letters as if they revealed the writer's character, so that, if intercepted, letters could destroy a person's reputation. Sending entailed risk. For instance, in an unsigned review of *The Correspondence of Leigh Hunt*, which appeared in the May 1862 issue of the *Atlantic Monthly* (one month after Higginson's "Letter to a Young Contributor"), the writer states: "A man's letters betray his heart,—both those he sends and those he receives" (653). Yet early on Dickinson insists that letters are for her not unmediated expression. In 1853 she declared that her letters are not typical: they do not contain news. To Austin she wrote: "You know it's quite a sacrifice for *me* to tell what's going on"; "I shall have to employ a Reporter"

(L141, L145). Two years earlier she had written to Austin that "If I had'nt been afraid that you would 'poke fun' at my feelings, I had written a *sincere* letter, but since the 'world is hollow, and Dollie is stuffed with sawdust,' I really do not think we had better expose our feelings" (L42). So, as she had already admitted in an 1850 letter to Abiah Root, the stories that she tells in her letters are "fictions," designed to "lead astray foolish young women"; they are "flowers of speech, they both *make*, and *tell* deliberate falsehoods" (L31). Dickinson's early letters are thus aware that truths are discursive constructs, sometimes even calling attention to the "disguise" that takes place "in all human intercourse," as Hugh Blair said in his well known 1783 lecture on "Epistolary Writing" (298).[10]

In 1854 Dickinson wrote to Austin: "I'm so tired now, that I write just as it happens, so you must'nt expect any style. / This is truly extempore, Austin – I have no notes in my pocket" (L165). To write "just as it happens" was appropriate to authentic "not for publication" letters. But Dickinson makes a point here of reminding Austin that her letters were usually deliberate compositions, not "of the moment" but constructed out of the "notes in my pocket" that accumulated through the day. From those slips of paper came her poems and her letters. If Dickinson's letters were, as this evidence suggests, not of a private nature but rather performance oriented, then her editors were faced with two choices when they presented them to the public: they could describe the extent to which Dickinson wrote with an audience in mind; or they could describe Dickinson's idiosyncratic life. Of course they chose the latter.

Copy Control

In 1875 Dickinson sent a letter to Helen Hunt Jackson that included a seemingly enigmatic verse. Jackson replied asking for an explanation; she included Dickinson's letter, adding this claim: "This is *mine*, remember, You must send it back to me, or else you will be a robber" (L444, note). Jackson's stand was not legally admissible—by law the letter remained Dickinson's—but she articulates the common feeling that a letter sent becomes public property. Jackson could copy Dickinson's poems and send them to others, which she did. And Dickinson knew that she did. The fate of posted letters and poems were, practically-speaking, very often out of the writer's control. They are "Fast-Fish," Herman Melville might have said.[11]

Modern copyright protection for writers was first developed in England in 1710. In the following decades, however, when a case went to court, booksellers and printers were still likely the ones awarded ownership, not the writers. Only by the mid to late eighteenth century did writers really become the owners of their work, even after publication. In the epistolary world, these changes meant that ownership of letters shifted from the possessor (usually the addressee, but possibly someone else entirely) to the writer. As Harriet

Martineau would observe a century later, the "law vests the right of publication of private letters solely in the writer, no one else having any such right during the author's life, or after his death, except by his express permission" (5). Perhaps the most decisive moment in copyright history for authors occurred in 1741, when the question of letter ownership was resolved. In *Pope v. Curll*, as Mark Rose has explained in *Authors and Owners: The Invention of Copyright*, Pope sued the printer Edmund Curll to stop the sale of a book of Jonathan Swift's correspondence which included many letters from Pope. The case asked whether the writer of a letter held copyright or the printer who had the actual letter in possession—and Pope won.[12]

Eighteenth-century British copyright laws did supply the precedents for early American copyright law, but as Meredith McGill has argued, the situation in nineteenth-century America was in large part determined by an 1834 case, *Wheaton v. Peters*, which held that published work was public property.[13] Republican ideologies of the time promoted wide dissemination over individual rights, so that the reader was in effect the owner. Wide dissemination of texts would result in an educated citizenry, it was thought. McGill writes: "an author could maintain absolute control over his text only insofar as he did not attempt to publish it" (42). In other words, writers could assert their rights as long as they used only the post office and refused to print. Not until the 1890s did American writers gain control over what they published in print.

"Once in the public realm," McGill observes, "the text is susceptible to uncontrolled copying because it is, itself, a copy" (43).[14] Dickinson's habitual production of multiple versions of the same poem as new epistolary occasions arose meant that she followed a practice of what I would call "controlled copying."[15] She rigorously controlled the means of production in her own home, but at a certain point, once a letter or poem had left and was in another's hands, she seems to have regarded the text as published. Sending was a form of publishing, though publishing was not printing.[16] That these multiples are extant has led to an almost insoluble problem for editors and scholars who feel forced to make choices that Dickinson herself refused to make. There's no easy answer for the question: Which is the original and which is the copy?

The collection of poems that Dickinson kept at hand constitutes what Barton Levi St. Armand has called her "portfolio." The typical New England portfolio, Dickinson's included, was a "sourcebook whose sketches could be worked up into more finished products when the occasion demanded" (5). However, Marta Werner's argument in *Emily Dickinson's Open Folios*, an edition of forty late fragments, implies that Dickinson would not have "worked up" a poem when it accompanied a letter: the version posted was as much a "sketch" as the version at home. Werner's comment on the late fragments, that they are the "symptoms of the processes of composition that can never be said to achieve closure," describes Dickinson's poems in general, I think (55). Pope had suggested that a sketch was an original: "an Author's hand" is "more distinguishable in a slight sketch than in a finish'd picture" (xxxix). It would seem, then, that St. Armand labels some of the poems "sketches" and some "finished products" because he wants Dickinson to have carefully retained ownership of the original versions. But if all of the poems are "sketches," if Dickinson was sending multiple "originals" through the post, then her correspondents would have shared in ownership.

The "editor" of Jean-Jacques Rousseau's *Julie* says in the prefatorial "Conversation": "I put my name at the head of the collection, not to claim it as mine; but to answer for it" (19). I like to consider Dickinson alongside the authors of epistolary novels; on questions of ownership, she, like Rousseau, is often playful. Leah Price has discussed Samuel Richardson's difficulty reconciling his various signatures (author, editor, printer and publisher) when it came to epistolary novels such as *Clarissa* (1747–1748). Richardson thought through, Price says, the problem of "how to claim ownership of texts while disclaiming authorship of their contents" (36). As a printer for commercial gain, Richardson differs from Dickinson, but similar issues would have surfaced for her. Her "natural" style definitively attributed authorship to her—she would "answer for it"—though claiming it as hers seems a less assured point. Giving her work to a printer would involve attributing ownership. Was she unwilling to sign a book as hers alone?

Who owns a letter when the writer cannot claim to be the origin any more than the addressee? In some ways, Dickinson must have regarded her work as a collaboration, or at least dependent on the response and the initiative of others.[17] In 1870 she wrote to Higginson, her correspondent of eight years: "The Vein cannot thank the Artery – but her solemn indebtedness to him, even the stolidest admit and so of me who try, whose effort leaves no sound" (L352). The correspondence began when Dickinson wrote to Higginson—but in response to his article. She refuses to differentiate between his public "Letter" (published in the *Atlantic Monthly*) and her private letter (sent by post). Moreover, her 1870 letter follows Higginson's recent visit to her in Amherst. He (artery) came to her (vein). Ultimately she would not sign more than her letters, and the posthumous production of "Emily Dickinson" was a collective endeavor. Others would claim ownership.

Paper Routes

Appearing in the same 1862 issue of the *Atlantic Monthly* with Higginson's "Letter to a Young Contributor" was Emerson's essay "American Civilization." In it Emerson observes that telegraphy borrows "the might of the elements. The forces of steam, gravity, galvanism, light, magnets, wind, fire, serve us day by day, and cost us nothing" (505). In contrast, letter "couriers could not go fast enough, nor far enough; broke their wagons, foundered their horses; bad roads in spring, snow-drifts in winter, heats in summer; could not get the horses out of a walk" (504–505). We "found out," however, "that the air and earth were full of electricity; and it was always going our way,—just the way we wanted to send" (505). Ordinary letters thus depend on human and animal nature—unreliable resources, and no match for "the might of the elements." While roads bounce left and right, electricity follows a direct line. Emerson's "portfolio" poet, for whom publication was "a secondary aim," thus composed not in a telegraphic or electric environment but in a paper one.

Dickinson was apparently unmoved by Emerson's enthusiasm for the "invisible pockets" of the telegraph system. Paper was her medium and people were her couriers. She saw with Emerson that letters followed a crooked, wandering road; letters departed in one state and arrived in another, if they arrived at all. The elemental conditions—muddy roads, snow, heat—they met on the post road marked them. The other side of Charles Dickens's "*be* the message," letters were themselves travelers and would suffer detours and delays.[18] The unpredictability of letter travel—and therefore of letter writing itself—gives to letters their mortal qualities.

A letter travels from writer to addressee through mediated space. Movement always encounters resistance, and anything in motion is perishable. Dickinson not only sent true perishables—flowers and fruit—with her letters, but defined the letter itself a perishable object. In an 1850 letter to Jane Humphrey, whose father was mortally ill, Dickinson wrote: "*Can* I console so far off, wont the comfort waste in conveying and be *not*, when my letter gets there?" (L35). In an 1851 letter to Susan Gilbert, she noted: "I want to send you *joy*, I have half a mind to put up one of these dear little Robin's, and send him singing to you. I know I would, Susie, did I think he would live to get there and sing his little songs" (L92). And later, in 1877, to Mary Higginson she wrote: "I send you a flower from my garden – Though it die in reaching you, you will know it lived, when it left my hand –" (L512).[19] What happens during the trip compares with the process of translating manuscript into print. It is at least metaphorically true to say that as print rewrites a handwritten text, so does a letter's route rewrite a letter; what an addressee receives is not what the writer had sent, though it is a resemblance.

Delayed letters are still gratefully received—they are, Dickinson wrote to Austin in 1853, "always new to us" (L115). In 1881 Dickinson wrote to her Norcross cousins: "After infinite wanderings the little note has reached us" (L727). And in 1882 she wrote to Otis Lord: "To write you, not knowing where you are, is an unfinished pleasure – Sweeter of course than not writing, because it has a wandering Aim, of which you are the goal –" (L750). Perhaps her letter has "a wandering Aim" because she cannot be certain of Lord's present address. Her letter, then, may travel indirectly—first to one person, then to him. Similarly, all of the hundreds of poems that Dickinson sent with her letters had "a wandering Aim." First the poems went to her correspondents, who may have copied them for others. Then the 1890s publications *read-dressed* those poems to a wider audience. Publishing was a forwarding on. Thus Dickinson, like Dale and Ventnor in Wharton's "Copy," did publish indirectly during her lifetime: while they plagiarized their correspondence for their books, she sent her poems through the post.

Dickinson was intimately connected with the world, enmeshed in a totalizing grid of always moving carriers. She knew that the act of writing presupposes an already existing means of distribution. To Abiah Root in 1852 Dickinson acknowledged that they were "separate indeed, and yet how near, bridged by a thousand trusts and a 'thousand times ten thousand' the travellers who cross, whom you and I may not see, nor hear the trip of their feet, yet faith tells us they are there, ever crossing and re-crossing" (L69). A few months earlier, in a letter to Austin, she commented that "the world is full of people travelling *everywhere*" (L53). With this world of "travellers" at her doorstep Dickinson could be at home without being separate. Perpetually departing things gave her her words to tell: "Were Departure Separation, there would be neither Nature nor Art, for there would be no World – Emily" (PF52). Departed, yet connected.

I want to conclude with a reading of "A Route of Evanescence" (Fr1489), a poem about letter travel that Dickinson sent to at least six correspondents between 1879 and 1883. The six addressees were Helen Jackson (L602: 1879), Louise and Frances Norcross (possibly L610: 1879), Sarah Tuckerman (L627: 1880), Thomas Higginson (L675: 1880), Mabel Todd (L770: 1882), and Thomas Niles (L814: 1883). A seventh copy was Dickinson's own, what Franklin calls a "record copy." Each of the seven copies is different, mainly in the punctuation; "revolving" has four variants, and one copy has the poem in two quatrains.

Suzanne Juhasz has argued persuasively, I think, that for Dickinson the "external contexts or referents or recipients can vary, because they are not the originary occasion for [the] lines of poetry; they are, rather, stimuli and echo" (435). I agree with this as a general characterization; it should be noted, however, that "A Route of Evanescence" was first sent in response to a request from Jackson for more bird poems. Dickinson refers to the poem as a "Humming Bird," and would sign it "Humming Bird" (an example of Dickinson eschewing ownership). In 1862 she had written to Eudocia Flynt a letter that she characterizes as "a Humming Bird," which had "sipped just Me" (L270). In "A Route of Evanescence," a hummingbird is a courier. "Humming Bird" is thus used by Dickinson to refer to poems and letters, to the letter writer herself and her couriers.

Dickinson knew Higginson's 1862 essay "The Life of Birds," in which he meditates on the hummingbird. As well, "A Route of Evanescence" was one of four poems that Dickinson shared with Higginson as she considered which ones in her collection she would donate to a local church benefit. And Niles, who would publish Dickinson posthumously, had recently written saying that he would like a "collection of your poems, that is, if you want to give them to the world through the medium of a publisher" (L813b). (Instead she gave them to the world through the medium of the post office.) Each of these factors was, no doubt, as Juhasz suggests, a stimulus and an echo. Dickinson copied this poem again and again, sending it to people (Jackson, Todd, Niles) she knew wished that her work would reach a wider audience. Her re-sipients are thus figured as hummingbirds too, passing on the poems to others.

A Route of Evanescence
With a revolving Wheel –   [revolving: renewing / delusive /
A Resonance of Emerald –   dissembling / dissolving]
A Rush of Cochineal –
And every Blossom on the Bush
Adjusts it's tumbled Head –
The mail from Tunis, probably,
An easy Morning's Ride –

                            (Fr1489D; Tuckerman copy)

Higginson's "The Life of Birds" describes the hummingbird as an extraordinary hybrid: gem, flower, insect and bird all in one. The green gem ("Emerald") and the red insect ("Cochineal," which comes from the cochineal insect, a cactus-feeder) references do allude to the colors of that elusive creature, the hummingbird. And while "revolving" and "renewing" suggest a material "Wheel," the other three variants (delusive / dissembling / dissolving) strongly connect the hummingbird courier's "wheels" with the "Route": both are evanescent. It seems a mix of the telegraph system's speed—able to collapse the distance between continents in mere moments—with a material post road.

In describing the scene of a postal vehicle having just raced by, the poem is thus a companion to her early letter in which she observes that "the world is full of people travelling *everywhere*" (L53). Only a few hours before in Tunis, the vehicle has knocked against the roadside bushes, and the spring blossoms momentarily register the effect. Things foreign are intimate with things local: the mail has come from northern Africa, and neither "Emerald" nor "Cochineal" are native to Amherst. Nothing moved faster in Dickinson's time than the postal system, which was synonymous with speed. To Elizabeth Holland in 1881, Dickinson sympathizes with a child who saw no difference between

"Vermont or Asia": both are far from Amherst (L685). And yet both are near—only "An easy Morning's ride." To use the postal system was to be connected with all of the people who were using it too, and working for it, wherever they were. Again: in "The Way I read," with a letter in her hand, Dickinson asks that we "Peruse how infinite I am."

"An easy Morning's Ride": in a letter to Susan in 1852, Dickinson writes that "there will be romance in *the letter's ride* to you – think of the hills and the dales, and the rivers it will pass over, and the drivers and conductors who will hurry it on to you; and wont that make a poem such as can ne'er be written" (L77; my italics). In "A Route of Evanescence," the route and the couriers do write a poem, I believe; Dickinson regarded their involvement in epistolary production as more than a metaphor. What happens to the landscape as couriers pass by makes the poem; the terrain and weather conditions inscribe their own (post)marks. The variants cast beside or beneath the lines are likewise so many signs of travel and her "wandering Aim." The poems with variants (either on the page or across multiple versions) thus have a "ride" too, like her letters; and in that way they have in some sense a life of their own, as "travellers who cross" and are "ever crossing and re-crossing" (L69). The bushes that adjust their tumbled heads in "A Route" are like the lines on the terrain of her pages. A poem with variants has been in a kind of epistolary exchange, sent back and forth between past and present writers. What may appear as signs of effusion, then, are instead determined by Dickinson's well rehearsed epistolary aesthetics.

Notes

1. Mark Rose quotes Hardwicke in *Authors and Owners* (63–64).

2. Howard Erskine-Hill has discussed how Pope often significantly revised his letters before publication: "Sentences were omitted, words changed, allusions altered"; his revisions "sometimes went so far as to take an earlier letter addressed to one person and print it in revised form as addressed to another" (xxiv–xxv). A century later Edgar Allan Poe was following Pope's lead in a series he called "Marginalia"—taken, he claimed, from the actual margins of his books. In marginalia, he says, we "talk freshly—boldly—originally" and "with no eye to the Memorandum Book" (1309). The extant pages, however, show that Poe made "extensive corrections" prior to publication (Miller xi).

3. One epistolary novel, for instance, was Jean-Jacques Rousseau's *Julie* (1761), which opens with a "Conversation about Novels between the Editor [R] and a Man of Letters [N]." When N complains that the letter writers in *Julie* abuse the rules of grammar and rhetoric, R replies sardonically: "I see that you would rather have Letters written to be printed" (9). Broken rules should prove the authenticity of the letters: "It is not a Novel," R insists, "It is a Collection of Letters" (9). Thus the not being "written for publication" caution applied to fictional letters too.

4. Higginson wrote the preface to the first volume of poems; Todd thereafter supplied the prefaces.

5. Altman has said that Madame de Sévigné's seventeenth-century letters practiced an "aesthetics of negligence" (30). I want to borrow that phrase: in her letters and poems, I think, Dickinson too cultivated an "aesthetics of negligence."

6. Wall's interest in "the bizarre fact that public writing was introduced to its larger readership by being scandalized" leads her to argue that "the prefatory language found in published works [relied] on the sonnets' language of courtly love" (202, 198). Renaissance sonnets also "thrive on the contradiction between public and private": "Sonnet cycles are insistently concerned with disclosure, privacy, interiority, and public representation, issues that culminate in the theme of illicit sight" (189, 191). Both the sonnet and preface, Wall argues, take as their founding text the Diana and Actaeon myth, in which Actaeon inadvertently sees Diana naked as she bathes, and is then torn apart by his own hounds after being transformed by Diana into a stag. A print text thus corresponds with the naked female body of Diana, and Actaeon with a buyer. Reading becomes "associated with the detection of scandal" (217).

7. See Gabrielle Dean's "Emily Dickinson's 'Poetry of the Portfolio'" for a reading of Emerson's essay in its publication context, the October 1840 issue of *The Dial*. Dean argues not only that Higginson remembered the essay 50 years later, as he tried to make sense of Dickinson's fascicles, but also that both *The Dial* issue and the fascicles determined some aspects of the 1890 volumes. My thanks to Marta Werner for sharing Dean's essay with me, and for our Dickinson conversations during the early stages of my essay.

8. Because the book was organized into ten sections, with each section containing letters to one or more addressee(s), and almost 50 addressees listed by name, Dickinson was to an extent portrayed as a social person. On the other hand, a chronological arrangement, with dates only listed on the "Contents" page—as the Thomas Johnson and Theodora Ward edition (1958) does—implies a solitary life.

9. Louis Renza makes the same point in *Edgar Allan Poe, Wallace Stevens, and the Poetics of American Privacy* (25). His subject is Poe and Stevens, but some of what he says in his "Going Private" introduction applies to Dickinson. He asserts that neither "writer naively presumes to foreclose his text's communicative impulses or residual effects"; instead, both "writers eschew an either-public-or-private binary" (16). Further, "their aestheticism lies not in a withdrawal from cultural concerns, but in engaging culture on private poetic grounds" (20).

10. Her later letters are no different. In an 1891 journal entry, Mabel Todd stated that "my own opinion is that she thought sometime her own verses might see the light of print, only by other hands than hers. As to the letters, that is different. Those to Mr. Higginson are not of a private nature, and as to the 'innocent and confiding' nature of them, Austin smiles. He says Emily definitely posed in those letters, he knows her thoroughly, through and through, as no one else ever did" (Bingham 166–167).

11. In *Moby-Dick* Melville explains that there two types of whales in the ocean: a Fast-Fish, which belongs "to the party fast to it," and a Loose-Fish, which is "fair game for anybody who can soonest catch it" (446). To continue with Melville's whaling terminology, Jackson has figuratively "waifed" Dickinson's letter.

12. I included as an epigraph the verdict of Hardwicke in the *Pope v. Curll* case. That Pope won his case means that, unlike Saintsbury, Hardwicke found Pope's letters "fresh" enough, to use Pope's own language in his 1737 preface: his letters were effusions, and "proof of what were his real Sentiments, as they flow'd warm from his heart, and fresh from the occasion; without the least thought that

ever the world should be witness to them" (xxxviii–xxxix). This establishing that letter writers were the legal owners of their work must have had, I think, an effect on how poets regarded their work. If they could demonstrate that their poems were versions of their letters, not "finish'd pictures" but instead "fresh from the occasion," copyright would likely be secured.

13. Poe's article on "Anastatic Printing" is certainly a response to the fallout of this 1834 case: authors of handwritten books, he surmised, would have been better able to claim ownership than authors of print books. Poe's idea suggests that the privileged legal status of letters is in part due to their handwritten aspect.

14. The article I have citing became Chapter 2 in McGill's *American Literature and the Culture of Reprinting, 1834–1853*, a fascinating re-evaluation of the two decades prior to the emergence of a "national literature." In that period, when "the republication of foreign works and particular kinds of domestic texts was perfectly legal," editors attached "national ideals not to texts or authors, but to publishing formats and methods of distribution" (3, 23). This was Dickinson's inheritance, one that she obviously embraced—copying and distributing her work through that truly democratic system, the post office.

15. Dickinson sent poems with letters to at least 99 correspondents (Smith, "Suppressing" 105).

16. Martha Nell Smith makes this point throughout *Rowing in Eden: Rereading Emily Dickinson*. "Reconceptualizing notions of 'publication' to include Dickinson's circulation of her poems to her correspondents," she says, "places her in an active, cultured network" (92). Dickinson's publishing activity is a very late form of what Harold Love calls "scribal publication" in *The Culture and Commerce of Texts*. Love's book details the circulation of texts in seventeenth-century manuscript culture.

17. In *Open Me Carefully: Emily Dickinson's Intimate Letters to Susan Huntington Dickinson*, for instance, the editors Ellen Louise Hart and Martha Nell Smith describe Susan as a collaborator. For proposals on Dickinson's "workshop," a social writing space, see Smith's *Rowing in Eden* (155–205) and the Dickinson Electronic Archives website: http://www.emilydickinson.org/safe/pwkshop.html.

18. Richard Menke cites Dickens's *Book of Memoranda* (1862) in "Telegraphic Realism": "Open the story by bringing two strongly contrasted places and strongly contrasted sets of people, into the connexion necessary for the story, by means of an electric message. Describe the message—be the message—flashing along though space—over the earth, and under the sea" (977).

19. Mail can be subject to "highway robbery" as well. To Mary Higginson in 1876 she wrote of her desire to send some springtime buds: "You should own my own, but the Orchard is too jocund to fold and the Robins would rob the mail" (L460).

WORKS CITED

The following abbreviations are used to refer to the writings of Emily Dickinson:
Fr *The Poems of Emily Dickinson*. Ed. R. W. Franklin. 3 vols. Cambridge, Mass.: Harvard University Press, 1998. Citation by poem number.

L *The Letters of Emily Dickinson*. Ed. Thomas H. Johnson and Theodora Ward. 3 vols. Cambridge, Mass.: Harvard University Press, 1958. Citation by letter number.

PF Prose fragments in *The Letters of Emily Dickinson*. Ed. Thomas H. Johnson and Theodora Ward. Vol. 3. Cambridge, Mass.: Harvard University Press, 1958. Citation by fragment number.

Altman, Janet Gurkin. "The Letter Book as a Literary Institution 1539–1789: Toward Cultural History of Published Correspondences in France." *Yale French Studies,* 71 (1986): pp. 17–62.

Bingham, Millicent Todd. *Ancestors' Brocades: The Literary Discovery of Emily Dickinson, and the Editing and Publication of Her Letters and Poems.* 1945. (New York: Dover, 1967).

Blair, Hugh. *Lectures on Rhetoric and Belles Lettres.* 1783. Ed. Harold F. Harding. Vol. 2. (Carbondale: Southern Illinois University Press, 1965).

Dean, Gabrielle. "Emily Dickinson's 'Poetry of the Portfolio'." *TEXT,* 14 (2002): pp. 241–276.

Emerson, Ralph Waldo. "New Poetry." *The Dial* 1.2 (October 1840): pp. 220–232.

———. "American Civilization." *Atlantic Monthly* 9.54 (April 1862): pp. 502–511.

Erskine-Hill, Howard, Ed. *Alexander Pope: Selected Letters.* (New York: Oxford University Press, 2000).

Franklin, R. W. *The Editing of Emily Dickinson: A Reconsideration.* Madison: University of Wisconsin Press, 1967.

Hart, Ellen Louise, and Martha Nell Smith, eds. *Open Me Carefully: Emily Dickinson's Intimate Letters to Susan Huntington Dickinson.* Ashfield: Paris Press, 1998.

Higginson, Thomas Wentworth. "The Life of Birds." 1862. *Outdoor Studies, Poems. The Writings of Thomas Wentworth Higginson.* Vol. 6. (Cambridge: Riverside Press, 1900): pp. 137–163.

———. "An Open Portfolio." 1890. *Emily Dickinson's Reception in the 1890s: A Documentary History.* Ed. Willis J. Buckingham. (Pittsburgh: University of Pittsburgh Press, 1989): pp. 3–9.

———. "Preface." 1890. *Emily Dickinson's Reception in the 1890s: A Documentary History.* Ed. Willis J. Buckingham. (Pittsburgh: University of Pittsburgh Press, 1989): pp. 13–14.

James, Henry. "Robert Louis Stevenson." 1900. *Literary Criticism: Volume One.* Ed. Leon Edel. (New York: Library of America, 1984): pp. 1255–1273.

Juhasz, Suzanne. "Materiality and the Poet." *The Emily Dickinson Handbook.* Ed. Gudrun Grabher, Roland Hagenbüchle, and Cristanne Miller. (Amherst: University of Massachusetts Press, 1998: pp. 427–439.

Love, Harold. *The Culture and Commerce of Texts: Scribal Publication in Seventeenth-Century England.* 1993. (Amherst: University of Massachusetts Press, 1998).

Martineau, Harriet. *Harriet Martineau's Autobiography.* 1877. Ed. Maria Weston Chapman. 2 vols. (Boston: Houghton, Mifflin and Company, 1885).

McGill, Meredith. "The Matter of the Text: Commerce, Print Culture, and the Authority of the State in American Copyright Law." *American Literary History* 9.1 (Spring 1997): pp. 21–59.

———. *American Literature and the Culture of Reprinting, 1834–1853.* Philadelphia: University of Pennsylvania Press, 2003.

Melville, Herman. *Moby-Dick, Billy Budd, and Other Writings.* New York: Library of America, 2000.

Menke, Richard. "Telegraphic Realism: Henry James's *In the Cage.*" *PMLA* 115.5 (October 2000): pp. 975–990.

Messmer, Marietta. *A Vice for Voices: Reading Emily Dickinson's Correspondence.* Amherst: University of Massachusetts Press, 2001.

Miller, John Carl. Introduction. *Marginalia*. By Edgar Allan Poe. Ed. John Carl Miller. Charlottesville: University Press of Virginia, 1981.

Poe, Edgar Allan. "Anastatic Printing." 1845. *The Complete Works of Edgar Allan Poe*. Vol. 14. Ed. James A. Harrison. (New York: AMS Press, 1965): pp. 153–159.

———. "Marginalia." 1844–1849. *Essays and Reviews*. Ed. G. R. Thompson. (New York: Library of America, 1984): pp. 1309–1472.

Pope, Alexander. "Pope's Own Prefaces to His Letters, 1729–1742." *The Correspondence of Alexander Pope*. Ed. George Sherburn. Vol. 1. (Oxford: Clarendon Press, 1956): pp. xxxiv–xli.

Price, Leah. *The Anthology and the Rise of the Novel: From Richardson to George Eliot*. New York: Cambridge University Press, 2000.

Renza, Louis A. *Edgar Allan Poe, Wallace Stevens, and the Poetics of American Privacy*. Baton Rouge: Louisiana State University Press, 2002.

"Review of *The Correspondence of Leigh Hunt*." *Atlantic Monthly* 9.55 (May 1862): p. 653.

Rose, Mark. *Authors and Owners: The Invention of Copyright*. Cambridge: Harvard University Press, 1993.

Rousseau, Jean-Jacques. *Julie, or the New Heloise*. 1761. Trans. Philip Stewart and Jean Vaché. Hanover: University Press of New England, 1997.

Saintsbury, George, Ed. *A Letter Book*. London: G. Bell, 1922.

Smith, Martha Nell. *Rowing in Eden: Rereading Emily Dickinson*. Austin: University of Texas Press, 1992.

———. "Suppressing the Books of Susan in Emily Dickinson." *Epistolary Histories: Letters, Fiction, Culture*. Ed. Amanda Gilroy and W. M. Verhoeven. (Charlottesville: University Press of Virginia, 2000) pp. 101–125.

St. Armand, Barton Levi. *Emily Dickinson and Her Culture: The Soul's Society*. New York: Cambridge University Press, 1984.

Wall, Wendy. *The Imprint of Gender: Authorship and Publication in the English Renaissance*. Ithaca: Cornell University Press, 1993.

Warren, Samuel D., and Louis D. Brandeis. "The Right to Privacy." *Harvard Law Review* 4.5 (15 December 1890): pp. 193–220.

Werner, Marta L. *Emily Dickinson's Open Folios: Scenes of Reading, Surfaces of Writing*. Ann Arbor: University of Michigan Press, 1995.

Wharton, Edith. "Copy." 1901. *The Collected Short Stories of Edith Wharton*. Ed. R. W. B. Lewis. Vol. 2. (New York: Charles Scribner's Sons, 1968): pp. 275–286.

SHIRA WOLOSKY

Public and Private in Dickinson's War Poetry

Ralph Waldo Emerson, in his essay "The Poet," declared that "the poet is representative. He stands among partial men for the complete man, and apprises us not of his wealth, but of the common wealth."[1] Within the norms of the nineteenth century, this would seem to relegate women poets to the status of "partial men." In the much accepted division of life into separate spheres, women were barred access to the "common wealth" as public space. Instead, women remained officially restricted to the domestic sphere—what Tocqueville describes as "the narrow circle of domestic interests and duties"—while men found their places in the "public" world.[2] Women thus could seemingly never achieve Emerson's representative stance—neither in its often overlooked sense (but the one most fully realized by Whitman) of the poet as public figure, nor in the more familiar sense of a rich and powerful autonomous subjectivity, which, however, finds and asserts itself in speaking for and to the wider community. In contrast, women seem at most to reflect in their work their own domestic imprisonment and its costs. In this circumscribed state, the woman poet seems cut off from history, more or less idle and more or less impotent with regard to the public course of events. She thus seems unable to address herself, as poets should, to a surrounding community, representing its true nature and direction while also lacking that strong sense of self and of

A Historical Guide to Emily Dickinson, ed. by Vivian Pollak (Oxford: Oxford University Press, 2004): pp. 103–131.

identity which gives the poet his authority—what makes him, in Harold
Bloom's quite conscious phrase, the central man, whose words can represent his world.[3]

In the case of Emily Dickinson, these assignments seem almost hyper-
bolically justified. If ever there were a private poet, surely it is she—a woman
famous in her own lifetime for reclusion: accompanied by a full array of se-
ductive, eccentric concealments and retractions: refusing to go out, dressing in
white, refusing to see guests, or even to address her own envelopes. Dickinson
seems the ultimate emblem of that modest retreat so urged on American girls
and women, rigorously restricting them to the privacy of their own homes. Yet
Dickinson's modesty, even while it conforms in many aspects with expected
and prescribed female behavior, does so with such extremity as to expose and
radicalize gendered norms. Dickinson's is modesty with a vengeance, more
explosive than obedient, more challenging than conforming. As to the se-
questering of Dickinson from public life, the reading of her work as hermetically private—a mode of self-investigation at its most interior—is in many
ways an imposition on her of this gendered paradigm rather than evidence
for it. It is a view of her work through the geographies of public and private
which are highly gendered and which block from sight her full engagement,
and address, to the central concerns of her culture. This decisively includes the
Civil War—that crucible of American claims and counterclaims, of violent
cultural crossings and transformations, whose implications penetrate every
sphere of American cultural identity.

To begin with biography, despite her peculiar behavior, every circumstance of Dickinson's social existence argues against severe detachment from
public affairs. Her family had a tradition of involvement in civic life. Her
father, after many years of prominence in town meetings, at Amherst College,
in the Home Mission Society, and the railroad project, was elected representative to the General Court of Massachusetts in 1838 (where he came to
know Herman Melville's politically controversial father-in-law, Judge Lemuel
Shaw. This seems to be the reference in Dickinson's poem "I had some things
that I called mine – / And God, that he called his" [J 116 / Fr 101] where she
retains him in her quarrel with God: "Jove! Choose your counsel – I retain
'Shaw'!") Edward Dickinson was twice elected Massachusetts State Senator
in 1842 and 1843; was delegate to the Whig National Convention in 1852;
and in the same year was elected to the United States Congress. His term
in Congress spanned the period of the Kansas-Nebraska Act, the Fugitive
Slave Act, and the first attempts to found the new Republican Party (with
meetings to discuss this issue taking place in rooms he shared with Thomas
D. Eliot, granduncle to a later American poet).[4] Both her father, Edward, and
her brother, Austin, were active recruiters and outfitters of Amherst soldiers,
involved in raising both funds and morale.

Many of Dickinson's other acquaintances were directly involved in political reporting and public affairs. Samuel Bowles, a long-time intimate of the family and herself, was editor of the *Springfield Republican*—which published soldiers' letters home and a column on "Piety and Patriotism." (Among the few Dickinson poems published anonymously in her lifetime are those which appeared in publications that aided the war effort.) Dr. Josiah Holland, another close friend, was a columnist for the *Springfield Republican* and editor of *Scribner's Magazine*. He also wrote one of the first biographies of Lincoln. And Thomas Wentworth Higginson, so central in the drama of Dickinson's own unpublication history, was a radical abolitionist (even to the point of supporting the John Brown conspiracy), an activist in women's rights, and colonel to the first black regiment of the Union army when Dickinson first wrote to him. As Hawthorne wrote in "Chiefly About War Matters": "There is no remoteness of life and thought, no hermetically sealed seclusion, except, perhaps, that of the grave, into which the disturbing influences of this war do not penetrate."

This is not to claim that Dickinson was herself a public activist, as many women indeed were. Despite the rigors of the ideology of the separate spheres, the boundaries between public and private were, in fact, extremely volatile, with women not only active but also in many ways the central actors in a variety of public-sphere ventures. These included education, religion, and many forms of what would be today called social services, such as hospital work, work with the poor, with orphans, with immigrants; urban planning, sanitation; abolition, temperance; purity reform and women's rights. Such activity generally belies the relegation of women to a "private" and "domestic" sphere—terms that were nevertheless applied to their community activities as seen to be continuous with the sorts of things women did inside the home. Many of these commitments, however, are neither domestic nor particularly like what women do in houses: urban planning, for example, or preaching. Some activities are political according to any imaginable criteria, even when, as in the case of abolition, the campaigns were (also) conducted in the name of the sanctity and integrity of family life against the constant assault of sexual slavery and the slave market's very denial of family existence. Nor were most of these ventures undertaken within the confines of the household. Domesticity, in fact, is only figurally geographic, since many women's activities took place outside the domicile. The geography of domesticity, so powerful in ascribing women to the private sphere, proves to be a gendered rubric applied to activities not because of their location but exactly because women performed them (when men performed such activities, they were not considered private but public.)[5]

Among these central areas for this women's activism, Dickinson directly experienced only the new realm of education—albeit with a strong exposure to the religious-civic sphere with which it was so forcefully intertwined. Her headmistress at Mount Holyoke Female Seminary, Mary Lyon, had founded the college in dedication to mission work and civic activism in the context of the enormous revivalism sweeping through Dickinson's religiously quite conservative home-county through much of her girlhood and indeed her lifetime. Even publication, a major and immensely consequential new venture for women, remains tensely ambiguous in Dickinson's case. Publication offered many women an avenue into public discourse. This emergence into publicity Dickinson declined, lacking both the economic contexts (most women moved into publication by way of either financial motive or financial excuse) and, apparently, the desire. Her fascicle nonpublication remains ambiguously poised between textual inscription and its own effacement and certainly evades publicity—although the circulation of her poems in letters to friends suggests something close to the coterie circles of shared poetry in earlier, Renaissance, courtly worlds.

Despite these almost unique removals from the mainstreams of American women's poetic lives, Dickinson's own writing career remarkably aligns with the enormous and traumatic political events surrounding her. More than half of her poetic production coincides with the years of the Civil War, 1861–1865. The years immediately preceding the war, when the possibility and rhetoric of conflict ominously intensified, were also the years which Thomas Johnson identifies with "the rising flood of her talent," as well as with the beginning of her reclusive practices. Her correspondence is similarly marked by public consciousness, with at least fifteen references to the war in the seventy-five letters she wrote between 1861–1865. Some are passing mentions, some are concerned with the fate of Amherst boys who had gone off to fight, including, notably, Frazar Stearns, over whose death Dickinson especially and personally grieved. But some letters are more general. Thus, to Louise and Frances Norcross, she wrote that "Since the war began" she has an increasing sense that "Tis dangerous to value, for only the precious can alarm. I noticed that Robert Browning had made another poem, and was astonished—till I remembered that I myself, in my smaller way, sang off charnel steps" (L 298).

Dickinson here places many of her most deeply felt poetic impulses into the wider context of the national agony enveloping her world. Dickinson's sense of the precariousness of possession, of the assault of time, contingency, and above all death on all that is precious and valuable, only acquired dire confirmation in the assaults of war. One might say that Emily Dickinson disapproved of reality, and for excellent reasons. What has long seemed a merely eccentric and highly gendered withdrawal from exposures to the world, takes on both motive and defiance once historical context is admitted.

Poetry in the nineteenth century directly participated in the discussions, arguments, claims, and counterclaims of the most pressing questions facing

America. For women, it provided a particularly powerful avenue for engagement in issues of public concern and entry into public debate. Dickinson's case is certainly most oblique. Yet her poetic engagement with her wider culture, and the importance of her work as a major response to the issues most central to nineteenth-century American cultural definition, can be investigated through a variety of methods—and without reducing the texts to mere historical document, ideological program, or political tract. Recent work, for example, has begun to probe how Dickinson uses the words of her culture, and how they import, into the arena of her texts, the associations, implications, often contested meanings of their general usage. This can involve her uses of various kinds of political language, or her images of whiteness against the backgrounds of their racial meanings.[6] One moving poem of desperation and appeal, "At least – to pray – is left – is left" concludes: "Thou settest Earthquake in the South – / And Maelstrom, in the Sea – / Say, Jesus Christ of Nazareth – / Hast thou no arm for Me?" (J 502 / Fr 377). "South" here is surely a political-geographic marker, no less than "south" is in Whitman's "Out of the Cradle Endlessly Rocking." There are scattered through the verse references to emigrants and settlers, showing Dickinson's awareness of contemporary demographic movement. Death is described as democratic in a poem which meticulously lists the demarcations of social division – "Color – Caste – Denomination" that "He" so equably ignores (J 970 / Fr 836). Another poem firmly declares that "Not any higher stands the Grave / For Heroes than for Men –." In a radical assertion of the unique worth of every individual, Dickinson brushes aside all conditions, whether historical heroism or economic status—the poem goes on to equate "The Beggar and his Queen"—before the "Democrat" death (J 1256 / Fr 1214).

A quite interesting set of poems use canny electoral puns. These include the famously isolating "Soul selects her own Society," which figures self-selection as a "Majority" chosen from "an ample nation" (J 303 / Fr 409). Another poem declares "The Heart is the Capital of the Mind / The Mind is a single State," with "One" a "Population – / Numerous enough" for the "ecstatic Nation" of the self (J 1354 / Fr 1381). There is the pervasive yet almost unnoticed use of economic imagery—of stocks and options and properties and ownerships—that weaves Dickinson's work into the volatile and increasingly defining American commitment to money ("Myself can read the Telegrams" reports Dickinson as following "The Stock's advance and retrograde / And what the Markets say" [J 1089 / Fr 1049], to take one example.) The vicissitudes of her own family fortunes—her father's financial reversals and then recovery—is of course a matter of biographical record (and altogether common in a period with little financial regulation). Still another avenue toward a historical Dickinsonian poetics is her position in the gendered distributions of her society, as, for example, through the representations in her work (and indeed in her life) of modesty—including the obscurities and obfuscations of her "slant" poetic truths—which so powerfully defined femininity in her period.[7] There is, as well, Dickinson's continued and intensive engagement with contemporary religious culture, then undergoing volatile and explosive transformation. Finally, there is the exploration of Dickinson's notions of selfhood in relation to models emerging in nineteenth-century America, with enormous consequences for American political, social, economic, and cultural life.

In all these cases, Dickinson's poetry becomes not only the powerful expression of her personal sensibility but also a centrally important representation of her society and her culture—a dimension which has been repeatedly neglected due, not least, to assumptions about gender. Through her work as a whole, I will argue, at stake in Dickinson's poetry is the possibility of interpreting her world at all, within her given paradigms of understanding and their promises of intelligibility and coherence. These the Civil War directly tested and contested. The trauma of the war put extraordinary pressure on the norms, and fundamental faiths, that had promised to structure Dickinson's world and render it meaningful. The result is a work deeply marked by the strains of reality around her and their implications for poetic expression and, specifically for poetic language.

The question of war penetrates Dickinson's work both through specific historical events and, more hauntingly as a general, framing context (which of course it unquestionably was). In terms of specific references, there are numerous poems that invoke war, either indirectly or directly.[8] Indirect imagery of war takes many forms. Nature is represented in battle imagery as "martial Trees" that "Barricade against the Sky ... with a Flag at every turn" (J 1471 / Fr 1505). Soldiers drop "like flakes" (J 409 / Fr 545) and sunsets spread in the uniform colors of blue and gray (J 204 / Fr 233) or as "Gulfs – of Red, and Fleets – of Red / And Crews – of solid Blood" (J 658 / Fr 468). Or war becomes a figure for Dickinson's contested interior life, a "Battle fought between the Soul / And No Man" (J 595 / Fr 629), a "Campaign inscrutable / Of the Interior" (J 1188 / Fr 1230), a soul "Garrisoned ... In the Front of Trouble" (J 1243 / Fr 1196). "To fight aloud, is very brave" but it is still *"gallanter"* to "charge within the bosom / The Cavalry of Wo" (J 126 / Fr 138). Or "My Wars are laid away in Books" (J 1549 / Fr 1579).

There are, however, poems that directly treat the Civil War in imagery and still others that are fully structured around it (as well as poems that may or may not be). For example, in one poem of equivocal consolation—"If any sink, assure that this, now standing –" (J 358 / Fr 616)—"the Worst" presumably gives way to some positive attainment or at least endurance, which however, turns out to be death itself: "Dying – annuls the power to kill." The ultimate image of such "Dread" is "the Whizzing, before the [cannon] Ball."

Then there are the elegies on specific war-dead. These include "It dont sound terrible" (J 26 / Fr 384); probably "It feels a shame to be alive" (J 44 / F 524); "He gave away his Life" (J 567 / Fr 530, probably); "Robbed by Death" (J 971 / Fr 838, probably); "Victory comes late" (J 690 / Fr 195). These are poems mainly in connection with the death of Frazar Stearns, the son of Amherst College's president. "When I was small, a Woman died" (J 596 / Fr 518) stands at least partly in memory of Francis H. Dickinson, the first of Amherst's war-dead (the poem may be a composite memorium). More general was memorials (as far as we know) are "Some we see no more" (J 1221 / Fr 1210), "My Portion is Defeat – today" (J 639 / Fr 704), "My Triumph lasted till the Drums" (J 1227 / Fr 1212). "My country need not change her gown" compares the present with the Revolutionary War (J 1511 / Fr 1540). Other poems no doubt remain to be detected; still other poems change in aspect once the context of war is admitted. Among these, notably, is "My Life had stood – a Loaded Gun," a poem that figures violence as firearms, and concludes with an ambiguous measuring of the power to kill against the power to die. There is also the wonderful and apparently early "Success is counted sweetest" (of course, martial language was already current right before the war) which carefully weighs gain against loss, deeply identifying with defeat in battle. Success itself becomes defined through its loss, to one

> defeated – dying –
> On whose forbidden ear
> The distant strains of triumph
> Burst agonized and clear! (J 67 / Fr 112)

The first striking feature of these war poems is the fundamental and commanding place they give to the problem of theodicy. Dickinson's war poems are persistently structured around the problem of justifying evil or suffering, or rather, of justifying a God who permits, at the very least, so much evil and suffering to pervade his world. The war seemed to her an agony of suffering and love. As she wrote to her Norcross cousins (cited above) announcing the death of Amherst's Frazar Stearns: "Let us love better, children, it's most that's left to do" (L 255, 1862). In her next letter to her Norcross cousins, she remarks: "I wish 'twas plainer, the anguish in this world. I wish one could be sure the suffering had a loving side" (L 263). In 1864, she writes the cousins again: "Sorrow seems to me more general than it did, and not the estate of a few persons, since the war began; and if the anguish of others helped with one's own, now would be many medicines (L 298).

Dickinson's war poems generally attempt to make out "the anguish in this world" and to decipher whether it has "a loving side." This would mean its fitting into some wider schema, some purpose that would justify the suffering, giving it place and hence significance. Yet in text after text, Dickinson marshals her own forces, ranging positive against negative, gain against loss, good against evil. In text after text, she assesses whether good triumphs over and justifies evil, whether gain outweighs loss, such that all find their place in a coherent, meaningful, and hence ultimately positive pattern which places and thus redeems the negative. And yet, in text after text, such measures do not come out. In, for example, "If any sink, assure that this, now stand-ing" (J 358 / Fr 616), the apparently consoling terms prove, as we have seen, to be only death, as the cancellation rather than the redemption of dread. The answer to "Dread" as "the whizzing, before the ball" is nothing other than a death that "annuls the power to kill." In "Success is counted sweetest," the fullest appreciation of victory is granted to one denied it—an intensified negative rather than a positive claim. Dickinson's elegy for Francis Dickinson, "When I was small, a Woman died (J 596 / Fr 518) imagines the mother's re-union with her son in "Paradise." Yet, while she has sympathy for the mother and admiration for the son, the conditions of heaven remain something the poet "cannot decide" and in uncertain relation to the all too certain "Scarlet Maryland." Other war poems focus on the accidental nature of winning or losing, dying or living. "He fought like those Who've nought to lose" (J 759 / Fr 480) portrays a soldier who, though courting death, is somehow de-nied it; while other soldiers, "Coy of Death," somehow suffer the "Doom" which eludes him. A paradigmatic "After Horror" is nevertheless represented through warfare, where uncertain death, or uncertainty in general, is figured as looking down a gun-barrel:

> Is like a Face of Steel –
> That suddenly looks into our's
> With a metallic grin –
> The Cordiality of Death –
> Who drills his Welcome in – (J 286 / Fr 243)

Far from fitting into an ordained and significant plan, war shows death to be arbitrary and recalcitrant.

Some texts give elaborate and immediate consideration to the chal-lenges of war, to its meaning—or, dreadfully—its meaninglessness. "My Por-tion is Defeat – today –" (J 639 / Fr 704) vividly represents war's violence, in deeply felt distress and despair at consolation. Dated 1862, the poem was written during the long and disheartening years of Northern defeat in battle. For Dickinson, picturing herself walking among scraps of body—and, signifi-cantly, of "Prayer"—on the battlefield, the vision of "Victory" is something remote—"somewhat prouder, Over there –." This delusive image of victory only makes worse the pain of defeat. But Dickinson is equally disturbed and dissatisfied by victory when it is achieved. "My Triumph lasted till the Drums" progressively erases any consoling or atoning value to victory, in distress for the "finished Faces" (of either side?) it cost: "And then I hated Glory / And wished myself were They" (J 1227 / Fr 1212).

This poem very significantly then opens into a general meditation on patterns of time and perspectives that promise to place, integrate, and hence redeem chaotic moments:

> What is to be is best descried
> When it has also been –
> Could Prospect taste of Retrospect
> The Tyrannies of Men
> Were Tenderer, diviner
> The Transitive toward –
> A Bayonet's contrition
> Is nothing to the Dead – (J 1227 / Fr 1212)

In a pun on "diviner," Dickinson intersects foresight with Godhead, divining with divinity. Julia Ward Howe, in her "Battle Hymn of the Republic," claims to 'have seen" the glory of God and to "read" a fiery gospel in the scenes of war she witnesses. Dickinson too seeks to descry, to witness current events as placed within a larger vision of time's whole, as in God's eternal perspective. This is in faith that the "Transitive" so seen becomes "Tenderer," that time's motion finds its pattern and hence meaning in a visionary and encompassing "Retrospect." Yet Dickinson eschews such a visionary grasp of the whole, remaining caught instead in a fragmentary present. And her ultimate image of repudiation is a "Bayonet," whose contrition offers "nothing" to the dead it neither redeems nor restores.

Dickinson's work brings to awareness the importance of theodicy as a core literary (as well as philosophical and religious) structure, in, for example, Aeschylus, Augustine, and Milton, Herbert and Donne, or, closer to Dickinson, Melville and Hopkins. In Dickinson, the problem of theodicy is at once personal, historical, metaphysical, and textual. In Dickinson's war poetry, what emerges is the way the problem of suffering is at once most acutely personal and yet also broadly and fundamentally historical. The theodicean questions about suffering and its justification are surely Dickinson's private ones, but they are not private only. They belong to her wider community. Indeed, it is, oddly, just where poems are most personal in terms of Dickinson's suffering, that they are also most culturally engaged. For the problem of suffering is essentially the problem of history. This is expressly and centrally the case in Christian terms, whose metaphysics continued to frame Dickinson's own experience and understanding. In this model, earthly events find their place and their meaning in a providential history that is both comprehensive and redemptive. Each experience is thought to find its corollary, and hence its significant place in a meaningful order, eternally present to divine vision. This divine order was specifically revealed through biblical pattern, focused in the life of Christ. In Christ, and especially in his suffering, death, and resurrection, earthly travail gained its full significance and justification—justification exactly in its significant reference to Christ's own suffering as the path and means to redemption.

This biblical and providential vision, encoding events in nature, history, and the self in an overarching divine pattern, continued to be strongly felt in the habits of orthodox, antebellum Amherst. Here was Jonathan Edwards country, a land of religious revivals, where, as Dickinson puts it in one poetic reference to Edwards, a "Martial Hand" urges "Conscience" (J 1598 / Fr 1640).[9] For Dickinson, the problem of suffering remains deeply tied to the paradigms of her religious inheritance (with Thomas à Kempis's "Imitation of Christ" a favorite text). But this was no less the case for her broader cultural world and not only in conservative Amherst. Very generally and normatively, the Civil War itself was interpreted through religious reference directly and potently felt, indeed vigorously invoked. The war was widely seen in the North as enacting apocalyptic scenes of punishment and retribution, whereby the nation would be judged and cleansed of the sin of slavery.[10] The war witnessed incredible outbursts of organized missionary activity. It was the object of intense prayer in churches throughout the nation. As Dickinson wrote to Thomas Wentworth Higginson, then serving in the South as colonel to the first black regiment: "I trust you may pass the limit of War, and though not reared to prayer—when service is had in Church, for Our Arms, I include yourself" (L 280). The rhetoric of contest itself resonated with the language of holy war and religious drama. Dickinson's father put it thus in a published plea of 1855: "By the help of Almighty God, not another inch of our soil heretofore consecrated to freedom, shall hereafter be polluted by the advancing tread of slavery."[11] Even Lincoln, with his exquisite restraint, could speak on one of the many days of fasting and Thanksgiving, which made up a public religious ritual throughout the war, of Union victories as "the gracious gifts of the most high God, who, while dealing with us in anger for our sins, hath nevertheless remembered mercy."[12]

Although not all of the numerous references to war in Dickinson's letters and poems can be certainly and directly related to immediate historical events, there is a continuity between martial imagery in political and religious contexts that makes them impossible entirely to separate in her work. But the same is true for her historical world. Attempts to find redemptive responses to the most daunting, violent, historical events would have been, in Dickinson's context, completely current. It is more than a coincidental curiosity that

Dickinson began writing intensively, and wrote over half of her poems, during the American Civil War. The Civil War reached levels of carnage before unknown, made possible both by new technology and new strategies of total warfare, in combination with a profound ideological challenge to American national claims and self-identity, political and religious.[13]

With regard to the latter, the war represents a crucial, although by no means unique, arena in which Dickinson enacted her ongoing and intensive religious anguish. Emily Dickinson's is very much a poetry of the religious imagination. Religion continues to be a fundamental paradigm through which she interpreted her world. This is not to claim that Dickinson is an orthodox religious poet. On the contrary, her work offers a forceful and original critique of traditional metaphysics in ways that recall her near contemporary Friedrich Nietzsche. Religion in many ways is a paradigm that fails Dickinson, and yet, she never completely discards it. If she is not devout, she is also not secular. Dickinson's work repeatedly rehearses her reasons for both asserting and denying a divine order, in constant countertension. In this sense, Dickinson's work does not take shape as a quest. Rather, it engages in endless disputation, which is endlessly inconclusive. There is a perpetual clash in which different positions challenge each other, with each one found ultimately wanting. In this disputation, religious questions confront religious answers, which do not, however, adequately resolve them. The result is a world that remains unsatisfactory without God, but equally unsatisfactory with the God of her fathers. In this light, readings of Dickinson as though she had comfortably settled into a post-Christian enlightenment, substituting art and the powers of her own mind for faith in divine orders and meanings, are both historically anachronistic and untrue to her verse. Historians underscore how religious institutions, hermeneutics, and sensibility continued forcefully to frame nineteenth-century life, especially the lives of women. As the century advanced, religious norms may have been boiling away, but they had by no means evaporated. Across America—in the North, and, differently, in the South—providential histories continued in strong, if also in transformed ways, marking not only American Romanticism with its demons of analogy but also the historical culture at large. The events of America continued to be understood as moments in a universal drama of redemption, even if such redemption was increasingly claimed for history rather than eternity. Dickinson's poems repeatedly operate with this framework and its promise of transcendent reference. In her terms, time should represent eternity; earthly experience, even or rather especially when involving loss and death, should find transfigured meaning within a structure of transcendence.

In certain moods, Dickinson's poems declare just such transfigurations, making hers a "compound Vision . . . The Finite – furnished / With the Infinite. . . . Back – toward Time – / And forward – Toward the God of Him –"

(J 906 / Fr 830). More often, however, Dickinson exhibits difficulties with her inherited metaphysical system, which prevent her from enjoying its promises. Readings of Dickinson that see her poetry as converting limitation to infinity, pain to joy, suffering to redemption, and death to poetic immortality replicate and transfer fundamentally Christian structures to the realm of art. But these basic structures of conversion, whether in religion or in art, appear to her to be faulty. In this regard, the claim that Dickinson freed herself from Christian orthodoxy while transposing many of its most constitutive structures into aesthetic experience and activity remains very problematic. On the contrary, Dickinson's work exactly explores just how problematic such transpositions can be. She questions to what extent art can indeed serve as figure for faith and, conversely, exposes how religious assumptions persist even beyond specific dogmas, to continue to exert pressure on both social and aesthetic ideologies. Her poetry repeatedly and painfully attests to misgivings that prevent her from reading her world as signs for any redemptive meaning whatsoever. It traces her resistance to making experiences types for each other in a chain of transferred meanings that point ultimately to some redemptive realm. This does not, however, make transcendent meaning dispensable. In text after text, she returns again to religious premises and promises; again finding them wanting; again finding them necessary.

Dickinson thus shares with her wider culture the imperative to make sense of suffering, disorder, disruption, through reference to coherent, overarching, redemptive patterns. The war focused her pressing need for interpretive transfiguration, in order to put together a world that was breaking apart—quite literally, in the American sectional strife and ideological warfare. And yet the war also pressingly and gravely ruptured the very paradigms needed for such justification. Dickinson in one letter presents her war effort as a poetic one, in contrast to the extensive and activist provisioning of soldiers most women engaged in: "I shall have no winter this year—on account of the soldiers—Since I cannot weave Blankets, or Boots—I thought it best to omit the season—Shall present a 'Memorial' to God—when the Maples turn" (L 235). Instead of blankets and boots, she offers poems. But Dickinson's poetic "Memorial" remains deeply equivocal. In this, Dickinson remains a rare case among her contemporaries in withstanding the impulse to defend and explicate suffering in terms that claimed for it metaphysical justification and redemptive value. Only Melville seems comparable, and even he, "Battle Pieces," seems (slightly) more palliative, on the political grounds of the evil of slavery and the good of the Union.[14] (Whitman's case is multiply complex, with brave affirmation offered across stark qualms.) Dickinson, in fact, is rarely political in the sense of engaging directly in issues of public policy.

Yet there is another sense in which Dickinson's war writing engages with the political, and that is in the sense of the polis–of public space and the life of the community within it. War is proposed not only as a historical-metaphysical problem—where metaphysics and history intersect—but also as a problem of selfhood, of the place of the self in the culture and community which surrounds it. For, as Sacvan Bercovitch has shown, it is in the life of the community that historical experience as providential pattern unfolds.[15] This was explicitly and dramatically the case for the original Puritan settlers, who conceived themselves as a federal people in covenant to God, whose fulfillment (and chastisement) would be directly revealed and experienced in the course of a divinely ordained providential history. This American habit of regarding itself as a chosen nation, a beacon on the hill, whose histori-cal events resound with cosmic and divinely ordained significance, evolved through the Colonial and Revolutionary periods, into the nineteenth century. It then emerged with a vengeance in the ideologies, and the rhetoric, preced-ing and exploding in the Civil War. The course of the community, its ultimate test and ultimate vindication, comes through as a history deeply imbued with transformed religious significance.

Dickinson is acutely conscious of this public and communal histori-cal dimension. And, as with religion and religious histories, she is deeply disturbed and conflicted regarding it. For in war, not only the status of the community and its historical course is ultimately tested, but also the status and claims of the individual self are equally so tested. In war, above all, the self is called upon to place life second to, or in service of, community, in the name of a greater purpose. War is above all the time when community commands and supersedes the self, for and within larger historical ends. At issue are not only the claims of the community but also the definitions of selfhood itself. These topics are engaged in one of Dickinson's specific war elegies, "It feels a shame to be Alive – / When Men so brave – are dead," written for Frazar Stearns, who had himself written to his father, Amherst College's president: "How can you terrify one who can look death in the face and has made up his mind that his life is his country's and expects it at any time? If I can serve my country better by dying now than living I am ready to do it."[16]

The Stone – that tells defending Whom
This Spartan put away
What little of Him we – possessed
In Pawn for Liberty

The price is great – Sublimely paid –
Do we deserve – a Thing –
That lives – like Dollars – must be piled
Before we may obtain?

Are we that wait – sufficient worth –
That such Enormous Pearl
As life – dissolved be – for Us –
In Battle's – horrid Bowl?

It may be – a Renown to live –
I think the Men who die –
Those unsustained – Saviors –
Present Divinity – (J 444 / Fr 524)

On the one hand, Dickinson pays great tribute to individual value and sacrifice. On the other, there is great tension between the self and the community for whom self-sacrifice is made. These variant senses of the self, and its very definition, emerge as contested, complex, under scrutiny. The soldiers themselves are honored and even exalted, as "unsustained – Saviors" who "Present," and in whom is made present, divinity in this world. Yet the soldier stands in strained relation to the community for whom his sacrifice has been made. The structure of justification is again invoked and again refused. "It feels a shame to be Alive," the poem opens, "When Men so brave – are dead." And it then asks: "Are we that wait – sufficient worth." It is noteworthy that Dickinson here brings herself in, at least as a member of the community at war. And, despite women's removal from direct participation in warfare, she effectively combines the domestic world with the public conflict in the striking image of "Battle's – horrid Bowl."[17]

Noteworthy as well is the measure of value in units of money—the importance of economic and indeed monetary terms. Such economic imagery is surprisingly pervasive in Dickinson. Here it is elaborate. The soldier is a "Pawn for Liberty," where pawn is both a sacrificial piece in a chess game and a property ceded but not yet sold. His sacrifice is a "price" that is "Sublimely paid." More abrasively, the men's lives are likened to "Dollars" in piles (a macabre reference to the piles of dead and wounded in the newly circulating war-photographs?). Dickinson here engages the emerging ascendancy and power of money in defining value and the self in America.

This overlay of economy, theodicy, and war is prominent in other war poems. "He gave away his Life" describes the sacrifice of self in war as "Gigantic Sum." This poem again concludes with a tribute to heroism and the infinite value of the transfigured individual (J 567 / Fr 530). The community, however, is in a compromised position: "Tis Our's – to wince – and weep – / And wonder – and decay." "Victory comes late" is less generous still. In this poem, even if victory is achieved or granted, it comes too late for the dead who suffered for it. One of Dickinson's few poems in free verse, the text is an outcry for those dead, without consolation from whatever the community has gained. Above all, it is an indictment of the divine, whose penury refuses the grace and love, care and charity inherent in the very notion of divinity:

> Was God so economical?
> His Table's spread too high for Us –
> Unless We dine on Tiptoe –
> Crumbs – fit such little mouths –
> Cherries – suit Robins –
> The Eagle's Golden Breakfast strangles – Them –
> God keep His Oath to Sparrows –
> Who of little Love – know how to starve – (J 690 / Fr 195)

Victory, rather than enclosing the event of suffering in its redeeming pattern, remains disjoined from the experience of sacrifice. Instead of serving as a sign of divine intention and intervention, it stands as a sign of divine denial, not only of his creatures but also of his own promised nature: a God of parsimony rather than of constant providence, who betrays, rather than rescuing, a sparrow in its fall. The bird emblems here are suggestive. The robin Dickinson had associated with herself as seeing "New Englandly" (J 285 / Fr 256). Here, it is excluded from the divine, communion table, while the Eagle—perhaps the American emblem?—who is apparently served is instead strangled. Providence becomes perverse economy.

Economic language was, to be sure, part and parcel of the rhetoric of American religion since its Puritan foundings. Dickinson registers this in many poems, where God appears as "Burglar! Banker" (J 49 / Fr 39); as "Mighty Merchant" (J 621 / Fr 687) and Swindler (J 476 / Fr 711); as "Exchequer" (J 1270 / Fr 1260) and "Auctioneer of Parting" (J 1612 / Fr 1646). "Paradise" is an "Option" one can "Own in Eden" (J 1069 / Fr 1125). The language of covenant and the notion of heavenly reward serve to represent spiritual matters in human language and human terms. But as Dickinson's work almost mercilessly exploits, analogies are disconcertingly unstable and can ultimately be converted in either direction, toward either term of comparison. Money may be an image of divine things, but divine things may conversely be reduced to money.

Money also, with accelerating power, is coming in Dickinson's century to define the individual as well—as Thoreau, for example, laments long in Walden. "Pawn for Liberty," Dickinson writes with complex punning (J 444 / Fr 524). The solder-self as sacrifice for liberty is the Union's ideology. But liberty also—as is quite explicit in the original Lockean formula that underwrote Jefferson's *Declaration*—means possessions. The liberal contract in Locke's terms pledged itself to uphold life, liberty, and property—which is to say liberty as property. Jefferson opened thus Lockean term to a more multiply constituted "pursuit of happiness"; but liberty itself retains a basic sense of the individual's right to what he owns against tyrannical attempts to take it from him without his consent, with the self itself a kind of property, proper to itself, determined by the self. [18] (Here it is necessary to remark that the gender is purposely male. Women were not accorded such liberal rights to property or the individuality it constituted, but rather were incorporated into the property of the male individual.)[19] Here further tensions emerge within the liberal polity. The self thus self-determined stands in strained relation with the community constituted by it precisely in order to protect and uphold just such individual rights and liberties. For absolute assertion of individual interests against any communal commitment would lead to endless centripetal forces unto dissolution. This, of course, is exactly the issue which exploded as civil war—with the South and North each claiming "liberty." In the Southern case, liberty is each individual state's right to secede against the tyranny of centralized power, but in the second, Northern case, liberty is the right to self-determination for each individual, which slavery was increasingly felt to betray.[20] That defense of this Northern claim nevertheless necessitated constraining individuals to a common cause was acutely grasped by Lincoln. In a Special Session of Congress, in 1861, he spoke:

> And this issue embraces more than the fate of these United States. It presents to the whole family of man, the question, whether a constitutional republic, or a democracy—a government of the people, by the same people—can, or cannot, maintain its territorial integrity, against its own domestic foes. It presents the question, whether discontented individuals, too few in numbers to control administration, according to organic law, in any case, can always. . . break up their Government, and thus practically put an end to free government upon the earth. It forces us to ask: "Is there in all republics, this inherent, and fatal weakness?" "Must a government, of necessity, be too strong for the liberties of its own people, or too weak to maintain its own existence?"[21]

Can government maintain or grant such liberty to the individual as to fulfill its promise of self-government, yet not thereby dissolve into fractured chaos? Can the pull to each self be prevented from becoming a mere pulling apart of the community? This, of course, is a core question of the Gettysburg Address, where Lincoln asks whether a nation "conceived in liberty . . . can long endure."

Emily Dickinson's poetry, like the Civil War itself, can be said to show the strains of these potent, intimate, and conflicting impulses and claims of American cultural life. The poem "Robbed by Death" describes dying in war as being "Robbed by Liberty / For her Jugular Defences" (J 971 / Fr 838).[22] Here the curious, if subtle use of a legal and economic term—robbery—verges into oxymoron: liberty quintessentially involves the protection from being robbed, the assertion of self-possession and its rights at the heart of individualism. (One more often thinks of being robbed *of,* not *by,* liberty). It is as if Americans' basic premises are consuming themselves, shown to be at odds within or between poems. "I'm ceded – I've stopped being Their's –" (J 508 / Fr 353) turns on a political pun, asserting selfhood radically against the authority of society. In the language of secession, the poet claims the right of withdrawal and independence from normative social-religious claims. In this defiant and solitary selfhood, she takes possession of a "Crown" of Queenship as self-sovereignty. Yet absolute selfhood can also leave the self isolated and frozen. In another poem with reference to war, "The Soul has Bandaged moments," the soul is wounded (J 512 / Fr 360). Its movement toward some complete "Liberty" of "escape" is fraught with danger, when the soul "dances like a Bomb," only to plunge back into "Horror."

The Civil War thus emerges as stage, motive, and image for Dickinson's deeply conflicted relationships to her cultural world, in religious, historical, as well as personal senses of the self. The consequences for her art and its language are momentous and profound. One poem very curiously stakes out these connections.

> Step lightly on this narrow Spot –
> The Broadest Land that grows
> Is not so ample as the Breast
> These Emerald Seams enclose.
>
> Step lofty, for this name be told
> As far as cannon dwell,
> Or Flag subsist, or Fame export
> Her deathless Syllable (J 1183 / Fr 1227)

In this poem of homage to the war-dead, what is absent defines and dwarfs what is present. The "narrow" grave is ampler than the "broadest Land," which however takes shape through it. The hero's sacrificial death, in turn, is significantly made into a trope for poetry itself. The image of "Seams" which enclose the hero's burial place recalls Dickinson's own sewn fascicles. And this death, like poetry and art, bestows a "name" that is lofty and immortal. "Cannon," "Flag," and "Fame" become mutual reflections, all gathered into the final enduring image of poetics itself as "deathless Syllable."

This poem offers a number of arresting alignments. The self is, on the one hand, invested with great significance. Yet this significance is tied to, and measured by, its relation to others and the sacrifices made for them. The value of the self emerges not simply in itself but in terms of others. Dickinson here situates herself at the very clash of contending impulses. Her self, on the one hand, remains independent, even defiant, of society's claims, with a courage of judgment that is unwavering. On the other hand, she is also skeptical of selves that are invested only in themselves, without reference, or devotion, to anything beyond the self. She is critical, that is, of both social authority and also of absolute selfhood. This contention ultimately informs her sense of her own vocation, of poetry and of herself as poet, as can be seen in one text with arresting conjunctions with her war poetry:

> The Martyr Poets – did not tell –
> But wrought their Pang in syllable –
> That when their mortal name be numb –
> Their mortal fate – encourage Some –
>
> The Martyr Painters – never spoke –
> Bequeathing – rather – to their Work –
> That when their conscious fingers cease –
> Some seek in Art – the Art of Peace – (J 544 / Fr 665)

The poet here, like the heroes in many Dickinson war-elegies, is a sacrificial figure. As in many war poems, the self is at once granted enormous value, and yet a value that emerges in self-effacement—indeed, in martyrdom, as witness to others at the cost of the self. Here Dickinson verges toward gendered senses of selfhood as self-denial. Indeed, the self in this poem is deeply strained, as is the poem's poetic, stretching tensely between declaring and denying its own poetic venture. Here are poets who do not tell, painters who do not speak. The self is at once affirmed and negated, with a painfully high cost to the self in both its assertion and renunciation—a strain Dickinson dramatically enacted in her own refusals to publish, even while circulating and preserving her poems in letters and fascicles.[23] There is a terrible burden in these denials, a severe disjunction from the audience the poem yearningly addresses. Yet, for all Dickinson's solitude and self-veiling, the poem is placed resolutely in a place of exchange, addressing and bequeathing to others. Even the immortality of poetic fame remains grounded in the limited mortal self, in an art undertaken in service to others: to "encourage Some," to bequeath "their Work."

This poem does not speak of war but rather of peace, which emerges as a strange trope for or strangely implicating art. It seems a kind of space standing beyond the turmoil of the historical world, yet also in close relation to it.[24] As an "Art of Peace," poetry does not escape suffering but rather renders it "in syllable." Here a certain relation between art and war, between language and rupture, becomes suggested. At issue is the strained and extraordinarily disrupted textuality of Dickinson's poetry, which, as in "The Martyr Poets," so often stretches between utterance and revocation, assertion and denial, claim and disclaimer, in ways that penetrate every poetic element and indeed basic linguistic structure such as grammar and punctuation. These textual ruptures, I would venture, suggest a final implication of Dickinson's war poetry. Many have been struck by Dickinson's apparent modernity; by how her strained and difficult forms—at once contained with in and yet strenuously recasting hymnal meters and modes—seem to foreshadow the radical experimentation of twentieth-century poetics.[25] This homology seems to me rooted in the ways Dickinson's work represents an intersection between historical, metaphysical, and aesthetic forces when these are under extraordinary pressure, and specifically, when long-standing, traditional assumptions regarding the basic frameworks for interpreting the world are challenged to the point of breakage. Dickinson's work is among the first directly to register the effects on poetic language of such breakdown. Articulate language depends on, even as it expresses and projects, the ability to conceive reality as coherent and meaningful. Dickinson, like Nietzsche and increasing numbers of poets and writers from the late nineteenth into the twentieth century, makes this power of language to assert order, and this vulnerability to disorder, central to her aesthetic. As one critic writes of Gerard Manley Hopkins, when reality and paradigms for interpreting it seem secure, "language need not carry a very heavy burden. The greater encompassing harmony is preestablished, as it were. Call this harmony into question . . . and the burden on language immediately becomes greater. It has to exert itself to hold things together."[26] Such "splitting apart of the communion" between paradigm and world, metaphysics and history, marks modern experience.[27] It deeply penetrates Emily Dickinson's poetic language, where disjunction penetrates grammar and line, word and image, often setting each against the other in strained and contested utterance. The breaking apart of metaphysical confidence and model, as interpretive framework for explosive historical events, and in conditions of radically changing senses of society and self: all these come together in the exquisite, painful, and proleptic register of Dickinson's language and poetics.

This certainly was the impression of one of the twentieth century's most radical experimental poets, Paul Celan. Celan, a Jewish, German-speaking Holocaust poet, is removed from Dickinson in place, religion, gender, and historical moment. Nevertheless, he deeply recognized himself in her, as attested by his translations of her work. His renderings propose and disclose the mutual implication and dependence of metaphysical, historical, and linguistic experience projected in her writing. For Dickinson, the Civil War raised problems not unlike those Theodor Adorno ascribes to the Second World War: "Our metaphysical faculty is paralyzed because actual events have shattered the basis on which speculative metaphysical thought could be reconciled with experience."[28] What Dickinson's work reveals and dramatizes are the consequences of such paralysis and assault on the very structure and language of poetry.

Emily Dickinson's texts are battlefields between contesting claims of self and community, private and public interest, event and design, metaphysics and history, with each asserted, often against the other. The contest finally penetrates the very construction of her poems, in their contentious image systems, their ambivalent and conflicting stances, their complicating grammar, and strained, often disjunctive language. And it penetrates into her sense of herself as poet, her role and vocation, and the very possibility of expression. Sequestered in her home, refusing to publish, bounded by gender roles that conventionally forbade her a direct representative or public position (although also under contest during her period), Dickinson nevertheless not only explores her world in her work but also addresses it. Dickinson's poems of war are never poems only about a specific historical event. They always reach into figural spaces beyond any immediate referent. At the same time, to deny them historical reference is to deny them, and to deny her, that representative status of speaking to and for others in a mere poetic of isolation. In the context of war, her poetry emerges as scenes not only of personal conflict but also confronting the most imperative concerns of her—and our—culture, in a poetics of contest and strain and concealment, but also of address and courage and revelation.

NOTES

Dickinson's poems are quoted from *The Poems of Emily Dickinson: Variorum Edition*, ed. R. W. Franklin, 3 vols. (Cambridge, Mass.: Harvard University Press, 1998). I also supply their Johnson numbers from *The Poems of Emily Dickinson, Including Variant Readings Critically Compared with All Known Manuscripts*, ed. Thomas H. Johnson (Cambridge, Mass.: Harvard University Press, 1955). Subsequent references are cited as (J) and (Fr) in the text.

Dickinson letters are quoted from *The Letters of Emily Dickinson*, ed. Thomas H. Johnson and Theodora Ward, 3 vols. (Cambridge, Mass.: Harvard University Press, 1958). Subsequent references are cited as (L) in the text.

1. Emerson, "The Poet," in *Selections from Ralph Waldo Emerson*, ed. Stephen Whicher (New York: Riverside, 1957): pp. 222–240, 223.

2. For discussion of Tocqueville's image and an overview of the separate spheres, see Linda Kerber, "Separate Spheres, Female Worlds, Woman's Place: The Rhetoric of Women's History," *Journal of American History*, 75 no. 1 (June 1988): pp. 9–39.

3. Harold Bloom, "The Central Man: Emerson, Whitman, Stevens," *The Ringers in the Tower* (Chicago: University of Chicago Press, 1971): pp. 217–234. Bloom, of course, is quite conscious of the gender-implications of central manhood, and purposively includes Dickinson in the category.

4. I review these and other historical connections more fully in *Emily Dickinson: A Voice of War* (New Haven: Yale University Press, 1984).

5. For fuller discussion, see Wolosky, "Public Women, Private Men," *Signs*, 28, no. 2 (Winter 2003): pp. 665–694.

6. See, for example, Vivian Pollak, "Dickinson and the Poetics of Whiteness," *The Emily Dickinson Journal*, 9, no. 2 (2000): pp. 84–95; Daneen Wardrop, "The minute Domingo': Dickinson's Cooptation of Abolitionist Diction and Franklin's Variorum Edition," *The Emily Dickinson Journal*, 8, no. 2 (1999): pp. 72–86; Domhnall Mitchell, "Northern Lights: Class, Color, Culture, and Emily Dickinson," *The Emily Dickinson Journal*, 9, no. 2 (2000): pp. 75–84. See also below note 22 on Critanne Miller.

7. See Wolosky, *Poetry and Public Disclosure*, vol. 4 of *The Cambridge History of American Literature*, ed. Sacvan Bercovitch (New York: Cambridge University Press, forthcoming).

8. This is in contrast with, for example, Thomas Ford's early, and for long unique, article on "Emily Dickinson and the Civil War," *University Review of Kansas City*, 31 (Spring 1965), which estimates four poems as directly deriving from the war (199).

9. Cf. Letter 712, in (L 3:701).

10. For one treatment, see Ernest Lee Tuveson, *Redeemer Nation*, (Chicago: University of Chicago Press, 1968).

11. Jay Leyda, *The Years and Hours of Emily Dickinson*, 2 vols. (New Haven: Yale University Press,1960), I, p. 333.

12. "Proclamation for Thanksgiving, Oct. 3, 1863," *Selected Writings and Speeches of Abraham Lincoln*, ed. T Harry Williams (New York: Hendricks House, 1980): p. 228.

13. George Fredrickson, *The Inner Civil War* (New York: Harper Torchbooks, 1968): pp. 79–80.

14. Dickinson here stands in contrast with, for example, Timrod and Lanier, James Russell Lowell and Longfellow, Julia Ward Howe and Helen Hunt Jackson, as well as the countless versifiers collected in *The Rebellion Record* or, more recently, in Alice Fahs, *The Imagined Civil War: Popular Literature of the North and South, 1861–1865* (Chapel Hill: University of North Carolina Press, 2001). Whitman reserves his skepticisms mainly for the postwar period.

15. Sacvan Bercovitch, *Puritan Origins of the American Self* (New Haven: Yale University Press, 1975), as well as his subsequent works: *The American Jeremiad* (Madison: University of Wisconsin Press, 1978) and *The Rites of Assent* (New York: Routledge, 1993).

16. Quoted in Polly Longsworth, "Brave among the Bravest: Amherst in the Civil War," *Amherst Journal* (Summer 1999): pp. 25–31, 28.

17. See Margaret Randolph Higonnet, ed., *Behind the Lines: Gender and the Two World Wars* (New Haven: Yale University Press, 1987), for discussion of the effects and complexities of women as (seen as) removed from battle.

18. C. P. Macpherson, *The Political Theory of Possessive Individualism* (London: Oxford University Press, 1962).

19. An enormous literature exists in political theory on this topic. See especially, works by Carole Pateman and Susan Moller Okin. Also Wolosky, "Public Women, Private Men," in note 5 above.

20. See Wolosky, "North and South," in note 7 above. *James McPherson's Battle Cry of Freedom* (New York: Oxford University Press, 1988) makes the differing senses of this crucial term a broad context for discussing the war.

21. Abraham Lincoln, *The Political Thought of Abraham Lincoln*, ed. Richard Current (Indianapolis: Bobbs–Merrill, 1967): p. 181.

22. This poem is elaborated in Cristanne Miller's thoughtful discussion on the term "liberty" in Dickinson and her surrounding culture, "Pondering 'Liberty': Emily Dickinson and the Civil War," *American Vistas and Beyond: A Festschrift for Roland Hagenbuchle,* ed. Marietta Messmer and Josef Raab (Trier, Germany: Wissenschafflicher Verlag, 2002).

23. In my own view, Dickinson, on the one hand, dreaded publication as an exposure that both her gender roles and her personal sensibility prohibited (and lacking, as mentioned above, both the economic reasons that motivated or allowed publishing by other women, as well as other such contexts, such as religious calling or political activism). On the other hand, I believe Dickinson believed in her gift as a poet, that she imagined her sister finding her carefully preserved texts as well as their eventual publication through the coterie she had created among highly literary correspondents such as Thomas Wentworth Higginson, as indeed occurred. Her deadline was not publication but immortality. Again, one recalls Whitman with his ventriloquist addresses to his future readers. Dickinson's relationship to audience is, I feel, deeply inscribed in her acts of writing, her self-conception as a poet and woman poet, the way her texts are constituted, even without her directly addressing an immediate concrete audience through publication.

24. There are, in fact, scattered references in Dickinson to "peace" in ways that seem to oppose it to war, as in the poem "I many times thought Peace had come" (J 739 / Fr 737), dated 1863.

25. On hymns, see Wolosky, "Rhetoric or Not: Emily Dickinson and Isaac Watts," *The New England Quarterly,* 61, no. 2 (June 1988): pp. 214–232; and Cristanne Miller, *Emily Dickinson: A Poet's Grammar* (Cambridge, Mass.: Harvard University Press, 1988).

26. Sigurd Burkhardt, "Poetry and the Language of Communion," in *Hopkins: Twentieth Century Views,* ed. Geoffrey Hartman (Englewood Cliffs, NJ.: Prentice Hall, 1966): p. 163.

27. J. Hillis Miller, *The Disappearance of God* (Cambridge, Mass.: Harvard University Press, 1963): p. 3.

28. T. W. Adorno, *Negative Dialectics* (London: Routledge & Kegan Paul, 1973): p. 361. I have discussed Dickinson and Celan in my unpublished dissertation, devoted to his translations of her work (Princeton University, 1982). See also Wolosky, *Language Mysticism* (Stanford: Stanford University Press, 1995); Wolosky, "Apophatics and Poetics: Paul Celan Translating Emily Dickinson," in *Language and Negativity,* ed. Henny Fiska Hagg (Oslo: Novus Press, 2000): pp. 63–84; and Wolosky, "The Metaphysics of Language in Emily Dickinson" (as Translated by Paul Celan)," in *Trajectories of Mysticism in Theory and Literature,* ed. Philip Leonard (New York: St. Martin's Press, 2000): pp. 25–45.

DEIRDRE FAGAN

Emily Dickinson's Unutterable Word

It may be the hope of every poet to discover the one word that says it all, but for Emily Dickinson, the dash—invariably ambiguous, often inscrutable—comes close to the all-inclusive unutterable word. She confesses in a poem, "I found the words to every thought / I ever had – but One –" (Fr436) and we consider whether in Dickinson the dash represents, in Beckett's phrase, "Literatur des Unworts" (a literature of the unword) (Disjecta 54).

The handwritten dash has sometimes been referred to as a stroke of thought. Certainly there can be nothing slap-dash about the characteristic Dickinson stroke of thought: her dashes appear to be quite deliberate. But these are not just thoughts; they are the physical manifestations of thoughts, and time and again the poet redirects us to what these strokes might represent. The dashes become a thread between the sayable and the unsayable, a caesura between life and death, a pause, a gasp, sometimes a chasm over which one must make a leap of understanding, all of which critics have pointed out. As a poet who demands much of her readers, Dickinson may also be said to use her dash to embody the role of the blank Scrabble piece, in that it mosaically takes on the position and fortitude the reader grants. Her dash is at once both reductive and encompassing, as is the best of her poetry.

Paul Crumbley, in *Inflections of the Pen: Dash and Voice in Emily Dickinson*, correctly observed that the dashes "disrupt" conventional thought pat-

Emily Dickinson Journal, Volume 14, No. 2 (Fall 2005): pp. 70–75. © The Johns Hopkins University Press.

terns and, in doing so, not only disrupt the thought pattern of the reader, but are strangely suggestive of the thought pattern of the poet (2). The point some other critics have made that such thought patterns on Dickinson's part could be indicative of a disrupted psyche seems far-fetched; there is little evidence that Dickinson's mind was anything but lucid. One considers, however, the possibility that the dash was simply a quirk, an absent-minded sort of twitch. Judith Farr pointed out that the dash was the most "used and abused" punctuation in the Victorian era (328). This might contribute to the possibility that Dickinson's use of it is not at all times as deliberate as it seems. While the dashes may appear to be intentional, given that they are a characteristic of Dickinson's poetry and prose, it is difficult to assign to them the depth of meaning one gives to the unconventional punctuation of other poets. When one thinks of Keats spending a day speculating whether to put a comma in or take a comma out, one is reminded of the precision of poets. But when one encounters Dickinson's copious dashes, one wonders how intentional the mark, at all times, could really be.

In his study of the manuscripts, Crumbley devised something of a translator's guide to the dash. He clarified the visual features of Dickinson's work in order to develop a system of analysis that illuminates shifts in voice. For this purpose he distinguished between various dashes in terms of length, height, and angle. While this is an intriguing approach and Crumbley draws some compelling conclusions, such visual attention to the dash would seem to suggest that Dickinson herself had such a guide, and that when she intended a dash to have a certain purpose, she was sure to use the "correct" dash to suggest as much. But no such notebook of dash translation is found among Dickinson's work, so one would have to resolve that dash "types" are something scholars have invented. Dickinson herself might have found these types surprising. As Timothy Morris points out in his piece on "The Development of Dickinson's Style":

> The state of Dickinson's surviving manuscripts confirms [a] picture of her as an inward-directed artist. There are no prose jottings on the construction of poems, no notebooks on art. We have no idea what her philosophy of composition was. We know that she revised carefully, sometimes taking great pains to find the right word. But she left no explicit clue to her creative process. (28)

When we are writing and use a dash ourselves, we hardly take a ruler to the task. Ask me to write a sentence twenty times, each time with a dash included, and I'm certain that at least a fair variety of heights, lengths, and angles would be found. While dashes seem to have undeniable significance in much of Dickinson's work, *how* they appear on the page seems to have little, as Cristanne Miller has suggested in *A Poet's Grammar* (50–53).

Crumbley notes at the start of his book that all the upward- and downward
-slanting marks are angled at twenty degrees, "not because Dickinson's angles
were uniform but because this angle fairly reflects the visual character of her
multiple angles." It seems, however, that the meaning of the dash, while various and eccentric, is not necessarily found in the slanting or length of a line,
but rather in that it appears at all. No word, however pervasive in Dickinson's
poems or letters, appears more often than her signature dash. Because of its
thousands of appearances, one can infer without careful study that the dash
did not have the same significance, relevance, or intentionality in each case.
Nor was Dickinson so focused on length and height as to be consistent in her
use of the dash each time she wrote a poem or letter. Indeed, her penmanship
was not very strong at a time when such a skill was prized, and it seems unlikely that she would have taken greater care with her dashes, a form of punctuation, than with her longhand. The amplitude of the dash is clear, then, but
its role is ambiguous. What must be determined is how important the dash is
to a study of Dickinson and, even more timely, whether the manuscripts are
important to any understanding of the dash at all.

It may be argued in certain instances that the dash is used for clarifica-
tion, either for the writer or the reader—a place where, rather than raising
her pen, Dickinson let it slide in contemplation and reflection. But this only
simplifies the other instances when its importance becomes undeniable, say,
for example, when she chooses to end a poem with a typically ambiguous
dash—as she does in "Because I could not stop for Death –" (Fr479) or "I saw
no Way   The Heavens were stitched –" (Fr633) or "I felt a Funeral, in my
Brain" (Fr 340)—as though to suggest that the poem has no end at all. The
punch of the dash, in these instances, comes from *where* the dash appears,
not from its shape. It is moments such as these that present readers with an
interpretive challenge.

However clever Dickinson was, her electric intellect consistently faced
an enormous task: finding precisely the right word to say all that she had to
say. While this is the quest of every poet, language often eludes when the unutterable intrudes. In Dickinson, the unutterable is represented by the dash.
To assert that the dash is often indicative of shifts in voice is to suggest that
the dash is not only used fairly consistently for similar purposes, but that it
can, in an important sense, speak. Yet the dash is silent. Even when it may
be indicative of a shift in voice, the disjunction can come from the dash itself, rather than from its form. The dash's capacity as punctuation is limited,
and its possibilities for meaning are forever obscured by its wordlessness. The
potency of the dash remains, nonetheless, and becomes, cataclysmically and
without words, emotion both expressed and unexpressed.

Steven Monte calls unarticulated ideas and emotions "embryonic words"
as they are "neither fully part of us nor fully developed," and it is to this em-

bryonic nature that I allude. He further argues that "focusing on the hand-written word . . . tends to privilege the poetry's appearance on the page over the sound the verse makes in the ear or the mind" (22). And Margaret Dickie reminded us that "concentrating on the paper, the script, the punctuation of Dickinson's manuscripts will take her work back to the point at which her sister, Lavinia, discovered the fascicles and from which every editor since Mabel Loomis Todd has tried to rescue her" (322). Take the words out and leave the dashes, and we haven't any poem. Take the dashes out and leave the words, and we have a poem that misses its mark. Put the dashes in, whether long or short, high or low, slanting upward or downward, and we discover an enigmatic poetic device that stands for every word and no word at once. It is the abyss that Dickinson emerges from and enters again and again, as she suggests in a letter to Susan: "Emerging from an Abyss and reentering it – that is Life, is it not?" (L1024).

Octavio Paz argues that "The poet makes a word of everything he touches, not excluding silence and the blanks in the text" (260). Dickinson expresses herself through silence. She anticipates the symbolist poets: a symbolist poem suggests, rather than defines, meaning. Dickinson describes her silence as one that she endures:

> There is no Silence in the Earth – so silent
> As that endured
> Which uttered, would discourage Nature
> And haunt the world –   (Fr1004)

Dickinson's silences do haunt: "Nature is a Haunted House – but Art – a House that tries to be haunted" (L459A). When she "only said the Syntax – / And left the Verb and pronoun – out –" (Fr277), she had the ability to haunt, almost more than with what she said. Robert Weisbuch wrote that the reader "must leave" Dickinson as "she rushes to and past the 'Dip of bell' where syllable grows into silence and the language ends" (177). Follow the dash beyond the dip of bell and we may find the all-inclusive unutterable word.

Dickinson's poetry is not comprised of one-sided singularity. She offers the dash as a space for the reader, but her poetry resists "meaning," or at least the sort of meaning that is so obvious it omits all other meaning. Crumbley rightly points out that "Dickinson's poems do not tell us as readers we must resist the impulse to locate specific, unified meanings; rather, the poems celebrate the positive pull toward unity by positioning it in the context of opposing impulses." And that, "Dickinson's writing consistently foregrounds the reader's choices, making it clear that any delight her poems afford is in some sense the product of negotiating tensions" (3). With the dash, the meaning lies in the absence; the meaning is what neither we, nor she, can know, but that the dash invites us to seek. Or as Gary Lee Stonum puts it: "meaning lies . . . only until it is securely or confidently grasped" (38). For Dickinson it lies in the abyss, and the poems become the only manual Dickinson left us on how to read the dashes, and the dashes the only manual on how to read the poems. For example, the dash appears as a thread that both joins and separates in the poem "From Blank to Blank –" (Fr484), where Dickinson speaks of a "Threadless Way." The "to" between the blanks is the thread between them. In "How the old Mountains drip with Sunset" (Fr327) the poetry is the dome that captures the reader; the dash indicates that the abyss lies within. In "Behind Me – dips Eternity –" (Fr743), where Dickinson posits herself as "– the Term between –," the dash functions as a caesura between life and death.

George Whicher once said: "Strictly speaking, the only adequate poem on the unknowable would consist of a blank sheet of paper" (298). Short of that, in Dickinson we get the dash as what she can and cannot say, of what can and cannot be said, of the thoughts and emotions for which we have no words. One is reminded of Wittgenstein's *Tractatus* in this regard: "Whereof one cannot speak, thereof one must remain silent" (31).

Dickinson's dashes insist on an audience, one "at its rare best," as Harold Bloom has put it, and one she never really had (296). Weisbuch wrote that Dickinson feared that the "demands of composition" would "limit the scope and obscure the outline of an individual thought," and it appears she utilized the dash as a way to resist such a limitation (12). As John Schmit advocated, "[e]veryone who reads Dickinson's poetry must eventually find the page she never wrote" (10). This is our task as critics and readers of her work—a task Dickinson did intentionally leave for us.

In the distant past, editors took liberties with Dickinson's dash; now it seems that theories of the dash have the potential to inhibit the poems in a similar way. If we are to embrace visual analysis, we need strong justification for its plausibility. In much the same way earlier that "revisions" of Dickinson's work interfered with understanding them, so might an over-reliance on manuscript study. Concern with the manuscripts seems to be more indicative of how literary theory looks at poetry in general than a specific revelation about the intentions of Emily Dickinson. Ultimately the manuscripts have little relevance to an understanding of Dickinson's use of the dash. It seems rather that this bounteous mark of punctuation, her signature mark as a poet, matters because it exists, not because of how it looks. The dash may simply have been a twitch of sorts, but if so, it is one she attempted many times to control, just as she sought to control everything else in her life. She made use of her twitch, demonstrating its significance clearly on certain occasions and not so clearly on others, and wanted us to make use of it as well. To suggest that it had the same sort of intentionality as her words, however, is to make meaning where even Dickinson herself can be found speechless.

WORKS CITED

The following abbreviations are used to refer to the writings of Emily Dickinson:

Fr *The Poems of Emily Dickinson.* Ed. R.W. Franklin. 3 vols. Cambridge, MA: Harvard UP, 1998. Citation by poem number.

L *The Letters of Emily Dickinson.* Ed. Thomas H. Johnson and Theodora Ward. 3 vols. Cambridge, MA: Harvard UP, 1958. Citation by letter number.

Beckett, Samuel. *Disjecta: Miscellaneous Writings and a Dramatic Fragment.* Ed. Ruby Cohn. New York: Grove Press, 1984.

Bloom, Harold. *The Western Canon.* New York: Harcourt, 1994.

Crumbley, Paul. *Inflections of the Pen: Dash and Voice in Emily Dickinson.* Lexington: University of Kentucky Press, 1997.

Dickie, Margaret. "Dickinson in Context." *American Literary History* 7.2 (1995): pp. 320–333.

Farr, Judith. *The Passion of Emily Dickinson.* Cambridge, MA: Harvard University Press, 1992.

Miller, Cristanne. *A Poet's Grammar.* Cambridge, MA: Harvard University Press, 1987.

Morris, Timothy. "The Development of Dickinson's Style." *American Literature* 60.1 (1988): pp. 26–41.

Monte, Steven. "Dickinson's Searching Philology." *Emily Dickinson Journal* 12.2 (2003): pp. 21–51.

Paz, Octavio. *The Bow and the Lyre: The Poem, the Poetic Revelation, Poetry and History.* Trans. Ruth L. C. Simms. Austin: University of Texas Press, 1991.

Schmit, John. "'I Only Said – the Syntax –': Elision, Recoverability, and Insertion in Emily Dickinson's Poetry." *Style* 27.1 (1993): pp. 106–124.

Stonum, Gary Lee. *The Dickinson Sublime.* Madison: University of Wisconsin Press, 1990.

Weisbuch, Robert. *Emily Dickinson's Poetry.* Chicago: University of Chicago Press, 1972.

Wittgenstein, Ludwig. "Tractatus Logico-Philosophicus." *The Wittgenstein Reader.* Ed. Anthony Kenny. Oxford: Blackwell, 1994.

Whicher, George. *This was a Poet: A Critical Biography of Emily Dickinson.* Ann Arbor: University of Michigan Press, 1957.

JAY LADIN

Meeting Her Maker: Emily Dickinson's God

It's common for secular academics to assume that religious belief—adherence to any religious system or ideology—is fundamentally at odds with the open-minded, exploratory enterprise of critical interpretation. That was certainly my assumption two autumns ago, when, as a new member of the English Department of the women's college of an Orthodox Jewish university, I led a seminar-style exploration of Emily Dickinson's poems about God. The question of Dickinson's religious beliefs—what, if any, beliefs she held and what, if anything, her poems reveal of them—has long been a subject of debate among Dickinson scholars. As I expected, the question was of great interest to my students, who had grown up practicing a modern Orthodox form of Judaism. What I did not expect was that these young women, who knew little about poetry, less about Dickinson, and nothing about Christianity or its nineteenth-century New England manifestations, would see so clearly through the tangle of Dickinson's contradictory portrayals of God and the equally contradictory conclusions scholars have drawn from them. I had assumed that the intellectual habits promoted by traditional religious belief and humanistic inquiry are inherently at odds, that while humanism encourages the exploration of complexity and contradiction, traditional belief encourages the opposite—simplification, homogenization, retreat from the messiness of existence into the comfort of tautological pro-

Cross Currents, Volume 56, Issue 3 (Fall 2006): pp. 338–346. Copyright © 2006 Association for Religion and Intellectual Life.

jection. But rather than inhibiting their ability to engage with Dickinson's challenging texts, my students' lifelong immersion in Orthodox Judaism helped them recognize dynamics at work in Dickinson's poems about God that my secular approach had obscured.

One of the nice things about teaching is the way it transforms vexing scholarly uncertainties into signs of professorial sophistication. Rather than feeling anxious that I didn't know the answers to the questions I was raising, I felt quite pleased to introduce the subject of Dickinson's religious beliefs by informing my class that scholars had been utterly unable to agree on them. For example, while Dorothy Oberhaus has argued that Dickinson wrote "in the poetic tradition of Christian devotion," Richard Wilbur and many others since have seen Dickinson's poems as expressions of an idiosyncratic, home-made relation to religious belief—what Wilbur calls "a precarious convergence between her inner experience and her religious inheritance" (Farr 105, 54). Other readers, focusing on Dickinson's most iconoclastic texts, see Dickinson as radically challenging Christianity and indeed all religious belief. This extraordinary range of opinions as to what Dickinson believed—and the abundance of textual evidence to support each of them—has prompted many scholars to adopt what we might call an agnostic attitude toward Dickinson's beliefs. As Denis Donoghue put it, "of her religious faith virtually anything may be said. She may be represented as an agnostic, a heretic, a skeptic, a Christian" (quoted in Yezzi 20). Wary that my students might simplify Dickinson's beliefs by filtering her contradictions through the lens of their own faith, I presented Donoghue-style agnosticism as the only intellectually responsible position possible—that is, the only position that confronted the entire range of beliefs presented in Dickinson's poems. To demonstrate Dickinson's irresolvable religious contradictions, I started my students off with poems that present completely incommensurate representations of God: the amputated absentee of "Those – dying then"; the withholding parent of the poem that begins "Of Course – I prayed – / And did God Care?"; the outgrown childhood God of "I prayed, at first, a little Girl"; the faceless, dematerialized "Infinitude" of "My period had come for Prayer"; the Disneyesque savior of vermin addressed in the poem that begins "Papa above! / Regard a Mouse / O'erpowered by the Cat!" No one, I assured them, could infer a coherent idea of God from this blizzard of conflicting evidence.

My students dutifully jotted down my words, relieved no doubt that I was excusing them from at least one measure of responsibility for understanding a poet they found so difficult. Having saved them from the humanistic equivalent of Original Sin—belief in absolute interpretation—I set my students to working their way through the poems line by line. They chose to begin with "Of Course – I prayed":

Of Course – I prayed –
And did God Care?
He cared as much as on the Air
A Bird – had stamped her foot –
And cried "Give Me" –
My Reason – Life –
I had not had – but for Yourself –
'Twere better Charity
To leave me in the Atom's Tomb –
Merry, and Nought, and gay, and numb –
Than this smart Misery.

At first we focused on grammar rather than theology. My students were baffled by the radical shifts in tone and perspective in the long sentence—or is it a sentence?—that begins "He cared as much as on the Air" and either concludes with "'Give Me,'" or with "Life." Or, since "My Reason – Life" can be read both as the end of the thought ("'Give Me' – / My Reason – Life") that begins the poem or the beginning of the thought that ends the poem, perhaps the sentence never really concludes at all. They were fascinated to discover that Dickinson uses this Moebius-strip-like syntax—an inelegant version of the technique Cristanne Miller calls "syntactical doubling"—to seamlessly shift from the melodramatic rage of the opening lines to the John Donne-like intellectual complaint of the last.

Once my students recognized that the poem represented two distinct attitudes, they began to find it easier to understand. Having themselves wrestled with God as both an inconsistent source of blessings and as the ultimate guarantor of the meaning of their lives, they found the opening lines' rage at God's refusal to respond to prayer quite familiar. For them, these lines were dramatizing a childish, egocentric relation to God, in which God is seen purely as a function of one's own needs. The end of the poem, they saw, was a more adult, intellectualized version of the same relationship. Though they weren't sure of the speaker's sincerity in stating that she would rather have been left in "the Atom's Tomb" as uncreated matter, they understood that God's unresponsiveness had provoked the speaker to question the value of consciousness.

Having identified both parts of the poems as forms of rage at God for failing to respond to prayer, my students found themselves back at the question of syntax. What, they wondered, was the relationship between these very different attitudes toward God? Why did Dickinson fudge the syntactical boundaries that would normally enable us to clearly distinguish them? Though they still couldn't figure out the sentence, they began to see that the defective syntax embodied a deeper problem: the difficulty, for the speaker and for anyone engaged in a serious practice of prayer, of separating the psychological from the theological. That is, the blurred syntax reflects the difficulty of distinguishing between subjective rage at a God who fails to personally respond to prayer, and the objective questions, such as the nature of God or the value of human existence, that Divine non-responsiveness raises. Perhaps, they speculated, the defective syntax was Dickinson's way of emphasizing the underlying similarity of these two very different theological tantrums.

I had guided my students through the syntactical issues raised by the poem, but to my astonishment, my students' discussion of its content had changed my own reading of the poem. Before our discussion, I read "Of Course – I prayed" as a deliberately incoherent critique of God. Now I saw it as a trenchant critique of an "immature" relation to God and prayer whose symptoms could range from childish rage to Metaphysical wit to a profound rejection of human existence.

I was both delighted by my students' ability to connect Dickinson's work to their personal experiences, and startled by the effectiveness of that connection. Rather than oversimplifying the complexities of the text, reading Dickinson through the lens of their religious experience had made my students more effective, subtler readers than they would have been had they adopted the humanist framework I offered them.

A fluke, I told myself. My students had transformed my reading of "Of Course – I Prayed," but my overall sense of Dickinson's indeterminate religious belief—a claim based not on individual poems, but on her work as a whole—was still unchallenged. Thus, it was not without a certain eagerness that I turned discussion to "Those – dying then," a poem whose "Nietzschean post-Christianity," as David Yezzi puts it, would demonstrate the essential instability of Dickinson's religious beliefs:

> Those – dying then,
> Knew where they went –
> They went to God's Right Hand –
> That Hand is amputated now
> And God cannot be found.
>
> The abdication of Belief
> Makes the Behavior small –
> Better an ignis fatuus
> Than no illume at all.

After the syntactical mishmash of "Of Course – I prayed," my students had little difficulty fleshing out the compressed spiritual history presented in the first stanza. "Those . . . then," they saw, referred to an earlier time, when belief in God and the afterlife was far more firmly and generally established. They also recognized the epistemological shadings in the stanza's phrasing—that is, that rather than making a statement about the actual organization of life, death and eternity, the statement that "Those dying then / Knew" they were headed to "God's Right Hand" was describing "Their" beliefs. With this understanding, it was easy for my students to see through the shock of the imagery of the amputated "Right Hand" to the deeper shock of moving from a description of beliefs (what "They" used to believe) to a statement of ontological fact (what God is now). They saw that, like the defective syntax in "Of Course – I prayed," this shock raises but does not answer the question of the relation between human belief and the nature of reality—whether the decay of human belief in some way led to God's amputated "abdication," or, conversely, whether "Those – dying then" were simply shielded by their belief from the harsh realities the last lines of the stanza assert.

This of course was the very sort of "Nietzschean post-Christian" perspective I wanted my students to glean from the poem, and I rather smugly pointed out that the vision of God this stanza presented was utterly unlike the God about whom the frustrated speaker of "Of Course – I prayed" complains. While the speaker of the first poem blames God for failure to respond, the second poem's image of God's amputated hand suggests a deity who is powerless to respond. Obviously, I concluded, the poems represent different theological universes—and demonstrate the inconsistency of Dickinson's beliefs.

Here, however, my students balked. Both poems, they argued, represent different takes on the same fundamental problem: the difficulty of establishing a relationship with God. One student startled me by pointing out that the statement "That Hand is amputated now" presents God's existence as ontological fact rather than simply a matter of belief. While the statement can certainly be read figuratively, as a metaphor for Divine ineffectuality in the face of modernity, it also presents a vividly physical image of God—an image that emphasizes rather than undercuts the sense of God's existence. They also challenged my claim that the poem's second stanza represents a Wallace Stevens-type assertion that humans need "supreme fictions" such as belief in God, even when we know they are fictions. Rather, they argued, the leap from "God cannot be found" to "The abdication of belief" suggests that God's absence may be a sign of human dereliction of duty (the peculiar verb "abdication" implicitly equates human "Belief" with royal obligation). Just because God "cannot be found," they said, doesn't mean that God is not there; after all, Jews have wrestled for millennia with the question of how human beings should respond to the "hiddenness" of God at times of personal and collective suffering. From their perspective, the second stanza laments not the absence of God but human acceptance of God's absence.

Though I insisted on the ambiguous relation between the stanzas, I could not escape the sense that my students were right: even here, at her most apparently nihilistic, Dickinson's poetry evinced a passionate engagement with God, an engagement that affirmed God's existence and importance even as it fretted or raged over God's inaccessibility.

My students had opened my eyes to the superabundance of evidence of Dickinson's relationship to God—evidence so strong that it appears to rule out the idea that Dickinson was an "agnostic" or a "skeptic." Though Dickinson wrote deeply skeptical poems, as my students demonstrated with regard to "Those – dying then," even these poems can be understood as reflecting a tumultuous but clearly ongoing relationship to God. Robert Frost, who wrote some of the bleakest verses ever penned in English, claimed he had a lover's quarrel with life. My students convinced me that the same could be said of Dickinson and God. Like Frost's quarrel with life, Dickinson's quarrel with God reflects the full panoply of human disaffection. But though Dickinson's God rarely seems to make her happy, she never breaks off the affair, never rejects the idea that, however incompatible we may be, human and Divine are made for each other.

Once I accepted my students' contention that Dickinson's belief in God was neither contradictory nor inconsistent, I also found myself agreeing that the nature of Dickinson's relationship to God was not, as I had insisted, "indeterminate." The relation to God my students found in Dickinson's poems is both simpler and more complex than most critical accounts suggest. Rather than contradictory religious beliefs, they recognized in her rhetoric and imagery a core assumption of God's existence—an assumption that underwrites and gives rise to a range of challenges and pleas. For them, what is at stake in Dickinson's religious poems is not God's existence, but God's accessibility, responsiveness, accountability, comprehensibility, and concern for the human condition.

From my students' perspective, the baffling array of religious attitudes Dickinson portrays in her poems reflect a clear, coherent and—to young women born along the fault-line between traditional religious belief and American modernity—quite familiar spiritual struggle. As a longtime ponderer of Dickinson's highly theatrical poses, I realized that I found her relationship to God familiar in a different way. Dickinson adopts a similar variety of moods and roles in her letters. For example, in her famous correspondence with Thomas Wentworth Higginson, Dickinson shuttles from flirt to adoring "scholar," condescending epigrammatist to eyelash-batting naïf. As in so many of the relationships she carried on via written language, Dickinson ceaselessly reinvented herself and her relationship to God. The list of Dickinson's theological poses is nearly as long as the list of her God-related poems: the lisping child of "I never felt at Home – Below" who anticipates wanting to run away from "Paradise" because "it's Sunday – all the time – / And Recess – never comes"; the beset but endearing rodent of "Papa above!"; the ontological adventurer of "My Period had come – for Prayer," who travels "Vast Prairies of Air" in an effort to face the ultimately faceless "Infinitude"; the sardonic skeptic of the poem that begins "It's easy to invent a Life / God does it – every Day." As in her letters, in her poems about God, Dickinson—or her alter egos—wheels from dominance to submission, from childish directness to arch sophistication, from loneliness to love.

In fact, the more closely one compares Dickinson's poems about God to her letters to acquaintances, the more typical of Dickinson her relationship with God seems. Both the poems and letters express an insatiable need for a level of response Dickinson's addressees rarely seem to supply. And in both poems and letters, whatever posture Dickinson adopts in her protean playacting, as my students noted, the focus, the drama, centers ultimately on her rather than her addressee, who recedes, despite the speaker's rhetorical grasping, into a life beyond her ken.

Perhaps that recession was the point of Dickinson's posturing. Though God and the others she engaged so passionately through her words always seem to fail her, their very distance secured the integrity of the self Dickinson kept so closely guarded. Many of Dickinson's religious poems dramatize her fear that God, unlike her human correspondents, would prove too present, too perceptive, too insistent to evade. The childish speaker of "I never felt at Home – Below," for example, worries that God, "a Telescope // Perennial beholds us." This nightmarish (for the reclusive Dickinson, at least) vision of an All-Seeing God obsessed with eyeing any soul foolish enough to attempt to hide itself rises to a pitch of post-Puritan paranoia in "Of Consciousness, her awful mate," which envisions a God as inescapable as consciousness itself, whose "Eyes" are "triple Lenses" that "burn" through any attempt at anonymity.

My students readily grasped Dickinson's rage at God's silence or absence; such feelings are common aspects of religious engagement. But as religious people focused on seeking rather than evading God, and as young women focused more on finding life partners than on maintaining personal boundaries, they found it difficult to understand Dickinson's horror of God's "triple lenses." A lifelong relationship involves endless negotiations over intrusiveness and distance, power and impotence, but even during the most difficult periods, there are moments when a couple's eyes will meet, and each will recognize the other and the difficult bond they share. For Dickinson and God, this moment seems to have come when both found themselves stranded face to face between Earth and Heaven, Eternity and Time:

> It was too late for Man –
> But early, yet, for God –
> Creation – impotent to help –
> But Prayer – remained – Our Side –
>
> How excellent the Heaven –
> When Earth – cannot be had –
> How hospitable – then – the face
> Of our Old Neighbor – God –

My students' readings of Dickinson's relationship to her "Old neighbor – God" do not constitute a conclusive account of her religious thought. But they do expose the fallacy of assumptions about the inherent intellectual limitations of religious belief. Rather than preventing my students from engaging with complexity, their beliefs helped them discern complexities I had sought to blend into the all-embracing, post-modernist vanilla of indeterminacy. For my students, as for Dickinson, religious belief is not a static answer but a lifelong pursuit of the most difficult existential questions, a pursuit that makes them supremely sensitive to the nuances and contradictions of the human effort to engage with that which is beyond us.

Works Cited

Dickinson, Emily, *The Complete Poems of Emily Dickinson*. Ed. Thomas H. Johnson. NY: Little, Brown, 1960.

Farr, Judith. *Emily Dickinson: A Collection of Critical Essays*. NY: Prentice Hall, 1995.

Yezzi, David. "Straying Close to Home: Author/Poet Emily Dickinson's Religious Beliefs and Spirituality," *Commonweal*, 125, Issue 17 (9 October, 1998): pp. 20–21.

JOHN FELSTINER

"Earth's Most Graphic Transaction": The Syllables of Emily Dickinson

"Emily was my patron saint," said William Carlos Williams. This essay comes from the manuscript of So Much Depends: Poetry and Environmental Urgency, *a field guide or handbook for the common reader. Essays on Williams and John Clare run in the January/February issue. Four more drawn from the 43 in this book—on Millay, Swenson, Haines, and again Williams—will appear in* APR *during 2007. My aim throughout this series is to face a crying need of our time by bringing alive the environmental imprint and impetus in familiar and surprising poems.*

"If I read a book and it makes my whole body so cold no fire ever can warm me I know I *that* is poetry. If I feel physically as if the top of my head were taken off, I know *that* is poetry. These are the only way I know it. Is there any other way." This could be William Blake in delirium, or Sylvia Plath, but not the "Belle of Amherst," as she once jokingly called herself, Emily Dickinson (1830–1886). In 1870 she gave her sense of poetry to Thomas Wentworth Higginson, man of letters, former Unitarian minister, champion of women's rights, and gun-running abolitionist who'd led the Union Army's first Negro regiment. After meeting the poet, the Civil War hero told his wife: "I never was with any one who drained my nerve power so much."

They'd corresponded for years, since 1862 when out of the blue, Dickinson sent him four poems, asking "Are you too deeply occupied to say if

The American Poetry Review, Volume 36, Number 2; (7–11 March/April 2007). © American Poetry Review.

my Verse is alive?," because "Should you think it breathed,. . . . I should feel quick gratitude." Higginson wrote back asking for a picture, and her response let him see an uncommon spirit: "I had no portrait, now, but am small, like the wren, and my Hair is bold, like the Chestnut bur—and my eyes, like the Sherry in the Glass, that the guest leaves—Would this do just as well?" A wren's small quickness, bold burr-like hair, and sherry eyes already seem vivid and peculiar. But sherry "that the guest leaves"? This signals a very rare bird.

About her writing experience, she also replied elusively (and slipping, as it happens, into her habitual four-beat three-beat iambic measure): "I made no verse, but one or two—until this winter—Sir." In fact she'd written almost 300 lyrics by then, including these lines transplanting the Holy Trinity into her garden: "In the name of the Bee— / And of the Butterfly—And of the Breeze—Amen!" Dickinson tells her mentor that her family are all religious "except me—and address an Eclipse, every morning—whom they call their 'Father'." And in this letter: "You speak of Mr. Whitman. I never read his Book—but was told that he was disgraceful."

Even before striking up a correspondence with T. W. Higginson, Dickinson had seen his judgment on poetic eccentricity: "It is no discredit to Walt Whitman that he wrote 'Leaves of Grass,' only that he did not burn it afterwards. A young writer must commonly plough in his first crop." She herself was nothing if not eccentric, and Higginson was unequipped to see how these audacious midcentury poets, like Hawthorne and Melville in the novel and Thoreau in the essay, were breaking new ground for American writing.

Emily Dickinson in Amherst could have missed seeing *Leaves of Grass* by "Walt Whitman, a kosmos, of Manhattan the son," which hardly sold at first. But there's one poem she must have encountered. Her household took the recently founded *Atlantic Monthly*, whose February and May 1860 issues it's known she read. That April the magazine published Whitman's "As I Ebb'd with the Ocean of Life":

> Nature here in sight of the sea taking
>   advantage of me to dart upon me
>   and sting me,
> Because I have dared to open my mouth to
>   sing at all . . .
> Ebb, ocean of life, (the flow will return,)
> Cease not your moaning you fierce old mother,
> Endlessly cry for your castaways, but fear not,
>   deny not me,
> Rustle not up so hoarse and angry against my
>   feet as I touch you or gather from you.

Voluble as ever, this sounds like nothing in Dickinson, yet by 1860 she'd already "dared . . . to sing," sounding her own breathtaking depths, as in "I taste a liquor never brewed":

> Inebriate of Air—am I—
> And Debauchee of Dew—
> Reeling—thro endless summer days—
> From inns of Molten Blue—

While it's easier to picture Walt tramping Long Island shoreline than Emily staggering home soused, that's not the point. Her language, her reeling imagination, gets something unheard-of out of summer's "Molten Blue."

The popular view of Dickinson gives us a wraith in white, seldom descending from her small wooden desk in the upstairs corner bedroom. Yet she had passionate friendships, and was no stranger to uncultivated nature around Amherst. "When much in the Woods, as a little Girl, I was told that the Snake would bite me, that I might pick a poisonous flower, or Goblins kidnap me, but I went along and met no one but Angels, who were far shyer of me, than I could be of them, so I hav'nt that confidence in fraud which many exercise."

Nor was she a stranger to the names of things. As an adolescent she kept a herbarium, a bound book with dried flowers labeled in English and Latin. Later she writes to young cousins about discovering a witch hazel shrub: "I had never seen it but once before, and it haunted me like childhood's Indian pipe, or ecstatic puff-balls, or that mysterious apple that sometimes comes on river-pinks." Puffballs, a mushroom-like fungus, do burst at the touch and discharge brown powder. But "ecstatic"? That sprouted from her own odd lexicon. At home she kept her conservatory in bloom all year long. One day she called someone in to see a chrysalis that "had burst its bonds, and floating about in the sunshine was a gorgeous butterfly," says the neighbor. "I did not understand all she said about it, but it was beautiful to see her delight and to hear her talk."

Often in her letters she'd enclose a flower, a hyacinth or pussy willow bud, or a bulb: "I have long been a Lunatic on bulbs." She once attached a riddle poem to a cocoon and sent it to her nephew. In illness the year before her death, Dickinson wrote a friend: "I write in the midst of Sweet-Peas and by the side of Orioles, and could put my Hand on a Butterfly, only he withdraws."

That reticent butterfly marks a difference between her and Whitman, who felt himself fundamental, centered in the natural world. A photo shows the Good Gray Poet on whose upraised fingers a butterfly has alighted; after his death a pasteboard butterfly was found among his belongings. Whitman spoke as easily for "beetles rolling balls of dung" as for "threads that connect the stars," but Dickinson felt no such certainty:

Touch lightly Nature's sweet Guitar
Unless thou know'st the Tune
Or every Bird will point at thee
Because a Bard too soon—

She'd rather slant-rhyme "Bard" with "Bird," and never wished to publish her work.

One of Dickinson's deftest lyrics acts out her glancing touch. "A Humming-Bird" exists in seven manuscript copies, all identical—she was that sure of it, sending it to several friends from 1879 on. After her death, the *Atlantic Monthly* printed what's now titled only by its opening line, as ungraspable as the creature itself:

A Route of Evanescence
With a revolving Wheel—
A Resonance of Emerald—
A Rush of Cochineal—
And every Blossom on the Bush
Adjusts its tumbled Head—
The mail from Tunis, probably,
An easy Morning's Ride—

For "revolving" she'd tried alternatives: "delusive," "dissembling," "dissolving," "renewing." But the clearest word best catches, or purposely can't quite catch, wingbeats so rapid they blur like spokes in a wheel, in a whir of repeating *r*'s through the first four lines. Swift evanescence leaves us in a sensory merge of motion, color, sound: a precious bright green humming, a scarlet or ruby-throated rush. Then without any notice the hummingbird—if that's what it was, we never hear its name—is gone.

Nothing's left to us, in the second quatrain, but every blossom astir, adjusting itself in the wake of a sudden visit. Then the witness speaks up, fancying how fast this happened. Whereas (in Shakespeare's *Tempest*) Tunis lies so far from Naples that no letter can arrive "unless the sun were post," here the hummingbird's passage is "An easy Morning's Ride." Flippancy tips the poem's angle of vision, dislodging any human dominion over nature.

Intimate with the flora and some of the fauna in her environs, Dickinson still doubted they were hers by poetic right. On Nature:

We pass, and She abides.
We conjugate her Skill
While She creates and federates
Without a syllable.

In another poem, butterflies (who appear 31 times in her work) again go distant from her, as does this singular bird:

A Bird came down the Walk—
He did not know I saw—
He bit an Angleworm in halves
And ate the fellow, raw,

And then he drank a Dew
From a convenient Grass—
And then hopped sidewise to the Wall
To let a Beetle pass—

He glanced with rapid eyes
That hurried all around—
They looked like frightened Beads, I thought—
He stirred his Velvet Head

Like one in danger, Cautious,
I offered him a Crumb
And he unrolled his feathers
And rowed him softer home—

Than Oars divide the Ocean,
Too silver for a seam—
Or Butterflies, off Banks of Noon
Leap, plashless as they swim.

Granted, Dickinson's bird "came down the Walk" close to home, not in wildness where Muir and Thoreau found the truth of things. This "Bird" (she capitalized any word she prized) lives far from Jonah's or Melville's whale, Beowulf's monster, Jack London's wolf, Ted Hughes's crow, though not far from Whitman's beetles. Dickinson, who'd read Charles Darwin on the survival of the fittest, found nature fierce even on her own turf.

Since it's humans who usually come down a walk, that phrase magnifies the beast biting a worm "in halves" and eating it "raw" (how else?). Her tough rhyme,

He did not know I saw—
. . .
And ate the fellow, raw,

links covert versus cannibal beings. Sounding for a moment like Peter Rabbit—"he drank a Dew / From a convenient Grass"—the poet intervenes again with an odd image for his "rapid eyes": "They looked like frightened Beads, I thought." Tacking on "I thought" admits that poetic adornment, despite the charming "Velvet Head," adds little to Nature, who acts "Without a syllable."

Now the poem turns on ambiguity. Does stanza three run on to four—"He stirred his Velvet Head // Like one in danger, Cautious . . ."—or does four begin a new gesture: "Like one in danger, Cautious, / I offered him a Crumb . . ."? It makes all the difference. Is the Bird or the speaker "in danger, Cautious"? Or maybe he's in danger and then she's cautious. Thanks to Dickinson's idiosyncratic syntax and punctuation, all these are possible, posing an endangered *human* species against an indifferent animal who "unrolled his feathers / And rowed him softer home" on a bluff off-rhyme with "Crumb."

Softer even than "Butterflies, off Banks of Noon / Leap, plashless as they swim." She might have ended with the bird, but no, Dickinson wades into the ocean toward creatures somewhere sometime out of mind. Do butterflies really leap from river-banks and swim, with or without splashing? In any event, "Banks of Noon" snaps our synapses, leaves us blinking into midday sun.

Birds, butterflies, and most often bees command Emily Dickinson's attention, acing out everything under the sun: "Buccaneers of buzz," "Baronial bees," "the goblin bee," "the lover bee," "When landlords turn the drunken bee / Out of the foxglove's door." She's in fine company here, from Plato likening bees to the imagination—they fetch abroad, then return and make honey—to Yeats fantasizing "a hive for the honey bee" at Innisfree. Or Coleridge's "Inscription for a Fountain on a Heath," opening on "This Sycamore, oft musical with bees." Or Keats's Autumn, conspiring with the sun "to set budding more, / And still more, later flowers for the bees..."

Still she looked askance at bees as at all things both great and small.

> To make a prairie it takes a clover and one bee,
> One clover, and a bee,
> And revery.
> The revery alone will do,
> If bees are few.

As often, her tongue-in-cheek rhyming undercuts human sovereignty. She scarcely credits Adam's gift of naming:

> "Nature" is what we see—
> The Hill—the Afternoon—
> Squirrel—
> Eclipse—the Bumble bee—

Nature is what we know—
Yet have no art to say—
So impotent Our Wisdom is
To her Simplicity.

What would she have made—*some*thing, no doubt—of a recent discovery in Burma, a 100-million-year-old bee found in amber along with four tiny flowers it was sipping?
She could be very bleak:

But Nature is a stranger yet;
The ones that cite her most
Have never passed her haunted house,
Nor simplified her ghost.

A late poem finds a double negative for nature, who is at once too mysterious and too actual for art:

Where melody is not
Is the unknown peninsula.
Beauty is nature's fact.

"Beauty is nature's fact": six syllables subverting ages of human presumption.
Nature's oldest fact, the snake, occasioned a brilliant poem wherein, as Rainer Maria Rilke put it, "Beauty is but the beginning of terror / We're just able to bear." Dickinson's friend Samuel Bowles, editor of the Springfield, Massachusetts *Republican,* had been asking to publish something of hers. On Valentine's Day, 1866, his front page carried "The Snake"—which was not her title, as she never gave any. Twice in this poem we learn she "met Him" or "met this Fellow," and how could a so-called recluse do so? Because her lifelong Amherst home had thirteen acres, including a meadow opposite her bedroom window on Main Street. In the woods as a girl, she was told a snake might bite her, "but I went along and met no one but Angels."
Here is the poem, properly known by its first line:

A narrow Fellow in the Grass
Occasionally rides—
You may have met Him—did you not
His notice sudden is—

The Grass divides as with a Comb—
A spotted shaft is seen—

And then it closes at your feet
And opens further on—
He likes a Boggy Acre
A Floor too cool for Corn—
Yet when a Boy, and Barefoot—
I more than once at Noon

Have passed, I thought, a Whip lash
Unbraiding in the Sun
When stooping to secure it
It wrinkled, and was gone—

Several of Nature's People
I know, and they know me—
I feel for them a transport
Of cordiality—

But never met this Fellow
Attended, or alone
Without a tighter breathing
And Zero at the Bone—

From A to Z, "A narrow Fellow" right down to "Zero at the Bone," she
shows *that* is poetry when "it makes my whole body so cold no fire ever can
warm me."

Only Walt Whitman before her, only someone whose "Verse is alive," as
she wrote Higginson, could come vulnerable yet alert upon "A narrow Fellow
in the Grass"—"narrow" meaning slim but also mean and constraining, plus
"Fellow," an associate or equal but more likely an ill-bred male in Shakespeare's
sense, a churl. Then her startling verb "rides," conjuring no reptile but a cavalier,
deepens the dread of this encounter, and the next line's verbs jar us off balance:
"You may have met Him—did You not" (she complained when the editor regularized her by putting a comma after "did you not"). Then "His notice sudden
is." That line too is unsettling, as a snake gives formal notice or suddenly notices
us, and the inverted "sudden is" scrapes its rhyme against "rides."

Eden is "always eligible," Dickinson once said, meaning choosable, at
hand—which suggests that evil is too. A sexual hint emerges like Original
Sin as the grass divides and "A spotted shaft is seen." Remember, there's no
title and no creature is named, though she knows him well enough:

He likes a Boggy Acre
A Floor too cool for Corn—

This made her editor Sam Bowles exclaim, "How did that girl ever know that a boggy field wasn't good for corn?" Then memory turns to childhood shock.

Yet when a Boy, and Barefoot—
I more than once at Noon
Have passed, I thought, a Whip lash
Unbraiding in the sun.

Her posthumous editors thought "Child" more seemly than "Boy," and also changed "Noon" to "Morn," smoothing the rhyme with "Corn." But they couldn't tame Dickinson's wild scene. This "Whip lash / Unbraiding" is no mere figure of speech but visionary menace: "It wrinkled, and was gone:" Compare a more predictable poem—"Sweet is the swamp with its secrets, / Until we meet a snake; / 'Tis then we sigh for houses . . ." —to see how arresting "A narrow Fellow" is.

Unsettling her meter as well, Dickinson's middle passage shifts from an 8 6 8 6 syllable count to 7-6-7-6, every other line ending on an unstressed syllable: *Bare*foot, *Whip* lash. Adopted from Protestant hymns she knew, this odd-even beat keeps us off balance and expectant, then assured again, even relaxed:

Several of Nature's People
I know, and they know me—
I feel for them a transport
Of cordiality—

Against the whiplash and Dickinson's sense of "unknown" nature, she risks a casual tone on "Several" and on "People I know," such as squirrels, deer. Likewise her rapture or sublime "transport" gets lightened by genteel "cordiality" ("Now Emily, be cordial to our guests!"). Except that the heart (Latin *cor*) at the root of "cordiality" will come back to end this poem on a kind of cardiac arrest.

In Dickinson's final stanza, "But" rebuts cordiality:

But never met this Fellow
Attended, or alone

No lout but somehow a fellow creature now, and still not named? In this biologic standoff, her word "or" turns dire when "alone" gets locked in by its rhyme:

But never met this Fellow
Attended, or alone

> Without a tighter breathing
> And Zero at the Bone—

Cordiality gives way to anguish (whose root is "narrow," like angst), tighter breathing cramping the chest on meeting this narrow fellow. In her own hand you can see a ripcord stroke crossing both *t*'s in "*Transport* of cordiality" and again in "*tighter* breathing."

"And Zero at the Bone": Emily Dickinson's most stunning line. After her "breathing" catches at the break, that firm last line feels all the more final, forcing "alone" to jibe with "Bone" in the poem's only perfect rhyme. Frozen at sight of a cold-blooded creature, the marrow goes null: "And Zero at the Bone." At this depth of awareness, opposites fuse, dread with pure recognition.

Another terrifying Dickinson lyric comes to mind, "After great pain, a formal feeling comes," where "Nerves" and "stiff Heart" are grown "like a stone." It ends:

> As Freezing persons, recollect the Snow—
> First—Chill—then Stupor—then the letting go—

"Snow" leads to "letting go," much as "alone" sinks into "Bone." At these moments a poem works as poem and not as some reportage after the event. "What's real *happens*," as her German translator Paul Celan put it.

Dickinson wrote a friend about choosing words, "as I can take but few and each must be the chiefest ... Earth's most graphic transaction is placed within a syllable, nay, even a gaze." Her syllables grip us: "His notice sudden *is*," "And Zero at the *Bone*."

Spasmodic, uncontrolled, wayward, Thomas Wentworth Higginson called Dickinson's verse. But yes, that was her genius and she had the strength of mind to tell him so: "Myself the only Kangaroo among the Beauty." To herself she said, "Tell all the Truth but tell it slant." In idiosyncrasy—omission, truncation, disjunction, opacity, illogic, semantic and syntactic and grammatic and prosodic and punctuational oddness and ambiguity—hers was the hummingbird's Route of Evanescence.

Unknowing riveted her, as with "Zero at the Bone," especially in her nagging sense of death. Some of Dickinson's most favored poems are her grimmest, bending your optic nerve:

> There's a certain Slant of light,
> Winter Afternoons—
> That oppresses, like the Heft
> Of Cathedral Tunes—

Heavenly Hurt, it gives us—
We can find no scar,
But internal difference,
Where the Meanings, are—

Touching bedrock despair she turns playful, running *"Cathedral Tunes"* into *"Heavenly Hurt."* As readily as Dickinson's "I heard a Fly buzz—when I died—" can darken,

And then the Windows failed—and then
I could not see to see—

she'll play at being Nature's stenographer:

Bee! I'm expecting you!
Was saying Yesterday
To Somebody you know
That you were due—

The Frogs got Home last Week—
Are settled, and at work—
Birds, mostly back—
The Clover warm and thick—

You'll get my Letter by
The seventeenth; Reply
Or better, be with me—
Yours, Fly.

Facing death in nature she goes jocular:

Apparently with no surprise
To any happy Flower
The Frost beheads it at its play— . . .
For an Approving God.

Dickinson's way of thought—by which she meant poetry—"keeps Believing nimble."

The young woman who told Higginson her family worships "an Eclipse, every morning" was not likely to share 19th-century sacramental ideas of nature, of skylark and sycamore and daffodil embodying divine spirit. Our ignorance and mortality, she said, make us "as exempt from Exultation as the

Stones." Yet "A Word that breathes distinctly / Has not the power to die," so we keep turning to finely timed lines such as these:

A Pit—but Heaven over it—
And Heaven beside, and Heaven abroad,
And yet a Pit—
With Heaven over it

. . .

The depth is all my thought—

That Pit would be mortal Earth, but again she refrains from identifying, and we're drawn in deeper than expected.

Reclusive and a spinster, but not sheltered, Emily Dickinson knew death dose up: women dying in childbirth, children from disease, Amherst's Union Army casualties returning throughout the war. Yet 1862 drew more poems from her than any other year. Losses studded her days: several older friends and mentors, Samuel Bowles, her mother, her father, and painfullest of all, late in life, her eight-year-old nephew Gilbert. Emily wrote a friend: "'Open the Door, open the Door, they are waiting for me,' was Gilbert's sweet command in delirium. *Who* were waiting for him, all we possess we would give to know." But "*is* there more?" she added. "Then tell me its name!"

At Dickinson's death on May 15, 1886, her sister-in-law Susan prepared the body for burial, putting violets and a pink orchid at her throat and flowers and boughs over the white coffin. An old family retainer remembers Emily's funeral wish: "She asked to be carried out the back door, around through the garden, through the opened barn from front to back, and then through the grassy fields to the family plot, always in sight of the house." Through the garden, through grassy fields, like the carriage in her best-known poem, "Because I could not stop for Death": "We passed the Fields of Gazing Grain."

Passing fields of grain, yes. But *gazing grain?*

Emily Dickinson Chronology

1830	Emily Dickinson born in Amherst, Massachusetts, on December 10.
1835	Dickinson begins four years of Primary School.
1840	Dickinson starts first of seven years at Amherst Academy.
1847	Dickinson enters South Hadley Seminary.
1850	Amherst College student newspaper anonymously publishes a Dickinson valentine.
1855	Dickinson visits her father in Washington, D.C.; meets Charles Wadsworth; family moves into the Homestead.
1856	Austin Dickinson introduces Emily to Samuel Bowles, publisher of the *Springfield Republican*.
1861	*Springfield Republican* anonymously publishes "I taste a liquor never brewed" under the title "The May Wine."
1862	Dickinson sends a letter and four poems to Thomas Wentworth Higginson; *Springfield Republican* anonymously publishes "Safe in their alabaster chambers."
1864	Dickinson in Boston for eye treatments.
1865	*Springfield Republican* anonymously publishes "A narrow Fellow in the grass."
1870	Thomas Wentworth Higginson first visits Amherst.
1874	Dickinson's father dies suddenly in Boston.
1875	Dickinson's mother suffers a paralytic stroke.
1876	Helen Hunt Jackson urges Dickinson to publish.

1878	Dickinson and Judge Otis Phillips Lord begin exchange of love letters.
1882	Mabel Loomis Todd and Austin Dickinson begin love affair; Dickinson's mother dies.
1883	Gilbert (bib) Dickinson dies, Emily and Susan Dickinson continue estrangement.
1884	Judge Lord dies, Dickinson's health declines.
1886	Dickinson dies on May 15; Lavinia discovers her sister's poems.
1890	The first of many volumes of Dickinson's poems is published, with Loomis and Higginson as editors.
1955	Thomas H. Johnson publishes three volumes of Emily Dickinson's poetry.
1958	Johnson and Theodora Ward as editors publish three volumes of *The Letters of Emily Dickinson*.

Contributors

HAROLD BLOOM is Sterling Professor of the Humanities at Yale University. He is the author of 30 books, including *Shelley's Mythmaking* (1959), *The Visionary Company* (1961), *Blake's Apocalypse* (1963), *Yeats* (1970), *A Map of Misreading* (1975), *Kabbalah and Criticism* (1975), *Agon: Toward a Theory of Revisionism* (1982), *The American Religion* (1992), *The Western Canon* (1994), and *Omens of Millennium: The Gnosis of Angels, Dreams, and Resurrection* (1996). *The Anxiety of Influence* (1973) sets forth Professor Bloom's provocative theory of the literary relationships between the great writers and their predecessors. His most recent books include *Shakespeare: The Invention of the Human* (1998), a 1998 National Book Award finalist, *How to Read and Why* (2000), *Genius: A Mosaic of One Hundred Exemplary Creative Minds* (2002), *Hamlet: Poem Unlimited* (2003), *Where Shall Wisdom Be Found?* (2004), and *Jesus and Yahweh: The Names Divine* (2005). In 1999, Professor Bloom received the prestigious American Academy of Arts and Letters Gold Medal for Criticism. He has also received the International Prize of Catalonia, the Alfonso Reyes Prize of Mexico, and the Hans Christian Andersen Bicentennial Prize of Denmark.

RICHARD WILBUR was named the second Poet Laureate of the U.S. in 1987. His books include *The Beautiful Changes* (1947), *Ceremony* (1950), *Advice to a Prophet* (1961), *The Mind-Reader* (1976), and a *New and Collected Poems* (1987). His *Walking to Sleep* (1969) was awarded the Bollingen Prize, and *Things of This World* (1956), won the Pulitzer Prize for Poetry.

DOUGLAS ANDERSON is Professor of English at the University of Georgia. His books include *A House Undivided : Domesticity and Community in American Literature* (1990).

TIMOTHY MORRIS is a Professor of English at the University of Texas at Arlington. He wrote *Becoming Canonical in American Poetry* (1995)

MARGARET DICKIE was the Helen Lanier Distinguished Professor of English at the University of Georgia. Her last book was *Challenging Boundaries : Gender and Periodization* (2000), published the year after her death.

DOMHNALL MITCHELL is Associate Professor at the Norwegian University of Science and Technology, Trondheim. His *Measures of Possibility: Emily Dickinson's Manuscripts* was published in 2005.

G. THOMAS TANSELLE is Vice President of the John Simon Guggenheim Memorial Foundation and Adjunct Professor of English and Comparative Literature at Columbia University.

DAVID S. REYNOLDS is Distinguished Professor of English and American Studies at the Graduate Center and Baruch College of the City University of New York. He is a respected Whitman scholar, whose books include *Walt Whitman's America: A Cultural Biography* (1995), winner of the Bancroft Prize and the Ambassador Book Award.

CAROLYN LINDLEY COOLEY has taught literature at the middle school, high school, and university levels. She wrote *The Music of Emily Dickinson's Poems and Letters* (2003).

LOGAN ESDALE is Assistant Professor of English and Comparative Literature at Chapman University.

SHIRA WOLOSKY is Professor of English and American Literature at the Hebrew University of Jerusalem. Her books include *Emily Dickinson: A Voice of War* (1984).

DEIRDRE FAGAN is Assistant Professor of English at Quincy University. She is the author of *Critical Companion to Robert Frost* (2007).

JAY LADIN is Assistant Professor of English at Stern College for Women, Yeshiva University.

JOHN FELSTINER, is Professor of English at Stanford University, where he teaches modern poetry. His books include *Translating Neruda: The Way to Macchu Picchu* (1980), *Selected Poems and Prose of Paul Celan* (2001), *Jewish American Literature* (2000), which he co-edited.

Bibliography

Anderson, Douglas. 'Presence and Place in Emily Dickinson's Poetry." *The New England Quarterly* 57.2 (June 1984), 205-224. Available from JSTOR.

Cooley, Carolyn Lindley. *The Music of Emily Dickinson's Poems and Letters*: Chapter 3, "Musical Qualities of Dickinson's Poetry: Nineteenth-Century Views." Jefferson, North Carolina: McFarland and Company, 2003: 59-69.

Dickie, Margaret. "Dickinson's Discontinuous Lyric Self." *American Literature* 60.4 (December 1988), 537-553. Available from JSTOR.

Esdale, Logan. "Dickinson;s Epistolary 'Naturalness.'" *Emily Dickinson Journal* 14.1 (Spring 2005), 1-23. Available from Project Muse.

Fagan, Deirdre. "Emily Dickinson's Unutterable Word." *Emily Dickinson Journal* 14.2 (Fall 2005), 70-75. Available from Project Muse.

Felstiner, John. "'Earth's Most Graphic Transaction': The Syllables of Emily Dickinson." *The American Poetry Review* 36.2 (March/April 2007), 7-11. Available from LION.

Hallen, Cynthia L. "At Home in Language: Emily Dickinson's Rhetorical Figures." *Emily Dickinson at Home: Proceedings of the Third International Conference of the Emily Dickinson International Society*, edited by Gudrun M. Grabher and Martina Antretter. Trier: Wissenschaftlicher Verlag Trier, 2001: 201-222.

Ladin, Jay. "Meeting Her Maker." *Cross Currents* 56.3 (Fall 2006), 338-346. Available from EBSCO: Academic Search Premier.

Mitchell, Domhnall. "Revising the Script: Emily Dickinson's Manuscripts." *American Literature* 70.4 (December 1998), 705-737. Available from JSTOR.

Mitchell, Domhnall. "The Train, the Father, his Daughter, and her Poem: A Reading of Emily Dickinson's 'I like to see it lap the miles.'" *Emily Dickinson Journal* 7.1 (Spring 1998), 1-26. Available from Project Muse.

Morris, Timothy. "The Development of Dickinson's Style." *American Literature* 60.1 (March 1988), 26-41. Available from JSTOR.

Reynolds, David S. "Emily Dickinson and Popular Culture." *The Cambridge Companion to Emily Dickinson*, edited by Wendy Martin. Cambridge: Cambridge University Press, 2002: 176-190.

Tanselle, G. Thomas. "Emily Dickinson as an Editorial Problem." *Raritan* 19.4 (Spring 2000), 64-80. Available from LION and EBSCO: Academic Search Premier.

Wilbur, Richard. "'Sumptuous Destitution.'" *Emily Dickinson: Three Views*, by Louise Bogan, Archibald MacLeish, and Richard Wilbur. Amherst: Amherst College Press, 1960. Reprinted in *Emily Dickinson: A Collection of Critical Essays*, edited by Judith Farr. Upper Saddle River: Prentice Hall, 1996: 53-61.

Winhusen, Steven. 'Emily Dickinson and Schizotypy." *Emily Dickinson Journal* 13.1 (Spring 2004), 77-96. Available from Project Muse.

Wolosky, Shira. "Public and Private in Dickinson's War Poetry." *A Historical Guide to Emily Dickinson*, ed. by Vivian Pollak. Oxford: Oxford University Press, 2004: 103-131.

Acknowledgments

Wilbur, Richard. "'Sumptuous Destitution.'" *Emily Dickinson: Three Views*, by Louise Bogan, Archibald MacLeish, and Richard Wilbur (Amherst: Amherst College Press, 1960). Reprinted in *Emily Dickinson: A Collection of Critical Essays*, edited by Judith Farr (Upper Saddle River: Prentice Hall, 1996): pp. 53–61. © 1996 Amherst College Press. Reprinted by permission of the publisher.

Anderson, Douglas. "Presence and Place in Emily Dickinson's Poetry." *The New England Quarterly*, 57.2 (June 1984): pp. 205–224. © 1984 *New England Quarterly*. Reprinted by permission of the publisher.

Morris, Timothy. "The Development of Dickinson's Style." *American Literature*, 60.1 (March 1988): pp. 26–41. © 1988 Duke University Press. Reprinted by permission of the publisher.

Dickie, Margaret. "Dickinson's Discontinuous Lyric Self." *American Literature*, 60.4 (December 1988): pp. 537–553. © 1988 Duke University Press. Reprinted by permission of the publisher.

Mitchell, Domhnall. "Revising the Script: Emily Dickinson's Manuscripts." *American Literature*, 70.4 (December 1998): pp. 705–737. © 1998 Duke University Press. Reprinted by permission of the publisher.

Tanselle, G. Thomas. "Emily Dickinson as an Editorial Problem." *Raritan*, 19.4 (Spring 2000): pp. 64–80. © 2000 *Raritan*. Reprinted by permission of the publisher.

Reynolds, David S. "Emily Dickinson and Popular Culture." *The Cambridge Companion to Emily Dickinson*, edited by Wendy Martin (Cambridge: Cambridge University Press, 2002): pp. 176–190. © 2002 Cambridge University Press. Reprinted by permission of the publisher. All rights reserved.

Cooley, Carolyn Lindley. *The Music of Emily Dickinson's Poems and Letters*, Chapter 3, "Musical Qualities of Dickinson's Poetry: Nineteenth-Century Views." (Jefferson, North Carolina: McFarland and Company, 2003): pp. 59–69. © 2003 McFarland and Company. Reprinted by permission of the publisher.

Esdale, Logan. "Dickinson's Epistolary 'Naturalness.'" *Emily Dickinson Journal*, 14.1 (Spring 2004): pp. 1–23. © The Johns Hopkins University Press. Reprinted with permission of the Johns Hopkins University Press.

Wolosky, Shira. "Public and Private in Dickinson's War Poetry." *A Historical Guide to Emily Dickinson*, ed. by Vivian Pollak (Oxford: Oxford University Press, 2004): pp. 103–131. © 2004 Oxford University Press. All rights reserved. Reprinted by permission of the publisher.

Fagan, Deirdre. "Emily Dickinson's Unutterable Word." *Emily Dickinson Journal*, 14.2 (Fall 2005): pp. 70–75. © The Johns Hopkins University Press. Reprinted with permission of the Johns Hopkins University Press.

Ladin, Jay. "Meeting Her Maker." *Cross Currents*, 56.3 (Fall 2006): pp. 338–346. © 2006 *Cross Currents*. Reprinted by permission of the publisher.

Felstiner, John. "'Earth's Most Graphic Transaction': The Syllables of Emily Dickinson." *The American Poetry Review*, 36.2 (March/April 2007): pp. 7–11. © 2007 John Felstiner. Reprinted by permission of the author.

Index

PS 1541 Z5 E38 2008
Emily Dickinson /

WITHDRAWN

Library & Media Ctr.
Carroll Community College
1601 Washington Rd.
Westminster, MD 21157

JUN - 5 2008